# BLØOÐ PØISONING

## C.F. KREITZER

MONSTER IVY
PUBLISHING

*To Alice Dassau and the many friends who helped open my eyes to my own privileges and prejudices.*

# CHAPTER 1

O ne solid line. For three weeks it has stared back at me so sleek and bold on the smooth, white Recipient paper. It's all I've been able to draw.
One line.

Every day I swear it looks more smug, more menacing and defiant than before. Like it knows something I don't.

I can't get over how unified the stroke is. No marbled texture caused by straggling pieces of charcoal trying to keep up with my hand like a herd of children unable to stay in line. No unplanned curves or loops from catching on the bumps of the recycled Donor paper.

It's perfect and it knows it's perfect.

Recipient pencils are like everything else here in Bloomfield, modified perfection. Altered and tested to perform at the highest possible satisfaction. Pleasing to the eye and to the president. Nothing out of place because they have a serum for that and a formula for everything.

I throw the pencil. The dim night-light by the bed across the room makes the shadows of the bouncing pencil dance across the floor.

My back aches with the way I hunch over, my body pinched into the corner of this Recipient mansion. The dark wooden walls and the slate-colored floor are even colder than they look. The sofa against the wall is too soft, the sheets on the bed too sleek.

From this angle on the floor, I have a perfect view of every beautifully nauseating feature. The bookshelves on either side of the window on the opposite wall, the giant bed in front of the shelves bookended by identical night-stands. All gorgeous, perfect, and new while donors fight over left behind furniture and abandoned war-ravaged homes on the other side of the wall. Even the door to the room is grander and bigger than any door I've ever seen. I like to always have it in sight, though I've never seen it open or close.

Food seems to be brought in either while I sleep or use the bathroom as if they are watching me. But for all I know, Recipients could have the tech to make it just appear on the table too. A levy straight from the kitchen to my room.

Torrin would know. My little brother knew how everything worked.

My first week here I slept through fitful nightmares and long stomach aches as I adjusted to the food. My second week I cried over Torrin.

I trace the line on the paper with one finger and push the worry away before the tears start up again. Perhaps a year ago I would have marveled at this simple line, the start of a perfect sketch, the endless possibilities of such a simple yet magical tool in my hands. Scars, even two months ago I would have jumped up and down like a little kid in front of a donation day feast to have materials like these. But now I know better. I know this is more than just a line. It's a bribe. And my cooperation is what they're bargaining for. I should be grateful I'm still alive; the price of mingling with a Recipient is death. I've had plenty of time to think over everything I should be feeling but what I feel is still rage.

Because even two months ago I thought I was in love. Before I knew who Marcus really was: their precious Recipient prince and future leader. Before I knew what he was capable of.

Murder.

I cover the line with my hand and close my eyes. I can almost hear the tinkling of crystal in my dingy home back in New Livonia as it shook in my cupboards against the wall that fateful day. The day I hid my high blood numbers from my family and told them I never wanted to donate. The day Papa's coworkers died in an explosion at the power plant. An explosion Marcus initiated.

A bump on the wall behind my bed makes me jump and my aching body instantly regrets it. The realization that it's not Torrin bumping down the hallways causes a different sort of ache.

There's another knock and I first think mice, but I'm not at home, and Bloomfield seems too clean to have a mouse problem.

My stomach lurches and growls. I hate how it already yearns for the food here like clockwork. The anticipation of seeing my food delivered, maybe seeing my enemies face-to-face again has me on my feet. As I cross the room to the window where Marcus stood, the cool breeze greets me and makes the curtains dance and sway. I like leaving the windows open. It makes me feel closer to home.

Another bump behind me makes the bedframe vibrate against the wall. More whispering. I'm certain this floor is not nearly as creaky as my home yet I don't move. I can make out enough to know there's a boy on the other side of

3

the wall. Younger and nicer sounding than an officer. His words are muffled at first, like he's farther away but coming closer. Is there another room next to mine perhaps? I strain to hear what he's saying.

"Stop it, Lecky!" the voice hisses loud and clear. "Stop it now, you rotten piece of mold, or you'll really get what's coming."

I move as quickly as my aching body allows, swiftly moving around the bedpost and toward the door to check on this poor "Lecky" fellow. I pause at the door handle for only a minute and am surprised to find it unlocked. Has it been unlocked this whole time? I'm too intrigued by the voices to laugh at my stupidity of not even checking my prison bars.

When I crack open the door, white glowing walls like the donation facility make me squint as I peer down the empty hallways. No one is there. A hissing electric sound fills my ears, and, as I lean further, a piece of my hair falls from behind my ear and suddenly lights up orange before turning black and smoking. I jump back from whatever invisible flame has me trapped inside.

Another bump echoes through my room, and I spin around. Slowly peering back at the empty space outside my doorway, I can only assume the sounds are coming from between these thick walls.

Inside them.

I shut the door a little *too* hard, and the voices stop. I hold my breath.

I make my way backward to the end of the bed, keeping my eye on the dark-brown paneled wall to my side. I'm too tired to think straight. Am I imagining things? I grip the wooden footboard, waiting for another sound—another bump to give away a clue to who is in my walls. I let myself take a much-needed but careful breath in, releasing the tension in my sore stomach. It's so silent I feel as if I can hear the wind pushing the quiet curtains.

Silence is what always breaks me. What cracks open the tears patiently waiting inside. The quiet makes me miss Torrin, and the missing leads to worry, and the worry gives way to fear.

The door opens. The shape of a woman, the maid, if I remember correctly, moves swiftly across the room like a small ghost. She pulls back the curtains, the metal rings on the curtain rod making a harsh, screeching sound, and then shuts the window.

"You should catch your death if you keep sleeping with the window open, miss."

I think of something sarcastic to say about how little it matters if my window is open or closed with the amount of sleep I'm getting nowadays, but I think better of it. I haven't spoken to a single soul in days, and suddenly all the questions I've had bubbling up inside me are gone.

The maid stops in front of me with her hands clasped at her waist. Her curls are flat like she slept on them, and her eyes have dark circles under them. Could she know something about the whispers behind my wall last night?

"Janice, is it?" I say.

"That's right, miss." She lunges for my covers, and I can't help but instinctively retreat. My body aches with protest.

"You're a Recipient," I say. Were we not trained to avoid each other? "You mustn't get too close."

She smiles at me in a way that instantly makes me start to sink back into the bed. "You needn't worry about me, miss. I'll be ok. Can I help you ready for the day?"

She tries again to remove my covers, and I reluctantly allow her. "Am I going somewhere?"

A pitying smile crosses her lips as she tilts her head. "I'm afraid not, miss. But you will be having visitors today. King Malloy wishes to see you himself, though I'm not told when. And the technician and head nurse will be in for your first donations shortly. You're his first month."

"First month?" The news of Adakin Malloy makes my palms sweat as I recall his scratchy voice from the prison cell, but I let the curious meaning of her words distract me.

"Yes. I'm not sure if this is my place to inform you, but I can't see what it would hurt. Prince Marcus will alternate months between Donors. A month with you while our scientists study his reactions, and then a month with your friend, Lazuli, to see the effects of her antibodies and presence."

I nod, expressionless, unsure of what I really think of this plan. I'm mostly just relieved that Lazuli is alright. And though I'm still certain a Donor in the "presence" of a Recipient is a fatal risk, I try not to think about Marcus at all. What do I care if he lives or dies from this stupid plan of his?

"I must say, you handled this news better than that dark-haired friend of yours. You two are complete opposites in every way," she says behind me. I don't turn to look at her as she continues. "Threw quite the tantrum, she did. Berty, her maid, has talked of nothing else since, and I'm sure it will be all over town by nightfall about how the low-numbered liar of a Donor wouldn't let a single Recipient so much as speak to her." I ball my fists as she gives a small chuckle. "She's a piece of work, that one."

"She's... been through a lot," I say, sounding more

6

defensive than I planned. I wonder if Gannet will rescue Lazuli as well as me? Of course he will. He must.

"And so have you, miss."

Janice moves in front of me again and stops. We make eye contact for a moment. Her green eyes are like a hypnotic potion calming me from the stare alone. I shake my gaze away and spread my palms against the waist of my satin blue gown.

"Yes, well..." I let the sentence go unfinished, and she moves again toward the tray by my bed.

I spot the small piece of donor paper sticking out from under a bowl of fruit. A secret note from Gannet, the sketch of a bird reminding me I'm not forgotten.Quickly, I grab it and slip it into my sleeve just as she comes to take the old tray of food away.

"Master Marcus will be in shortly with your breakfast, and I'm sure the technician will not be far behind. Ring if you need me, miss." She waltzes around the room in her white apron so quickly I spin when she nears the door.

"Janice."

She pauses with a smile showing her crooked yet white teeth. I don't know what I planned to say to her. I think I only wanted her to stay. I've been alone for so long and there is something about her, about the way she moves—or no, perhaps the way she talks or smiles—something about her reminds me of Papa. Something about her presence reminds me of the good parts of home. I don't know how to tell her this because, for scars' sake, she's a Recipient. How can a Recipient, the enemy, feel like home? Perhaps I am a lot more lonely than I realized.

Her steady smile gains a little understanding as her head tilts and her eyebrows raise, waiting for an answer. How different the smiles of these Recipients are. No drugs.

No control. No blue serum from donations sparkling behind their eyes.

"How do I ring for you?" I finally say.

Janice smiles and raises her eyebrows. "Of course. How silly of me. I forget you're not accustomed to our ways or our technology." Two steps from me, and she is by the wall closest to her. Balancing the tray on her hip, she puts out her hand and places it against the wall. It ripples at her touch, and when her entire palm is pressed up against it, a bright-white edge outlines her fingers.

"Every part of the room is blood activated. All you need do is place your hand on the wall and call for who you are in need of. It will send a message to where we are located. Or at least, for you, as long as we are in the same building. *Your* blood will not have long-range access."

I stare at her hand, and she smiles again at my reaction. A patient, non-patronizing smile. I step closer to her, never taking my eyes off the glowing wall under her hand.

"Scars galore..." I whisper in amazement.

The door opens behind us, and Marcus enters with a new tray in hand. Janice dips a curtsey with a bowed head. Something she never did in my presence, and it reminds me who Marcus really is. My hand automatically goes to the inner part of my elbow, seeking a bandage to pick at. But, all that's there is a group of scars that have completely healed. I picture the sketch of Gannet's to comfort me instead.

Janice's voice sounds weak when she speaks again. No more confidence. No more kindness. "I'll leave you two, unless there is anything more the Master is in need of?"

"That will be all, maid." His speech is short and abrupt I don't know why it makes me so angry to hear him speak like that, but it makes me wish for a glass wall between us.

One like at the ball separating the Donors and Recipients. I've never been more aware of exactly who and what he is. His blue eyes are cold.

"Her name's Janice." I scowl at him. I clasp my hands behind my back, squeezing, and wonder at why I would defend another Recipient like this. Just because she reminded me a little bit of home? Is it because I hate him so much?

Janice cowers at my words.

I clench my teeth while watching Janice shiver and hope I can be less vocal. A good Donor until the resistance comes for me. Just play along until Gannet rescues me. A sitting duck. Not just sitting. A mute sitting duck.

Marcus eyes me, and I look at Janice again. It has nothing to do with her. My biggest fear was being seen for merely a number, by my blood alone instead of my talents and qualities. That's what I thought made Marcus different. To me he was a sick donor who I thought saw me for who I was and not what runs under my skin. But here Marcus sees Janice by her station alone. A maid and nothing more. Would he have spoken to me on the streets if he hadn't known I had a number that would keep him alive? His face softens under my glare. He looks repentant and pitiful lifting his chin as if he is determined to prove to me that he has changed. With tray in hand, he swivels toward Janice and bows to her. She stands a little straighter in order to see him and looks as if she may crumble or whither to the ground at any moment.

"Excuse me," Marcus says with airs. "We are no longer in need of your hospitality, *Janice.* Thank you for your services."

Janice doesn't appear trusting of her voice as she pulls

both lips in, covering her teeth and biting them together. She nods before scurrying out of the room.

When the door shuts, Marcus walks across the room and places the tray on the small round table near the foot of my bed.

"That was unkind to put her in that predicament," he says in a low voice.

"Unkind? Of *me*? You're the one who called her 'maid.'"

"It's what she is," he reasons with a shrug. Sitting at the table as if it's the most natural thing to be in this room alone with me, he crosses his legs and leans back in the wooden chair.

Two people in one day. I'm so out of practice I huff and puff, making sounds for several minutes before actually finding my voice again. "Yes, she's a maid, but it's *what* she is, not *who* she is. We're all more than our station."

"Even me?" he says with a raised eyebrow.

At first I sink a little, thinking I've walked right into a trap. I know exactly what he's inferring. That I refuse to see past what he is, that it somehow excuses his decision to lie about who he is. But he used his station to do horrible things!

"Especially you," I stand a little taller trying to remember all the words I've wanted to hurl at him. All the rehearsed arguments and speeches that consumed me these weeks are gone.

Maybe it's all the memories flooding my tired, confused brain. Or maybe it's simply the shock of his presence when I'd become so accustomed to him before my prison sentence began. Whatever the reason, that habitual side of me that doesn't just remember his touch but expects it like muscle memory, makes my heart hammer at him sitting here in my room. Minds can be cruel things. Storing away moments only to torture us with them later. I hate how the memory of his arms holding me when he kept me from running to save Mrs. Price is what I think of now.

But the memory runs red as the knowledge of what he's done floods me. He murdered Greg. He put Oliver in prison. He stole my blood. He lied to me.

And then, he had the audacity to ask me to marry him.

I speak through clenched teeth, slow and rational. "Though our station does not make us who we are, we should all still be held accountable for our actions." I take a deep breath after such control. "What did she do to earn such critical judgment from someone so high?"

He leans forward over the tray of food and picks up a stack of plates.

"I don't know much about Donor laws, but it is against the law in Recipient territory to murder your husband." He pops a grape in his mouth to let his words sink in. Juicy, sour words that don't make much sense. "And no one is perfect"—he places a hand on his chest—"no matter how high they are. We all suffer the consequences of our mistakes."

Janice? Are all Recipients murderers? This information sobers the mood in the air. I tuck my dress under me as I sit at the other chair in the room where he has placed one of the plates.

Marcus doesn't offer me food; he just fills his own plate with cheese and more grapes. I study his perfectly manicured hands with strong protruding veins webbing underneath his tan, smooth skin. He reaches for a different kind of cheese. It's white with something speckled mixed in. The smells reach me, and I restrain myself from sighing, forgetting momentarily about his confusing accusation. Cheese. I've missed cheese. His hand pauses, and our eyes meet.

"Are you not hungry?" he says with concern.

Ignoring him, I finally fill my plate as well. I don't understand why I have to eat with him. From what I saw from the window, Bloomfield looks plenty large enough for him to eat somewhere else.

"Are all my meals to be supervised?"

"Is that how you view this?"

"I'm a prisoner, aren't I?"

"I'm sorry. I wish it was different. That you were free. That things were different between us. But it's the best I could get from the King."

I stand my ground, staring into his hurt-filled eyes. So blue they're almost translucent like the oceans before the germ wars. Too bad his soul isn't as clear and transparent, perhaps then I wouldn't have been so easily deceived. His brow clouds his eyes, and a twinge of regret wars inside me before I stamp it out quickly.

He made his own decisions. Now it's time for a lesson in consequences. Something I doubt he's ever had to experience.

Bending over his plate, he picks up a piece of fresh pineapple. Without looking up, he states as simple and robotic as possible, "For the experiment to be accurate, I've decided to spend a month with each of you Donors. During this time I will take advantage of every opportunity possible to be in the Donor's presence to see if the reactions are the same or have any adverse effects."

My smirk goes unnoticed. 'Adverse effects' indeed. We were taught all about the hereditary virus that can attack one's own flesh from the inside out. How Donors, with valuable antibodies, are immune yet can carry the disease without ever knowing, without a single symptom. A chill runs up my arms, and I shiver involuntarily at the memory of those symptoms; the images they forced upon us at such a young age. I already know what will happen. Lazuli and I will expose Marcus to the virus. While receiving Lazuli's donations, there won't be enough antibodies in his system to save him.

I grab a small cube of white cheese and roll it between my fingers, trying not to picture the white patches of decay that can develop into open wounds from the virus. I can feel Marcus's eyes on me now. Is there a chance he could be right? What if Adakin Malloy already figured out the cure years ago but loved power too much to give up this way of life? So much so that he wouldn't tell his own grandson, who sits here eating a variety of fruits that Donors can only dream about having? Or does he, too, already know there will be no "adverse effects"?

I angrily pop a piece of the white cheese into my mouth. As soon as the soft, salty square hits my tongue a tiny moan bubbles up my throat to greet it. Marcus laughs through his nose then clears his throat to try and mask it.

"I was hungry," I say tersely. "This cheese... It's amazing."

His smile is broad and though eerily familiar, like a memory from a different life, a different version of myself, it gives me no comfort. I curse myself for how long I stare at the way his cheeks dimple around his lips and how beautifully white his teeth are, but I can't make myself look away.

Marcus continues to grin, perhaps thinking we're sharing a special moment, but he couldn't be more wrong. Experiment indeed. Anyone can play scientist, and I have my own theories. He won't last more than a month.

The smile that once entranced me now sickens me. All I see now is a greedy, spoiled boy. A murderer grinning because he cares for no one. My face burns with contempt, and I bite my cheek, looking over his shoulder to hide my raging anger.

"Pepper-jack white cheddar," he says.

The rest of our brunch is spent in silence, and soon there is a knock at the door. It opens without us answering, and a young woman steps through. Her red hair is swept up in a loose bun, and her white lab coat along with a black bag in hand gives her away.

The technician.

# CHAPTER 2

I look at Marcus as the technician shuts the door behind her. He, however, is smiling at the beautiful technician like he knows her. He probably does. Something about thinking of Marcus having beautiful Recipient friends does something funny to my chest and has me questioning if he ever looked at me that way.

The technician dips her head, making loose strands of her healthy red hair fall forward. She gives a graceful, one-handed curtsey as she speaks.

"I'm Alexandria, but you can call me Alex. I'll be your technician for this experiment." Her voice is like honey, smooth and slow, yet with the hint of something sticky if messed with. She finally looks my way after a long appreciative grin for Marcus. He's probably the reason she took on this job.

"Thank you for taking this on, Alexandria," he says.

"Anything for you, sir."

Sir? I raise my eyebrows at Marcus as he looks my way and his cheeks redden.

"And please, it's Alex."

When she sets her bag down and opens its wide mouth, my heart starts to hammer. Gannet was my only technician except for my last donation as a contracted Donor. It was my first experience with the blue sparkling serum. The memory of having no control over my face or the words that left my mouth has my blood panicking. The constant smiling and the beautiful colors were both addicting and frightening at the same time. But I have no contract anymore. I stand and consider the window again. I'm not that far up, am I?

"Aston?" Marcus says. He is soon by my side, though still hesitant to touch me. Good.

I instinctively pick at my inner elbow where the needle will soon go, but it is clean and smooth, not sticky from bandages yet. Instead I rub my finger over the scar. Scars. How is this happening? The very thieves of my blood are going to stand in the room with me and watch it leave my body? It can't happen. I won't allow it.

Gannet was the only one with me through all my donations. I know now he was who kept me free to feel by giving me the drugs separately. I close my eyes and hear his words, "just breathe." I can almost feel his soft, cold hands on my arm prepping the site.

Marcus moves. I step back and he freezes. Gannet was the only thing keeping me free, but what's going to save me now? Why hasn't he come yet? I have never been very good at being quiet. Sitting and waiting has never been my strong suit. This imprisonment will be a trial of my patience, trust, and how willing I am to serve the resistance. I'll prove to them I'm worth rescuing and an asset. But what will stop these Recipients from drugging me now? Marcus? Ha!

"I have an allergy to the coagulant." My voice is airy

from my quick, shallow breathing. Of course the allergy was a ruse invented by Gannet to keep me from the controlling drugs given to Donors, but they don't have to know that. I look to Marcus then back to the technician.

He brushes his hand against my forearm and I flinch, grabbing my arm. I pull it to my chest. "The blue liquid. It has to be separated," I say.

"Aston, I'm sure this technician has been notified of everything in your file."

We both look to Alex, and she smiles like she is embarrassed by my outburst in front of the royal Recipient prince. "It has to be separate."

"I am well informed about your needs, Donor." She spits out the words with a tight smile.

"Her name is Aston," Marcus says. Our eyes connect again, and his expression seems to say, "Two can play this game," as if his little charade of calling Janice by her name was something for *me*. Something he did to earn points, and now he's shoving it in my face. My fingernails sting tight against my palm, and the lump of fear in my throat hurts worse from looking at him. His pointy cheekbones and blue eyes used to mean something to me. Now I can't even look at him without feeling sick.

"Yes, sir. I'm sorry, sir," the technician says. My eyes narrow as the technician continues, "I have strict orders on how the procedure should be performed, Aston, and I assure you they do not differ from what you're used to."

Flustered, I blink and look away only to realize Marcus has reached a hand toward the side of my waist. For comfort? To keep me steady? I do feel on the verge of fainting. I twist away from his touch and angle myself toward the chair at the table. Would he have really touched me? In Donor territory he was always so careful.

Never in public, never in front of others. When Lazuli found us, he nearly dumped me out of his lap. But here. Here he is all ease and comfort. Amongst his own kind it seems he couldn't care less who sees us together. In my land he is the enemy, but here he is the king.

"Where do you want me?" I'm determined to get through this.

"Where you were sitting is fine. We have better machines than the donation facilities. It won't take up as much space or take nearly as much time."

I retake my seat, and Marcus moves out of the way. He stands behind his chair, gripping the top of it and leaning forward with a brooding look that gives him the appearance of a worried old fart. His smoothed, hardened hair doesn't help.

"Would you rather I not be present, Aston?"

Alex looks up at him with admiration.

I want to say yes. I want to jut my chin in the air with a firm look and a disdainful glare. I want to yell and stomp and tell him to go away. Scars, *I* would rather not be present!

But I know that anything I do he would only chuckle at or compliment my pout or find some other way to discredit me. It would have the reverse effect on him. "Aston?" He steps away from his chair like he's thinking about coming over to me again. Since when do Donors ever get what they want? I shrug at him and look out the window before I say something stupid. Don't want to upset happy, adoring Alex now do we?

Alex sets a small black box on the table in front of the tray of food and connects clear tubing to it. Pulling up the sleeve of my dress, I lay my exposed arm on the edge of the table. Three round scars glisten under the light of the chandelier above, and Marcus makes eye contact with me again. The tension in the room is unavoidable. I should have risked saying something stupid. Should have said something. Anything. He shouldn't be here. This feels too intimate. Like we are about to partake in an unforgivable ritual or sin.

I feel too exposed to have him here watching this technician prepare her long needle and sanitize my naked arm with alcohol.

Alex is kneeling before me when she leans in with a needle in hand.

"Just a tiny pinch," she says as the cold needle rests within the crook of my arm. It reminds me of when a technician surprised me at my front door and told me it was just a tiny finger prick. When Alex's needle breaks through my flesh, I grip the armrest of the chair with my other hand.

Not as gentle as Gannet.

Marcus must see the pain on my face for he steps around the table, and his hand is soon on my shoulder. Again it feels wrong to have him here, but I'm literally a chained prisoner by the needle and tube; pulling away from him could splatter us all with my blood. So I sit, wincing, his hand burning on my shoulder, my insides twisting from the combination of it all.

I have nothing to compare this to, but the heat in my chest hates that he is here supporting me. He has too much to gain from this pain. Too much to profit for me to believe he cares about *me* and not merely what I am giving him.

I shut my eyes tighter at the pain in my chest. I cared about him. To think I even pitied him and his supposed low numbers. He cares more about what's in me than who I am. It's like... It's like... Mam.

I gasp a little at the realization, which makes Alex look

at me, and Marcus squeezes my shoulder. Mam is who I have to compare this situation to. Perhaps that's why this feels so wrong, because of the realization that he is more like Mam than I ever thought someone could be. He doesn't have low numbers nor need my pity; he only needs my blood. The rest of me is nothing to him.

The pain in my arm dulls.

Alex tapes the tube in place and leans back on her heels. She smiles at Marcus above my head before she looks at me. "Should just be thirty minutes."

"That's not *that* much less than the facilities," I grumble.

"It's about half the time." Her scowl makes me want to stick my tongue out at her like an angry toddler. Marcus thanks her and somehow graciously dismisses her. She gives me another glower as she slips behind the door and promises to be back to check on me in time.

"Can I get you anything?" Marcus asks.

I ignore his concern and stare at the dark tube that is stealing my blood from my body. When he gets no reply, he steps past me, giving me a perfect view of the windows, and walks across the room. For a moment I think he's leaving. I turn to see if it could be true, but instead he is on the far side of the room where he stops at a cupboard beside the blue sofa in the corner.

Opening the doors to the cupboard, he retrieves several boxes. He tucks them under his arm as he closes the cabinet door and returns. I stare at the door as he passes it, wishing he would leave. As he draws nearer, I recognize some of the boxes. Games. Gannet got out games during my donations also. I look out the window again. All I can see from my position is blue sky and the very tips of trees. The memory of how I treated Gannet makes my heart sink. I was certain he was drugged and robotic. I never knew he was a local resistance leader trying to recruit me. If I had, maybe none of this would have happened. If I had let myself trust Gannet maybe nothing would have developed between Marcus and me. My family would still be getting a contracted amount.

Marcus stops in front of me with a sheepish smile. "Records showed you played board games with your technician while donating? We have some here."

My head snaps up. "You spoke with my technician?"

"Not...exactly. Though we did consult one with another about your donations, he never brought up anything like this." Marcus shakes the game in his hands rattling the checkers pieces inside. "Gannet was a rather strange fellow, I will confess. Very formal. Not a very happy person which is strange on a Donor." I feel suddenly defensive about Gannet. Of course he doesn't smile like the other donors, he's a part of the resistance that found an escape from the Recipient serum.

Marcus eyes me, clearly surprised at my reaction. I recall the conversation Gannet had with me before I was thrown in prison. The story of Gannet's family farm being destroyed by Marcus and the royal family and anger rises up my arm, tingling with the blood leaving my body. How could Marcus speak about Gannet so nonchalantly as if he had nothing to do with his family's misfortune?

"I just reviewed footage," Marcus blurts out, misreading my discomfort. "All donation facilities have cameras."

My cheeks burn. What else did they see

"I swear I wasn't spying on you—not in a creepy way at least. I just wanted to make sure this experience was as normal as possible. Besides, you were always in the last cubicle so I couldn't really see you. I just saw the technician

21

regularly bring this in." Marcus grins and holds up checkers.

I stare at the game and a small lump forms in my throat. Gannet always took me to the same cubicle. He knew where the cameras were. He was always a step ahead of me. He'll come. Soon, I can feel it.

"Shall we?" He begins to open the box. "I think we have another twenty minutes at least. Do the games help distract you? Is it very painful?"

"I'm fine," I say, and I do not want to play that game with him.

He convinces me to play a game called chess. The game board looks identical to checkers and I place my free hand on my cheeks to hide their heat. Marcus notices though and questions me.

"I'm just not very good at these games," I say. "We didn't have games like these growing up. Only at the facilities." I don't tell him how old and ruined those games were. The facility games are falling apart and I wonder now— seeing these nice new Recipient game boards—if the facility ones are Recipient hand-me-downs.

Chess is much more complicated than checkers. Each piece has a different move, and I have to ask what each piece can do every single time. I don't like it. My head hurts, and I find myself rubbing at the tape over the needle much more than usual.

"Checkmate," he says and explains to me how the game is over.

I relax back into my chair, rubbing at my cold arm, happy that the difficult game is through. Really happy. I smile at my arm—at the tube returning the unneeded blood back to me. It sparkles.

"Marcus!" My voice is strained yet I already can't wipe

the smile from my face. All the smiling and all the colors. It's not fully in my system, and I'm panicking that I won't get to say anything before it's too late. My body, however, welcomes the drug like a long-lost friend that will relieve me of all my troubles. It will if I don't hurry up. "Alex didn't follow Gannet's orders. Get it out! Get it out!"

I lean forward in my seat, pointing at my arm and dangling the tube in the air. Marcus drops down to one knee in front of me.

"Are you sure?"

I look at him. His hair is gorgeous. *Gorgeously rotten*, I try to tell myself, but I can't deny how beautiful his hair is with all the many hues of yellow. How could I not have noticed these colors before? I could never paint his hair so perfectly. There probably aren't enough shades of yellow paint in the world to do this hair justice.

I don't answer him. I only smile, and my arm moves against my will. I stare wide-eyed at my hand. My head aches with the screaming inside—"Murderer! Recipient! Liar!"—but I'm not in control anymore. Soon my cold hand is caressing his soft, warm cheek. No stubble or hint of facial hair, just skin, hot and smooth. For a moment I give up the useless shouting inside and give in to the serum.

He doesn't relax under my touch. His face is hard and confused. Yet there's sadness there too. He wants this touch, I can tell he does, and so with a smile plastered on I let my hand run up the back of his head into his hair. Recipients always get what they want, right?

Inside I'm huddled in a corner wishing I could close my eyes and cut off my arms. My other hand reaches out to his neck, and I dip closer to him. My hands want to pull him closer, but all I want to do is rip myself away from him. He's betrayed me. He's a liar. I silently scream once more, but there's no one to hear me. There's nothing I can do.

When his hand slides down my forearm toward my hand, my smile falters. Yes, see? He's the enemy. Pull away!

"Aston? Something's wrong. What's going on?"

The door opens, and Alex is there, eyeing us questioningly as I caress the Recipient prince's hair. My smile broadens to see how she envies me.

"You didn't separate them," Marcus says sternly to her. "She's acting strange and breathing funny. Get it out now."

"I can't get it out," she says. "That's too much blood to take without putting any back. I thought for sure..."

Marcus looks again at me with sadness in his eyes. He pulls my hands away from him and puts them in my lap. I giggle.

"Yes. We mustn't in front of the technician." I give a tiny wink toward Marcus. The blue in his concerned eyes looks deeper and richer than I've ever seen it before.

"What's wrong with her?" Marcus whispers.

"I don't know. I've only dealt with Recipients. Is this not normal?"

The machine beeps, and Marcus tries to help the retrieval of the needle go faster, assisting Alex with bandaging. The smell of honey fills the room as some of my blood drips to the floor. Marcus dismisses Alex sternly, and I smile without effort as she leaves with a down-turned face. As soon as she's gone my arms find him again, but a small tear drips down my cheek. Make it stop, I whisper to myself.

Marcus helps me to the bed, and I flinch inside, noticing every touch. His hand on my waist and under my arms makes me groan internally. But all I do is smile at him and stroke his hair, which seems to make him more concerned. His hair is so hard and firm, like his arms. He apologizes at least three times as he tucks me in and instructs me to try and sleep it off. A chair scraping against the wooden floor close to my bed reminds me of Papa, but still I smile on. Papa says to sleep it off. I'm nothing but a dutiful daughter. Making him happy makes me happy.

"This is your destiny, little Ash tree," Grandma says a thousand times. Every year she brings me to this tree that is my namesake and says the same thing. This time the vivid details make Grandma look different somehow. Not younger but stronger, like a leader. "The answer to humanity lies here in this tree, and you have the key to its success. Keep it. Nourish it, and we all will survive."

# CHAPTER 3

My dreams turn more drab and frightening as the serum wears off and I start to wake. I'm standing on the tram with the outside world whizzing by faster and faster, yet I'm the only one struggling to keep my balance on the swaying car. My bent knees wobble, and I stumble a step or two while the gaunt woman in front of me only seems annoyed with my predicament.

The tram stops, and the doors slide open. I look around me at the angry passengers before I exit the tram. I wish I could help them. I quickly find my wooden cart. Its splintered handle digs into my palms but I can't pull away. Nothing is triumphant about the way I push my unknown merchandise. It's not like when I tried to bring my paintings to the marketplace so ignorantly full of hope. I had a naive bounce in my step then. Now each foot moves in front of me like they do not take orders from me, and I push the cart forward with a smile I cannot erase. The whole atmosphere around me screams that something is bloodcurdling wrong. The image of curdled blood makes my stomach lurch.

My heart pounds with my tramping feet like the drum to a death march. The market fills with shoppers. I park my cart and pull out a fine white teapot and place it on top. Three mismatching teacups join it in a half circle as if they are worshiping the tea kettle. One tea cup is old and worn with faded red roses circling the rim. Another has dark black stripes differing in width winding around the top and striping the curvy handle. The last cup is trimmed in gold, has a wheat pattern across the side, several chips, and a large crack down the center of the yellow image.

I don't look into the faces that approach my cart, I only pour as they gather around me. Blood flows out of the tea kettle. I am serving them my blood. My blood numbers pool in their cups. The white blood cells glisten like diamonds or melting sugar cubes floating in the tea. One hundred and fifty-seven of them to be exact, pumping through my body and out through the kettle, now a permanent extension of my arm.

My body grows weaker and weaker. I watch as my immune system leaves my body cup by cup. Soon my throat is on fire, and my head aches. Yet still they come with empty cups, and still I pour. My eyelids sting with fever, and my legs crumble beneath me, dropping me to the dirty broken road. With a lowered immune system, I'm now susceptible to the virus that kills Recipients. The virus that eats one's body from the inside out. The virus that, even if fought off, would be passed down to my children. Still, I don't turn anyone away, I only tip the kettle into their cups over and over again.

They crouch around me like vultures to a carcass, like I crouched by the Donor in the gutter so long ago, and the cups all wait patiently for their turn. The final cup seems to float in front of me, the wheat-colored one as yellow as Marcus's hair. I watch my dark-red blood stream slow, then thin, and then begin to drip. As my vision fades from red to black there is a deep, satisfying pride that warms me as my eyes close. I didn't spill a single drop.

It's dark again when I open my eyes. The whisperings and bumping are there again, but there's something *in* my room as well. Someone shifts in a seat, and I call out.

"Marcus?"

My next thought is Gannet. It has happened. He finally came to save me from the serum like he did last time. I sit up in bed, about to call his name. I'm still smiling when the lamp on the bedside table turns on, and I freeze. The chair Marcus was sitting in before now has someone else occupying it. Someone I've never met in my life, yet has stared back at me and spoken to me through port screens and magazines since I was a baby. His unnaturally yellow hair with almost glowing purple-white stripes on the sides makes the room light up even more. King Malloy's muck-colored blue eyes are more shocking than from his pictures. Piercing blue but with a hazel center. Everything inside of me has stopped. My heart, my blood, my organs—all my insides freeze yet my smile picks up in full force again. My mind knows it's from the serum, but my face doesn't care.

"Ah, Aston. Vazeto, is it?" His voice gives away his age. The rest of him has been through too much to lie as easily as his skin, which has been well-preserved. The truth is deep down—he's decrepit and ancient. The gravel in his voice is not the same as Grandma Bolgi's. It's more menacing and slimy. He pronounces my Hungarian name perfectly, though, and as I struggle to regain consciousness I let my eyes close and recall my grandmother's own sweet crackly voice as she once scolded me: "The way you New World young ones slaughter my Latzi's name—"Vah-zee-toe" with wide mouths. The Hungarian alphabet is longer because speaking is an art! Voh-seh-tu. When we move our mouths, we should put meaning in our words. Not slur them together with rapid stupidity and hope the listener can keep up."

"Why is she waking up already?" The old gargling voice returns, waking me again. I leave my eyes closed and listen to the harsh sound of his voice, like rocks in a blender. "You said this serum was better. Stronger."

A long pause makes my muscles tense with pain.

"She's not going to see what I want her to see at all, is she? What?"

As far as I can tell there is no other voice answering him. I open my eyes and stare at my lone visitor dumbly, wondering who he is talking to, why he is here, and how he knows Hungarian so well.

His worried face resolves into what is supposed to be a reassuring smile, although it is anything but comforting. "I'm glad you could join me," he says. "I hope you will forgive my intrusion with the serum."

My smile deepens on cue against my will, and inside I'm outraged. He made sure Alex got the donation wrong.

He gives a lopsided, lumpy old smile. "I take that as a yes, and I *am* sorry, but I couldn't risk your temper in our first-ever meeting. I have seen plenty of your outbursts over the past year. And let's not forget your quick, impromptu rescues. No, I needed the serum so you would listen. But don't worry, I will let you have your freedom soon enough. We all know the queen bee must be given enough freedom to rule in order for our plans to be executed."

My smile falters slightly. Partly because I have no clue

what he's talking about with queens or bees. The reference makes me think first of my recurring nightmare and second of Gannet, who was raised on a bee farm, and it instantly sobers me. But I'm also frozen in place, because it slowly sinks in that he seems to know everything about me. I remember the cameras Marcus spoke of but Gannet and the resistance kept our secrets safe. How much could he really know?

The King gives me a wrinkly wink that makes my stomach burn with anger and disgust. Was he calling *me* a queen bee? What does that mean? Does this have something to do with Gannet's family? My mouth becomes somewhat under my control, and I take advantage of this moment, unsure how long it will last. Is the serum already wearing off?

"Are you a beekeeper?" I internally cringe. Possibly my only moment free of the serum and that's what I ask?

His chuckle is unnerving, and right before the serum takes over completely, I shiver, then smile.

"You could say that, yes. I'm a keeper of many things, actually. Bees, secrets, power." He pauses. "People. But what I need to know now is about someone named Bolglarka."

I'm for once grateful my smile is unmovable. Without fidgeting, I stare right at his slush-gray eyes, not really blue, not exactly brown, just a mixture of colors like melting dirty snow. Bolglarka? Grandma Bolgi's wrinkled smile fills my vision. If he knows everything else about me, why doesn't he know this as well?

"I have reason to believe she is your grandmother."

So he does already know the connection. My smile finally falls slightly from the corners of my mouth, and my cheeks enjoy the rest.

"Yet even with all our spying and sleuthing, we can't seem to find her."

Grandma Bolgi's voice over the phone right before I was captured, right after I was informed that she was the leader of the resistance, comes to mind. "Tell them nothing," she said. I press my lips into as thin a line as my fighting smile will let me. I feel control coming over me again. I even muster a small scowl and take my chances trying to change the subject.

"Why did you let your grandson take on this foolish experiment?" I say. "You know it has nothing to do with being in my presence that's saved him, it's just my numbers that make him well."

Adakin looks at his watch and then smiles as if he is appreciating something. He looks back up at me with astonishment as he leans forward. I want to hide under my covers. "Amazing," he whispers. "You've only had the serum in you for a few hours..."

He doesn't finish his sentence, just continues to analyze my eyes and face. For being "amazing," he doesn't seem all too pleased with me. His sigh is ragged and slightly panicked as he crosses his arms and leans back into his chair. "Yes, I admit my grandson is delusional to think this will succeed. But his idea gave me one of my own. He inspired me to see you as more than just bait for your grandmother. Thanks to him, the dear boy, I was able to see your value. Perhaps you could lead me right to your grandmother and accomplish a few other tasks before everything goes back to normal." He seems to notice me shifting in the bed, leaning closer to him with yearning. "Yes, Aston. You could go back and live with your family. Your sweet Torrin would have you again."

My lip curls; he knows about my brother and how I

treasure him.

"All would be right, and we would all have what we want."

I try to act like that's not my one true desire when I answer him. "But when it's Lazuli's turn to play Donor, Marcus will be exposed to the virus, and without my antibodies... It's just, Lazuli's numbers are so low. It's too risky. We both know without the right antibody it doesn't matter what he does socially or emotionally. He will be exposed and won't have my blood to fight off anything." I can't tell if it's the serum speaking or if it's real care and concern that rips at my chest. I rest my hand there to calm it nonetheless.

Adakin shrugs as he unfolds his arms and sits up as straight as his curved back will allow. "There are casualties in every experiment."

"But he's your grandson."

"And she's your grandmother. How could she keep so much from you?"

"My grandmother loves me. She would do anything to save me."

Adakin leans forward, almost standing, and puts his hands on the bed, inching closer to my face. I lean back, but the smell of honey overtakes my senses and I smile with such force that it makes my eyes squint. Up close I can see Adakin's broken blood vessels webbing against his cheeks like bruises. "Aston, I know things about your grandmother that wouldn't just shock you, they would horrify you. Give you nightmares. She isn't here to save you now, and she probably never will be." His ghostly crackling whisper sends a chill down my back and goosebumps cover my arms. He's wrong. He has to be. She will send Gannet. He will come, won't he?

He smiles, happy with the effect he's caused and happy about something else as well. "So fascinating." He looks into my eyes then stands tall and towering. Putting his hands behind his back, he speaks again as if nothing freaky just happened. "I am glad you're staying with us, Aston. I look forward to getting to know you better. In the meantime, think about your grandmother and what you really owe her. I could give you more than she ever could. She is invaluable to the success of both our people. We need to find her."

As soon as he is done speaking, the light switches off without a sound, as if it read his mind. I wait for the sound of the door opening and closing to mark his exit, but it never comes. My body sinks into the covers as one tense mass while I smile into the dark. Every muscle aches with rigidness. A bump behind my bed lets me know the ghost in the wall is back. Was this person listening the whole time? I hear the whispers clear as day now.

"Someone's in more trouble than you this time, Lecky. Now move your butt, you dirty fuzzbucket." Another bump makes me wonder about this poor Lecky fellow. Did he get kicked? Why doesn't he ever speak? Thinking about the boys in the wall is easier than thinking about my own troubles.

I don't know how long I lie here waiting for Adakin to leave, but every inch of me hurts, and my mind is nowhere near sleep. My eyes are still open, my aching smile still plastered to my face, when a faded yellow glow starts to take over the room. The door opens and Janice tiptoes in, making her way to the curtains. Just as she's about to yank them open, I pull my hands to my dry eyes to rub and ready them for the light.

She approaches my bed, and I remember the things

Marcus said about her. Did she really kill her husband? She seems so nice. Her small round face and kind eyes don't seem like the murderous type. Though I didn't ever suspect Marcus either, and he murdered fifteen power plant workers. Perhaps I'm not a good judge of character.

"Would you like your breakfast now, miss? I could ring for it to come right away if you would like." Janice's hair is in an up-do, making her face look more round than normal. It's not round in an overweight sort of way but a pleasant, young sort of way. Like she never grew into her body.

"No, thank you. I'm not very hungry." I smile, hopefully my last smile, and my face relaxes for a moment. "But I would like to change clothes. Were you ever able to find any pants?"

She shakes her head. "I'll keep looking. Let's step into the bath again. Freshen up a bit, eh? You look like you didn't sleep a wink last night. Did the donations drain you a bit too much yesterday?"

She helps me out of the covers, and I only smile a weak, pitiful smile in reply. She has no idea. We step into the bright lights of the large bathroom bigger than my bedroom back home. Eyeing the bathtub skeptically, I look at Janice readying a bath towel and robe. Hopefully she didn't drown her husband to death. Why would they put a convicted murderer as caretaker of their invaluable Donor?

She turns a knob above the bath, and even though I hear the sounds of water, and every now and then catch reflections along the white ceramic tub that look like water, nothing is actually coming out of the faucet. I turn to Janice. She smiles at me. Something's different. The reflections are red. I recall the red lights that tortured a young girl named Gloria in the streets. What does Janice plan to do to me?

I speak before I think better of it. "The head nurse says you murdered your husband."

Janice's smile is erased as quickly as the light turned off last night when Adakin Malloy left. It must be true. There is guilt and torment written across the frown lines of her face.

"It is what I was convicted of, yes."

"Is it true?"

Her green eyes lock with mine, and we are at a standoff. As my mind clears, and I have more control over my thoughts and actions, I realize I don't want it to be true. I don't know exactly why, but I want to like Janice. Maybe I'm just missing Papa too much. Perhaps I am seeing too much of him in her because I want to. But she's a Recipient; they're takers only. My papa was the kindest, most giving person I've ever known. How could I see him in a Recipient?

"He was very sick, miss." Her soft whisper is laced with emotion.

"Did you kill him?"

"His donations weren't doing anything." A tear silently slips down her cheek and her eyes, though still on me, see something else. Someone else. "His skin was covered in bruises, and he stank something awful. We spent everything we had at the auctions for him. I couldn't afford to try again."

Couldn't afford it? The idea of a Recipient unable to afford anything doesn't make sense to me. As I think back on the auctions there were, of course, more wealthy Recipients who were bidding on the highest numbered Donors, but I assumed *everyone* was bidding at *some* scale. I never fathomed the idea that some couldn't afford to bid at all.

Janice lowers her head and stares at her hands. Tears drip past them to the ground. "I stopped giving him his donations. And he passed within the week."

A war rages within me, but I'm free of the serum now, aren't I? I have the urge to reach out and hug this woman. To embrace her, touch her in some way. But she's a Recipient. She stopped giving donations, which in our land means those Donors kept their blood, lived healthier and a little longer. But her husband died because of it. It could easily be a sob story played across our screens back home about how this family suffered because they didn't make it to the auctions in time. I teeter in place, not knowing which side to be on. If I disagree with Recipients, does that mean I don't value the Donor lives she saved? But how can I call her a murderer for trying to keep her loved one from suffering any longer?

It has to be the system's fault. They divide us, they pit us against each other until we are too confused to make sense of any of it. Our system is the murderer, not this woman. But I still don't know what the difference is. She's a Recipient yet just got a taste of their own laws. Why should I feel pity for her just because she's had a taste of what it's like for every Donor family out there? Recipients distort everything. I stand a little taller in front of this woman. She's still a Recipient.

She sniffs in the silent bathroom; the sound echoes. It reminds me of my own father's tears. My shoulders fall a little. He would comfort an innocent person no matter their kind. He always told me the test of our true nature would come when we were on our own without anyone to answer to. I don't have to be her judge. I can still show kindness.

"I'm so sorry, Janice." I put out my hand and step forward, giving her shoulder a squeeze.

Wiping her face with the back of her hand, she gives a weak, red-faced smile.

"It's okay, miss. He's not hurting anymore. And I got the

chance of meeting you. I wouldn't change anything about what I did, really." A moment of camaraderie passes. She *is* like my papa, I decide. She may be a Recipient, but she is also compassionate and strong.

"Off with your clothes and into the tub with you now, miss."

I look down at the empty tub again.

"But Janice, there's nothing in it."

She follows my gaze and then gives a giggle. With a touch of the wall by the faucet, glowing red bubbles appear like a red bubble bath. I step back from the odd electronic-looking display of a bathtub.

"Don't look so scared. It's the same bubbles that cleansed you your first night here."

"I must not have been completely coherent then, because I remember a full bath of hot water kissing my skin. This looks like it will torture me."

"We don't waste water anymore. The Lakes are too precious to waste on cleaning dirt off us. Now we use laser soap. It works similarly to how we bury our dead. The lasers scan the skin for any dirt or foreign objects then disintegrates them into the air. The tech has improved over the years so now it feels just like a normal bath. The heat of the lasers is better than any hot tub I've been in, and I'm old enough to remember them." She says the last part with a wink that makes me shiver, remembering Adakin's wink in the night.

"Go on. Step in."

I put my hand through the "bubbles" and their warmth tingles as I glide through them. How do they feel wet? I remove my hand and hold it up to my face. It looks the same. I make a fist, moving my fingers against my palm. It's still dry.

"Might want to remove your clothes first. It doesn't feel quite the same with them on." She giggles again.

I remove the blue dress and underclothes awkwardly, still not used to a maid being with me at all times. One foot goes in and then another. I slowly lower myself into the red glowing tub, and it is amazing. I don't understand how the Recipients have done it, but right now I'm impressed with them. How they can make this and not find the vaccine or cure for themselves is unbelievable. I close my eyes, and I smile on purpose now—a gentle, happy smile that doesn't hurt my face so much.

The smell of lavender fills the room again, but this time I can tell it doesn't come from the bath but the walls somehow. I sigh and dip further into the tub, letting my neck rest on the edge.

Janice laughs harder. "I think you're not scared of this bath anymore. What did you think it was going to do to you?"

"I've seen red lasers do worse things than clean you."

The room is silent before she whispers into it, "Aye. As have I, miss. As have I."

A rapid knock breaks out through the bathroom, and I sit up with a jolt. Thankfully, there is no water to slosh out onto the floor.

The door opens, and I get a glimpse of yellow hair that sets my heart racing. Has the late night unwelcome visitor returned already? My leader, ruler, and now interrogator it seems. Janice runs to block the door, yelling as she moves.

My breath is a prisoner caged in my throat as I'm locked in this strange place. The bubbles sting as I grow tense, and I can no longer smell the lavender.

# CHAPTER 4

"**M**aster Marcus, stop right where you are! The lady is in the bath."

My heart races for a different reason now as he stops in place, and I throw my hand across my bare chest since there's technically nothing but lasers covering me.

"Aston?" Marcus's deep, panicked voice rings through the tiled room. It cracks at the end and wavers with a hint of emotion. What is he so worried about? Does he know how his grandfather interrogated me last night? He sounds like someone just told him I'd been murdered.

Janice is at the door with her hand on the handle, but she doesn't close it. Marcus's foot is in the way.

"She's not in her room and the donation made her so... and I heard the King was..." Marcus pauses.

I sit and wait for what he could possibly say next. Why is he acting so strange?

"Let me hear her then, maid," he says roughly, giving up quickly on my plea for treating Janice humanely and calling her by her real name instead of her station. His voice is winded and frightened. "Aston?" he calls out again. "You there? Are you okay?"

"Yes, Marcus. I'm here." I roll my eyes, feeling stupid. "Where else would I be?" I lay the irritation thick on those words. It gains a tense sort of chuckle from the doorway, and he removes his foot. Janice does not close the door all the way.

"Right," he says. "Good point. I... I have breakfast. I'll just be here when you're done." His words are separated by heavy, relieved sighs. What did he think happened? Or rather, what did his grandfather tell him happened? Just the thought of the King makes me shiver in the fake bathtub.

"Okay," I say, rolling my eyes again. How awkward this all is. I guess I should at least be grateful there aren't uncomfortable sounds of me moving or dripping water mixed into the conversation. With lasers for a bath, my skin feels dry as soon as I leave the "water."

Janice holds the door and looks at me. She bugs her eyes and waves her hand toward the person behind the door. What does she want from me? I shrug my naked shoulders and shake my head.

Janice hisses with a hand around her mouth for discretion. "He just brought you food. Don't you know who he is?"

I wish I could splash dramatically and make a scene. I want to tell her that, in fact, for six months I did not know who he was. I want to tell her how, even though I now know, I still don't give a fig about who he is.

Marcus shifts his weight by the door, and Janice waves her arms at me again.

"Thank you," I grumble and try flicking at the bubbles in front of me.

Janice drops her hands by her sides and looks at me like a disappointed mother, but clearly that is what she was wanting me to say to the spoiled Recipient prince who is a true murderer but has the audacity to label Janice one.

Marcus makes a humph sound, and with that, the door is finally closed.

I have never been so self-conscious about the process of getting dressed. As I pull the liquid silk dress over my head, I try not to recall the last time I dressed in front of him when he escaped into my dressing room, but it's no good. I stare at myself in the giant bathroom mirror and his pacing in my room feels too close. Thick walls separate us this time, and I try to shake the memory from my head over and over again. There's something more intimate and unnerving about dressing near him this time. This time we are in his territory. In his very home even. Before he was just a sick and pesky Donor, but I know better now. I must repaint every memory with the image of who he really is. Sick, but not a Donor. Pesky, but not poor. Kind, but not genuine.

"How is my hair still wet if it's just lasers?" I ask Janice.

She removes the towel from my hair and brings out a comb. "I don't know everything about how the tech works, I just know it does."

Once my hair is slicked back, still stringy and wet, I step out of the bathroom. Marcus is looking through the window with his hands clasped behind his back. There is a lovely bouquet of flowers on the table next to the tray of food. Flowers like I've never seen before.

"The flowers here are different." I try to sound as nonchalant as possible.

"Yes." He turns to the table and away from me like I was hoping he would. "It was my mother's doing. She specialized in hybrid flowers that are now commonplace around Bloomfield."

"They're beautiful."

Marcus turns back toward me. His eyes are luminous and filled with mixed emotions like the strange combinations of Recipient flowers that can't make up their mind if they're a rose or a daisy. I grimace, remembering how I smiled at him. How I touched him. Is he remembering that now too?

I step back. "I'm sorry about yesterday," I say with clenched teeth.

"No. I'm sorry. I'll look for another technician to do the job somehow. I had no idea that was going to happen, but I can see why you need it done a different way now. As much as I loved your..." I make the mistake of looking at him when he stops talking. The longing on his face looks almost as tormented as I feel. "As much as I loved you near me, it felt wrong."

My heart skips at his mention of us near each other, and I want to strangle my own heart with my own two hands.

Marcus steps closer, and it surprises me that I don't instinctively step away from him.

"Find a new technician somehow?" I ask. "Do you not have many Recipient technicians?"

"None that are brave enough to take on this task is more like. They are all too afraid to be in the company of a Donor."

Too afraid to get sick, I'm sure. When Janice steps into the room to excuse herself for being late, I look at her differently. She is also risking much by being here. I thank her warmly, and when the door shuts behind her I turn to Marcus.

"My maid. Was she forced to be my caretaker because of her crimes against her husband?"

"No. She volunteered."

"Why would she do that?" There's something comforting about Janice *wanting* to be here, but I'll admit it also makes me very suspicious.

Marcus shrugs. We sit on the sofa on the far wall of my room and continue to have a very boring formal conversation about flowers. Marcus knows the name of every one of them and their classification. My interest only piques when he mentions the bees.

"We have many beehives and beekeepers across Bloomfield and all Recipient towns, really. It's the key to reintroducing a new species of plant, of course."

I make a humming sound as I think about what to say. "So are only Recipients beekeepers?" I remember Gannet telling me before I was captured that his family had been beekeepers in South Dakota before they were slaughtered for not following Recipient orders.

"No, we had a Donor section that were beekeepers as well. But it was very poorly managed and shut down not too many years ago." He eyes me now, and it makes me wonder if there is more to the story than what he is telling me. It makes me aware of how close I have scooted to him, and I lean away.

"You see, Aston"—he clasps his hands as he leans forward, elbows on his knees—"I was raised with the belief that Donors couldn't carry out such intricate orders. That they were only good for one thing." He stares down at his twiddling thumbs.

I know what the one thing he is referring to is. Does his ignorance change anything though? I'm telling myself it does, but I can't logically forget about the lives his ignorance took, the homes which his actions, no matter how innocent he thinks, destroyed.

Janice enters with a new tray and our uncomfortable silence is broken. She already has the old tray in hand as we move from the sofa.

"Lunch is served. Master Marcus, your grandfather would like to see you in his study."

"But I—"

"I'm instructed to take no refusal, and your lunch is with him."

This surprises me since there still looks like enough lunch on the new tray for three people. Marcus turns to me as if he is thinking about kissing my hand again or hugging goodbye. I fold my arms much too quickly and he frowns. There may have been a day I enjoyed those old gestures from my contraband books, but now is not one of them. I just want him to go. I walk toward the table without a word and pick up one of the small sandwiches. Marcus walks through the doorway and Janice follows.

"Janice, there's enough food here to feed an army," I say. "Won't you stay and eat with me?"

Her hesitation makes me fidget, and then I recall the risk Marcus made me aware of. The danger being in my presence causes her. How could I so quickly forget who she is and what I am capable of?

"I'm sorry I wasn't thinking. I don't want to put you in danger."

She looks back at the door as I speak but then shuts it and sets the empty breakfast tray back on the nightstand, and I let my words trail off into a smile.

"Well, you are right about that food," she says. "I don't know why cook sends so much. It just gets thrown away, and I know plenty in this town that would donate themselves to get ahold of some of this food." She flicks her eyes up at me with shock on her face. "Sorry, miss. I didn't mean—"

It's my turn to laugh, seeing how worried she is that she has offended me. "It's okay, Janice. And call me Aston. I insist."

"Thank you, mi— Thank you, Aston."

We both sit and grab the little sandwiches that have different colored spreads in them. One is orange and tastes like cheese though is creamier than anything I've ever had.

"You mention Recipients that are poor. But I thought all Recipients were wealthy. How do they survive, Janice? Why don't they have money?"

As she nibbles at her sandwich, she looks up from beneath her light-brown eyebrows. "There are plenty of poor, all right. Maybe not the kind of poor I hear is in your part of the world, but poor enough to hurt. Maybe like in the middle. Not quite poor, not quite rich."

"But how?"

"Wealth in royalty is inherited. But still some Recipients make bad choices with it." She draws circles in the air with her carrot as she speaks. "Some Recipients need more donations than others or some squander it on"—she squirms in her seat and then takes a crunching bite of the carrot before finishing her sentence—"unspeakable actions."

"Oh." I sit up straight and fidget with my bandage. "You mean like—"

"When I say unspeakable, it's because"—Janice's face turns bright red—"I don't wish to speak of it."

"Yes, of course." It's my turn to blush, and I apologize as she continues.

"There are also those who earn their money, the tradesmen who are descendants of Recipients who once found favor in the royal class. They pay rent to the estate their family belongs to. And then there's the ruling class which taxes the rich and bans the enemies."

"Enemies? I don't understand."

"We have strict rules in this territory. Those who go against the rules, or even so much as offend a royalty or ruling class, can be fined and punished. The likes of me, for instance. My husband was the fifth son of a Recipient earl, and with only two brothers left living, we would have made our way into some fortune eventually, if my George hadn't taken ill. He and his brothers were never close. Mark didn't even need the inheritance. He married the daughter of a viscount who had already come into her inheritance. But that's another story. We were content with the land he inherited and had enough money from his apprenticeship with the ambassador. Oh, George had great plans, but see, we were in the middle. Not royalty rich but not poor either. We were happy."

Janice takes a roll and holds it tenderly in her hands as if she made it herself. "When his regular donations stopped working, we spent everything at the auctions. But when that wasn't a match either, it became a race between brothers. If George could just outlive them, perhaps we could afford to go to auctions again. But in the end, I had no money left to defend myself in court after he died. And to make matters worse, I..." She looks at the roll angrily now and breaks it apart piece by piece, making a mess on her apron. A wisp of hair escapes her bonnet, and she curls it around her ear.

Without any pushing or prodding, she lifts her chin and continues. "I offended a duke while on trial. I was angry and had just lost my husband. I called *them* the murderers for not protecting my George. I lost my title, any claim to

have a mouse problem. She must be lying to me. "Cats that can talk?" I push.

"Perhaps the cats are what you heard. I hear they're causing quite a nuisance in the laundry rooms. Ghastly moaning sounds at night have scared Norman a great deal." She lets out an unladylike laugh. "Though hearing Norman scream like a girl is a fun trick. We don't get much entertainment around here." She laughs again and steps further into the hallway. "But with the telecom, these walls literally do talk. Good day, miss."

I watch her retreat down the hallway. It feels so normal all of a sudden. Standing at my bedroom door as if I could just waltz around the mansion, I almost forget I am a prisoner. I wonder where Lazuli's room is and how secure these grounds are. I reach my hand toward Janice, wishing she could take me with her. Out of the corner of my eye there's a familiar reflection of red. I don't register it fast enough, and as my fingers pass the threshold, an invisible wall of fire hits them. A wave of pain zings up my arm. I yank my arm back with a sharp gasp. I nurse my fingers and breathe heavily. Very much a prisoner.

Janice stops at the end of the hallway and looks back before rounding the corner. The pain starts to subside, and I think about the things Janice said. I know I heard a voice, not a cat, but why would she lie about that? At least she confirmed my suspicion that there are paths inside the walls. Now to find out who's in them.

# CHAPTER 5

It's been three weeks now since I first awoke in Bloomfield, locked up in this room like the prisoner that I am. I wonder if Adakin knows about my attempt to leave the room. I haven't dared try again.

Marcus is sitting in my room like he has been every day. I gave up trying to get rid of him or trying to ignore him. Other than Janice, he's the only visitor I get, and boredom can only feel heroic and rebellious for so long. We're playing the card game I am good at: gin rummy. I yawn as I lay out a run that empties my hand. We're on the floor for some reason, and I arch my back against the bed for a nice stretch.

Marcus throws down his cards. He is sprawled on his side, supporting his head with his hand. "Why don't you ever want to play checkers?"

"Hm?" I try to ignore his question by bending forward to gather and shuffle the cards the way he has taught me.

Marcus props himself up on his elbow, clasping his hands near his chest and crossing his ankles. "We've played every game we own except checkers. Why not checkers?"

He eyes the box across the room, and before I can say anything, he hoists himself up and walks toward it.

With cards in hand, I stand but quickly fall back onto the bed. My back aches from sitting crouched on the floor. "I don't know, Marcus. I'm just so sick of games. I want to do something else. I have never felt more like a lab rat, and I'm a Donor so that's saying something."

"Okay." He puts the checkers game back on the table. "What do you want to do then? What would you do if you were back in New Livonia?"

The question catches me off-guard. I try to imagine myself lying on my hard, hand-me-down bed back home instead of this giant white cloud of a bed. A strange hollow feeling gnaws at my gut. I haven't thought about home all week and realize there is a small part of me that's subconsciously enjoying the food and comforts of Recipient life. I feel too guilty to miss home now. Like it isn't genuine at all now that I've been forced to think about it. I pull my knees up, and the sleek fabric balloons away from me like a parachute. My stomach ripples in panic as I remember I'm in a dress. I quickly sweep the fabric under my knees. "Well, for starters, I wouldn't be wearing this. I would have jeans I could move around in." He steps closer to the side of the bed as he listens to me. Looking at the polished table by the bed, I picture my scratched up, unpolished nightstand at home and think of my treasured novels hidden in horrible textbooks. "I'd read if I were back home."

"You like books?"

"Some." I won't say which ones for fear of who's listening. The look on Janice's face that day when a voice came through the room right as she confessed that she has something to gain by being here has kept me on guard.

"Come on then." Marcus grabs my hand and pulls me

off the bed. He turns without looking back and without letting go of my hand.

"Marcus—"

He doesn't stop when he reaches the door. I pull against him and say his name again. Doesn't he know it will electrocute me to go through this door? He doesn't seem to notice my anxiety and pulls me through. I wince, bracing myself for the shock, but when no pain comes and Marcus is still moving excitedly, dragging me with him, I turn back, looking at the open door growing smaller by the second. I laugh at the idea of being free from my cage without a bruise or burn to show for it. My room looks so dark and brown amidst these white halls with nothing surrounding it. I wonder how someone would get into those walls.

"Where is Lazuli's room?" I feel bad at how long it has taken me to ask this question. Some days I forget she's here at all.

Marcus frowns and shows his first hint of worry. Does he think I will run away and try to find her?

"On the other side of the house."

We turn the corner and the walls are no longer white here. They are a deep mahogany wood like my bedroom. The floor is no longer white tile but full of red lush carpet. On the opposite side of the red carpet is an identical white hallway. As we fly past I can only assume at the end is a matching brown door and bedroom for another Donor girl. Lazuli. Marcus pulls me down the carpeted hallway, and it quickly turns into a large balcony with a dark wooden banister opening with a high vaulted ceiling. It reminds me of the ambassador's mansion with the giant chandelier ahead. On either side of the balcony are two sets of stairs larger than the one at the ambassador's ball.

"Down there is my bedroom." He gives me a wicked

grin that I can't interpret. I turn my head in the direction he points. Behind us, the hallway stretches out like a long red tongue. The two white prisoner hallways cast lopsided glows against the red carpet. At the end is a giant wooden door with gold trim and ornate carvings. I can't make out what the carvings are of. An animal maybe? A beehive?

The excitement of leaving the room blinds me to how he holds my hand. He tugs on me again like a little kid pulling me along to show something off. I match his pace as he skips down the stairs and rounds the banister going the opposite direction of the stairs. This long marble hallway is lined with doors. They're all so identical I don't know how anyone could keep them straight.

"These are the guest rooms," he tells me. "For visiting Recipients right before Auctions when my grandfather holds parties."

At the end of the hall is a double door, grand and beautiful, with carved wooden designs on the trim. These are definitely beehives. When he opens it, I smell them first. Just as I would recognize Grandma Bolgi from her sweet scent of mints and Papa's of gasoline and orange soap, I recognize this smell like another family member I miss. Books. The lovely, dusty wood smell of books. I want to close my eyes and enjoy the feeling of deja vu, of the comfort and familiarity it gives me, but I also don't want to miss a thing. There are rows and rows of them. As he opens the door wider, my mouth drops more as shelves tower to the ceiling and go deeper into the room than I can see.

"A library," I say, astounded, unable to look at him or register that his hand is squeezing mine.

"Who's your favorite author?" he asks.

I look at him now. He is as giddy as a Recipient on donation day, and the fact that this is what makes him so makes me happier than serum. But can I trust him? Can I tell him of my dearest friends that died long before our world, yet somehow knew everything we would miss and be without? These friends who have been banned by his grandfather and other Recipient authorities?

"You probably wouldn't have them," I say, and turn to admire the room once more. "But this is still so wonderful."

"I bet we do. What, are they banned?"

He says it so nonchalantly my smile drops, and I eye him critically.

"Aston, you forget where you are." He smiles smugly. "This is the very place where those who wrote up the bans studied the books. But we wouldn't just burn them. Now, who is it?" He drops his face lower to mine, and I can smell that soap smell once more, only now it makes sense why. He is a clean Recipient, not a sick, dirty Donor. "And later you will have to tell me how you found them and kept them secret." Another wink makes me shiver. Will I ever be able to look at a wink quite the same way?

"Austen," I croak and then gain my wits after clearing my throat. "I only know the name Austen."

"That's an easy one," he says as he pulls me along. "*Sense and Sensibility*? Or *Pride and Prejudice*?"

At first I think he's being rude. I am not prideful, and he's the one who has struggled with prejudice over a poor Donor nation, but then he puts in front of me a beautiful hard copy of a book. The title reads *Pride and Prejudice* and the author along the bottom is "Jane Austen."

I finally take my hand from his to cradle this precious book. "Jane," I whisper. It's as if I'm being united with a secret pen pal that kept me alive through the worst times imaginable. I want to hug this book and cry. Hide in a corner and devour it all over again. Of all the things to tear up about, a book is what sends me overboard?

"Oh, Aston." Marcus cups my chin and even he can't ruin this moment with my dear Jane. I love the name and want to say it over and over again. Jane, Jane, glorious Jane, how did you do it? How did you survive a money worshiping male-run society and still give women hope through something as silly as love?

"There are more written by her," Marcus says in a hushed voice as if realizing the reverence this moment deserves.

"More?"

He pulls out three other books all with Jane's name on them. I hug each one of them until my arms are full and heavy.

"Pick one and you can take it to your room to read. In fact, I will make it so you may come here whenever you wish, if you would like?"

"Like?" I'm glad these books are positioned between us, for I feel as if I could kiss him. "I would like that very much. But pick one? I could no sooner pick a favorite flower here in Bloomfield. How do I make such a choice?"

He grabs one from the pile titled *Northanger Abbey*. "I believe this was the first of her published works."

"Then I shall start from the beginning," I say, trying to mimic Janice's English accent. I don't know why, it just sounded like something Janice would say. He laughs and helps me put the others back.

We roam the library for an hour more, and I crack open Austen's book gently every now and then, impatiently peeking at what lies in store. The bookshelves reach the vaulted ceiling and have ladders that hover inches off the ground like maglevs leaned up against the top of the shelf.

Row after row—the number of books is unfathomable. There are rooms to study in with tables and chairs and rooms with books just about maps.

We reach a far corner with a large door. On it, a golden template reads simply "Office."

"What is that?" I point. "Whose office is it?" I've so quickly grown accustomed to roaming freely, forgetting all about the painful experience with my door. I step up to it and place my hand on the handle before getting an answer. A shock pulses up my arm. This time it's enough to make me tremor, and I grunt at the effort to jerk my hand off the source of electricity.

"Sorry," Marcus says as he runs up to me. He laughs when he looks at me. "Your blood doesn't have clearance for that room." Blood-activated doorknobs? "Actually, none of us do. That's Grandfather's private office."

I look at the door as I rub my hand. At first glance, it looks just like a regular door. As I study it now however, while nursing my throbbing fingers, I notice a sort of blurry aura around the handle. Like a mirage. Upon further investigation, a red glow from under the door clearly indicates lasers, and I doubt those are meant for cleaning.

"Are you fond of history? Our collection of historical accounts is much more extensive than any other library." Marcus walks away, and I move to follow him though my eyes don't fall away from the door quite yet.

I squeeze my numb hand as I finally peel my eyes off the dark wooden door. I pause a moment, however, as something catches my eye. There's a shimmer to the wood that reminds me of my walls. I glance at the surrounding walls and shelves of the library. Their wood seems darker and more solid. Old, even. Looking back at the door, I find that glimmer again as if the wood is dancing so quickly it's almost unnoticeable. It's a white screen underneath, I realize. Programmed to look like wood just like the walls in my room.

"Did you know," Marcus drones on, "that the last germ war was planned by one woman alone?"

His news brings my full attention. He smiles at my interest.

"I think her name was Eve or something like that, but the war began because of her studies and intricate maneuvers. She was part of an organization that called themselves IPC."

"What does that stand for?" I ask.

"I don't know, but I do know just the book to ask."

Before we round the corner of a far-off bookcase, I look back again at the guarded door. What behind that door is so secret that it requires so much security? It has more security than my own room. I've got to find out.

The sun is setting when we leave the library, making long shadows loom across the shelves of books. With my arms full of new friends and gateways to information, I silently whisper a goodbye to my friends on the shelves as Marcus closes the doors.

Walking down the long marble hallway with the click of our heels echoing in the silence, I find myself for the first time feeling somewhat safe. Maybe it's learning the new boundaries of this place. Like a child learning that stoves can burn and dogs can bite, I now know where to avoid and that the pain isn't as bad as I thought it would be. The feeling is still a surprise. I'm deep in thought about what exactly it means to feel safe around Marcus again when he steps past the stairs. Puzzled, I stop walking and he spins in front of me.

"You said you like our flowers. How would you like to see them up close?"

"This is turning out to be a bit more like a date."

He lifts one side of his mouth into a sly, crooked grin. "Are you complaining?"

I shift the books in hand so as to pick at the healing scar on the inside of my elbow. "Not at all *Master* Marcus," I say sarcastically, but he doesn't even seem to notice. Figures. "Merely pointing it out."

"Freedom is freedom," he says flippantly.

"I wouldn't call this freedom, to finally leave my bedroom." I'm back to scowling at him, which erases his smile. It really is a shame, he has such a lovely smile, but he is a little too quick to misunderstand my situation.

Irritated by his mocking of my imprisonment, I don't notice how we weave through the mansion and make it to a set of three French doors. Instead, I'm thinking about Gannet. Do they have ways of watching the palace? Will they be able to see when I am free of its walls and be able to snatch me up? Outside the doors is a patio with white ornate tables and chairs and beyond that is the garden that I can see from my bedroom window. At first, I'm checking the corners for surveillance before I remember it's in the very walls. I look to the sky for any signs of those coming to save me.

We step off the stone patio, and the strong fruity smell of pollen distracts me, embraces me. Fresh ground and musky dew—it's been so long since I've been in their company. Roses are the only flowers I recognize. The birds all sing their evening chirps as the setting sun gives a golden luster to the world. We step out from under the canopy of the patio, and Marcus points to a blue flower bush.

"Hydrangea lily," he says.

I don't know flowers well, but I can still appreciate the beauty of something so foreign to me. The blue flowers are large, and some of the petals are rounded, while some are pointed. Each flower has a long, yellow stick coming from the middle, something Marcus calls a stamen, and together they make a giant snowball of blue and yellow. Leaning closer, I can smell the strong, honeyed scent mixed with the thought of a tropical forest. This is the smell that fills the garden. Strong and beautiful.

We walk through pathways and over small bridges placed across a little creek that runs through the garden. We admire each plant in solitude, every now and then bumping hands, but nothing more. It's a Garden of Eden of sorts. Full of possibilities but strictly limiting at the same time. The departing sun gives the sky a range of dark and light blues and lights slowly turn on across the garden and within the creek, making a glowing river wind through the ground like an electric eel. A cool breeze toys with my hair and the smooth fabric of the dress is chilly against my skin. I rub my arms as I look into a large tree; its budding branches sway in the wind. Three spotlights circle its trunk, lighting up the base of the tree and casting shadows within its leaves.

The tree reminds me of a time in my youth visiting Grandma Bolgi in Canton. She always took me to the same tree by a swing set and told me the same thing each time. Hugging me close, she rested a hand on the tree and said, "I am sure you are the one that needs to know this, Aston. You are our little ash tree, strong and tall and important. Never forget that." Always different variations of the same sentiment. I am just like the ash tree. I am the ash tree, always remember the ash tree. I don't know much about trees.

Perhaps this one isn't even an ash, but something about its girth and height makes me think of Grandma. Of Bolglarka with evidently so many secrets. What will I tell Adakin Malloy when he returns? I would be a fool to think he will give up on something so easily. I will see him again. I'm sure of it.

As I contemplate Grandma Bolgi more, I realize visiting her was never visiting a home. She always met me at the tram station in Canton, took me to a park or a friend of hers for lunch. Now that I know what she is, perhaps those friends were early resistance leaders. But the day always ended with the same park with the same old tree swing. I realize now I have no idea where Grandma Bolgi lives. We house-jumped four times just in my lifetime, a common thing for donors since we could never own property. We just stole someone else's if left vacant. Grandma Bolgi mostly visited us and I think I just assumed she was always in between homes.

Marcus approaches and puts an arm around me. I step away from his side embrace.

"Scars knows what you must think of me, Aston. What can I do to prove to you I'm not the blood-sucking murderer Donors think I am?"

The sun is on its last leg of light and makes Marcus's agony look more intense, creating dramatic shadows on his face. The confrontation makes me shiver even more. I don't want to talk about this now, not here. I just want to go home. I want Grandma Bolgi and Gannet to come get me and take me back to where everything is dirty, yes, but home. Where I can name the plants and see the sky whenever I choose. What do I even say to Marcus?

"You can let me go home and give up this pointless study, Marcus."

He throws his hands up in disgust as he rolls his eyes in disbelief. "What does that—"

"This is all a joke. Your grandfather said so himself. Why can't you see that? You did well because my blood numbers are high. You don't know anything about what's going on!"

"My grandfather?" He sobers quickly and steps closer to me. "What else did he say to you?"

I ignore him and his proximity. "I do care about what's happening, which is exactly why I can't just sit around and enjoy embraces or stolen touches while my family is out there suffering." The panic induced by my own words makes my voice rise. "Especially when those arms are the very ones that killed people I knew and cared for. I care so much, Marcus, that I'm literally bleeding every day for the cause while you sit here with rich Recipients, condemning the poor and innocent of your own kind as wicked murderers when the spoil lies within its own royal castle."

"Oh yes, that's right. I'm the bad guy." Marcus runs his hand through his hair as he steps back and looks around.

How can he joke about this? I feel as if I may slap him.

He makes a forced kind of laugh like he can't believe what he's hearing. "I don't..." He laughs again.

When he turns back around the smile on his face is incredulous. I've never seen this kind of look on his face before and decide I don't like it at all. It makes me feel childish, like I'm about to be scolded. I fold my arms to keep from shaking.

"Surely you saw the Recipient updates on your port screen each day?"

He is speaking, of course, of the daily death toll and news reports of Recipient lives that were suffering. Always with sappy music and professional filmography. "Yes, I know very well the Recipients had good storytellers to show us how devoted we must be to the system. A way to play on our sentiments—"

"They're true, Aston!"

I've never heard Marcus raise his voice before. It makes me want to cry and run away, yet I'm so transfixed on what he has to say I only squeeze my arms together a little tighter.

"One of those stories was my mother! Those stories were meant as a way to save people like her that really needed it. Like me, her donations weren't working." He runs another hand through his hair and sighs as he collects himself. "Look, I don't blame you for thinking the way you do, about me, about your maid, about any of it. It's the way you were raised. I never met a Donor in my whole life, but every day I saw my sweet angel mother, who read me stories and sang me croaky ill-infested lullabies that still torment my nightmares. I watched her drift away like sand between my fingers and was told over and over again that these mythical Donors were the only thing that could save her."

Marcus looks across the garden, his eyes glistening in the last ray of light like he is seeing his mother before him. His words remind me of a day I called his people mythical too. Those Recipients over the wall wanting nothing but our blood. I look at the garden too. His mother's garden.

"Forgive me," he says in a quiet voice. The sun is no longer shining in our faces, so my eyes can rest, and I see the garden differently now. "You're right. It's my fault so many are dead. I should've acted sooner."

I don't know what I should feel about him finally admitting the truth. I stand motionless, staring at him in shock. He speaks before I can open my mouth.

"But is it really very different than you refusing to donate to help Recipients?"

"It's not the same," I find myself saying.

Marcus just raises an eyebrow. I squeeze my arms together even tighter and scowl at him. He's still a Recipient, masterfully trained to gather sympathy. To recruit our loyalty. It's why they try to take our emotions away, so they can control them more easily.

"How is this different, Aston?" His voice drips with impatience.

With my arms still folded, I grab pieces of my dress and squeeze the fabric like it can help me stay calm. "I didn't kill anyone!" I shout.

Marcus turns toward me and tugs my elbow until I face him. His face is hard and his words are fast. "You keep accusing me of murder " He lets go of my arm and throws a hand into the air. "But with numbers like yours, Aston, who knows how many lives you could have saved? Who knows how many lives were lost while you were playing rebel with your paintings." He paces away from me, then back as if he will say more before thinking better of it and walking away again.

His words cut me deep. His accusations ring through my bones with truth and sting my eyes with realization.

"You were selfish and naive and unforgiving, yet I still found a way to love you despite your actions. I found a way to love you no matter your upbringing or prejudices. Because you just didn't know, like I didn't know. And I still wish every day that you said yes to my proposal." He leans down to reach for my hand which is now limp and dangling at my side.

A single tear slips down my cheek, and I pull my hand away from him. "I. Am not. A murderer," I repeat. My voice is shaking and slow. My stomach twists at how much my words are trying to convince myself and not just Marcus. "My absence of action is not the same as you delivering a bomb to unsuspecting, innocent people. Not to mention the Bee farms that employed hundreds of Donor families, murdered by your hand. How many more deaths are you responsible for? How much more am I to forgive blindly or overlook?"

"Bee Farmers?"

"My technician knows you murdered his family."

"Gannet? That strange Donor who never smiled? What does he have to do with all of this?"

"Yes, Gannet. You made his life miserable and then mock him for being a strange unhappy Donor. He has every reason to be unhappy. The blood of his entire family is on your hands. He told me so himself how you were the cause of all his pain and sorrow. His loss. His home and loved ones burned to the ground right before his eyes."

Marcus goes rigid, and his jaw juts out from clenched teeth. He towers over me.

"I can't ignore the things you've done. Your actions are more than ignorance or upbringing can excuse. And this is my body, Marcus. It's still my choice! And even if you were the last Recipient on New Earth, I wouldn't save you on purpose." My shrilling voice quiets the crickets and the birds. As soon as the words leave my curled lip, my heart hurts a little. My face is hard, and our angry gazes hold us both hostage. The lights in the garden cast odd, angry shadows across his face, and the silence leaves the mood indecipherable.

Marcus turns his head and looks out over the garden. Somehow it doesn't make me feel victorious. He steps back.

He takes one long look at me like he wants to say more

but doesn't dare and then turns away. He says over his shoulder in a stiff and quiet voice, "No need to repeat that again. I'm sorry I can't do more to set you free." He pauses and turns to look at me again, his eyes in a tortured grimace. "But I do sincerely regret our past. Now that we know what we know, I hope..." He lets the sentence trail off with a sigh as he turns back toward the castle.

He's halfway across the garden when I remember that I only made it through my door unscathed because I was with him. I run to catch up to him but don't dare walk beside him. Instead, I follow him like a duckling following its mother. Unsure of the way or the dangers. Regretting a little of what I've said. I'm in a land I don't understand, sitting and waiting for a rescue or orders that I'm unsure will ever come, now following a Recipient who, I've realized, I still don't know anything about.

We walk the halls in silence, and when we reach my door, he lets me in and slams it without a goodbye.

My room is dark, and I use my hands to navigate. I don't want to see the room. I don't want to see anything. Tears blur my vision, but I ignore them. I don't want to see the tears, either, because I think a few of the tears are regarding Marcus, and I'm not ready to shed tears for him. Before I jump into bed with my dress on, the thumps behind the wall begin. I count three different sounding thumps as I slip off my shoes onto the floor. There's something comforting about the mysterious people in the wall. They found somewhere to not be seen. I envy them. There are no voices tonight, just the padding sound of tiny thumps and bumps that lull me off to sleep.

# CHAPTER 6

It's the last week of my time with Marcus, but I haven't seen him in three days. I guess we both needed our space. I've been thinking a lot about what he said. Everyone is partly who they are based on how they were raised. Didn't I notice that in my sisters? In Mam? Even Papa—he was against the system because of his resistance-leading mother. I grew up hating Recipients.

I've been sitting alone on my sofa, staring out the open window and thinking about the televised Recipients' sob stories. Trying to remember even one of them. At least one. Could I have seen Marcus's mother once and completely overlooked her merely because of what she was? I still don't address the issue of forgiving Marcus, though his words stay with me even in my dreams. Riding a tram that crashes off a cliff: "Forgive me." Running from an angry mob with technician needles in their hands ready to prick me: "Forgive me." Drowning in oceans of flowers that both scratch me with their thorns and choke me with their aroma: "Forgive me."

When the technician enters my room on Monday

morning to find me eating my breakfast alone, yet again, I find myself worrying.

"Is Marcus in good health?" I ask Alex.

"Yes, Donor, *Master* Marcus is as well as ever." She seems too cheery with the way things are. She's no doubt happy to have her dear friend and prince no longer so infatuated with a little, nothing Donor like myself.

Alex leaves without even a glance in my direction, and I spend the rest of the day rereading *Pride and Prejudice*. True to Marcus's word, I had access to the library, but discovered that any other door or part of the house gave the same shock as that doorknob in the library. When I first discovered my easy access to the library I felt smug and defiant. Scars, after that first nerve-wracking attempt to try my door handle again, wondering if I could trust Marcus, I opened my own door a dozen times just to prove I could. The more I opened and closed it, the more I got to laughing like a maniac in a psych ward that didn't know what doors could do for people. Open and close over and over again.

The library felt like such a dangerously mighty place. Reading empowers people. Marcus clearly didn't realize what he had done. I also used my library time, and materials from the desk in my room, to write down what intel I'd gathered so far. I ripped out blank pages in some of the books and drew graphs of the hallways. I marked the doors my blood did not have access to, and which windows hurt less than others when I tapped them. When Gannet comes, I'll be more than just a sitting duck to him. I'll prove my worth. I'll make my escape so easy for him they'll probably make me captain over some division of spies and technology.

As I stretch across the bed, stiff from hours of stillness, I freeze in place when the bumping picks up again. Like clockwork, almost every night my visitors come. Some nights I knock back on the wall but get no response. I've determined that there is a boy who bullies Lecky, and tonight it is mute Lecky that comes. Finally finding a way to escape his captor, I bet. I've grown quite attached to the mute creature, somehow found some solidarity with him in our similar circumstances. I silently root for him to have enough courage to once and for all speak up for himself! I tense when I hear the bully show up.

"Lecky, you old fart." I'm suddenly determined to save him. Perhaps Austen's book has influenced and persuaded me more than I realized. The shuffling behind the walls increases, and a big thump sends a vibration down through the bed I lie on. There's no possible way this is just my imagination.

The voice whispers louder this time. "You got me in so much trouble I'm not going to feed you for a week, you old turd. Get up, you filthy mongrel." The voice sounds younger than I originally thought. Could these be boys bullying each other? Why doesn't Lecky stand up for himself? Or herself for that matter?

"You'd find your own scraps though, wouldn't you? Ya rotten girl, you. Ya old hag."

Oh my heart. It pushes me right out of bed, and I knock on the wall right above my pillows. I pull the bed out and rub all across the screen made to look brown and wooden. Thumps and shoves abound from behind it as I keep looking for some sort of door or line showing a mark or some way to get back there. I will tear this wall down if necessary to save poor Lecky. That poor girl.

After an hour of pulling furniture away from the wall, rugs lay wrinkled and chaotic around the room, and I'm exhausted. The bumping stopped long ago. No one is there anymore. I slump to the floor with my back against the wall and come up with a plan of what to do the next time that rotten boy returns. Which forces me to realize something else. I have to find a way to get a message to Gannet. Having goals makes me feel a little freer. Number one: save Lecky. Then maybe I'll be that much closer to saving myself.

THE REST of my last week that was supposed to be with Marcus goes exactly the same way as Monday. I have read every one of Jane Austen's books and found a copy of a similar looking book by a Charlotte Bronte. *Jane Eyre* is a story that, though I love just as much, I find myself unable to read through very quickly. I catch myself reading a paragraph and staring at the wall or the ceiling and thinking about how similar we are. Charlotte Bronte gave words to my predicaments. I feel like she knows me, like she lived my life and gave me a voice. Today is my last donation of the month. I've been practically alone all week, because Alex doesn't count as company. Even Janice has been missing, and I worry that I got her into trouble when I invited her to share a meal with me.

I'm confused at why he's telling me this and roll my eyes. "Oh," I say with a "good for you" tone.

"I have convinced them to invite you. And Lazuli too. As our guests."

"Oh." Now that is a surprise. I raise my eyebrows and sit my book down.

"I know you hate Recipients, but this might give you the chance to ask for more from those who are funding you. A little more freedom, perhaps."

There is a long pause, and I begin to wonder if he has

left the conversation after all. The wall still glows around my hand, and I'm just standing here, thoughts swirling about what to say. Should I apologize? Should I thank him for the opportunity to finally socialize with others? Should I ask him questions of how to appropriately act in front of "prominent Recipients" since my only experience was a lie?

"Good day, Aston. I'll see you this evening."

With that, the wall goes dark under my hand and then ripples up into a glow again. I pull my hand away and hug it close to me.

Alex enters with a tray in hand and a black bag slung over her shoulder.

"I am very put out by this," she says. "I am not a servant. I'm a well-qualified technician."

She says this like I'm the reason she is pulling double duty. Perhaps I am, but the real reason Alex has been cranky all week is because Marcus is not here. I discovered another technician handles Marcus receiving donations, so being with me was the only chance Alex had to be near the royal prince.

She goes through the motions quickly, and I wince with each of her rough moves. Once the needle is in my skin, she leaves. My mind wanders as I eat with one arm and bleed out the other. The dinner party should be interesting. I've read about them in my books and wonder just exactly how fancy tonight will be. More than one fork and proper napkins that I place in my lap—I hope it's just like the parties in Jane Austen's books. If they are coming to dress me more appropriately it must be pretty sophisticated. I find myself both excited and terrified at the prospect of being around Recipient royalty. As long as I can control my temper and not make a fool of myself, perhaps I could help the resistance somehow. Gannet is bound to come for me soon. Maybe I can gather intel or create more sympathizers in the high Recipient ranks. It's a wonder Adakin Malloy would trust me in such a situation.

I drop my gaze onto the clear tube retrieving my blood. And then to the little black box doing all the work. Adakin *doesn't* trust me. I stiffen. My grip on the half-eaten apple tightens, and the juice in my mouth feels rancid as I stare at the little black box hooked up to me. Of course he doesn't trust me. I grab the box. It's like a time bomb—the wrong move could complicate things. If I tamper with it too much, I could hurt myself or contaminate the donation and make it unusable.

When Alex had to fix it once before, she did something to the handle on top. I move my finger across the curved black handle and feel a small clip. There are two matching clips on the side, and when I flip them over the machine opens like a folder. I notice it instantly. A clear vial connected to tubes and filled with blue sparkling serum. My face aches just looking at it, remembering the control it takes from me.

I rip it out and the machine beeps wildly. I don't know how to make it stop. Maybe it's because the tube it was connected to is still attached on the other end. I pull out the other end where it connects with a click and then see a little rubber stopper dangling on the place where it was connected. As soon as it is stopped-up the beeping ceases. With shaking fingers, I hide the vial under a plate on the tray. With a click, the box is back in place just as Alex walks in. I adjust myself in my seat, sweating as she walks across the floor.

"I heard beeping," she says, annoyed.

I shrug to mask my labored breathing. She picks up the box and turns it over. It makes the normal winding sound and soon the blood is returning cold but plain and non-drugged. I wonder if Alex knew the serum was in there. She examines my returning blood, and I hold my breath, waiting to see if she notices there's nothing sparkling within it. When she looks away, I relax a tiny bit. Looking over the box, she finds a place on the top where I forgot to lock it and flips it closed with a thud.

"That must have been all it was." She doesn't even look at me as she turns and leaves again. Where does she even go while I sit here bleeding?

I later move the vial to my bed, safely between the mattresses with the note from Gannet. And the rest of my long day is spent looking at the flowers from my window, playing checkers with myself, and thinking of Gannet. I was actually trying not to think of Gannet since I don't trust my own mind in a room this intelligent anymore, but the more I told myself not to, the more his baby face and soft brown hair appeared in my memory. Especially in contrast to such a careless, rough technician. How could I not long for his gentle hands today?

I've beat myself in checkers for the third time when the door opens and Janice walks through. I run to greet her, practically knocking her over.

"Oh, Janice, I was so worried. What happened? Why haven't you been here?"

Her chuckle feels like home already. "Give me room to breathe, miss, it's only been a week."

"I thought I got you in trouble for eating lunch with me."

"Nah, miss, we are allowed to eat." She laughs again as she moves across the room and makes the bed. "Are all Donors as strange as you?"

She has never really called me a Donor before. It shocks

me how much it stings. I am reminded that she is a Recipient. Somehow seeing her as a victim of Recipients helped endear her to me, and I saw her as my equal. I forget the virus runs through her body just the same. She is just as susceptible to the illnesses and bacterium that I may expose her to as the Recipient in the library. She said she works for her donations. I wonder how strong they are.

"I just came down with a small cold is all," she says. "Nothing to worry about. Fit as a fiddle now."

The reminder of her frailty sobers me.

"Oh, Janice." I take a step away from her. "It was from being with me."

"Nonsense. Now get in there and let's ready you for the party." She shoos me toward the bathroom.

I take another step away from her instead. "But being away from me is what made you better."

"No, sleeping for two days and getting extra transfusions is what made me better. Colds happen, miss. My virus is well-managed and under control. I am no more susceptible than the next Recipient."

She flaps her arms more toward the door and I hesitantly follow. The bath is no less enjoyable. It's amazing. Torrin would love it.

"Do you know, am I allowed to send letters? Back home to my family?"

"I doubt it, miss." She doesn't say anything more about it, and I don't ask again.

The dress she lays over me is not the plain-blue satin one that I have been wearing but a red ornate ball gown with a fitted sleeveless top. The skirt goes to the floor and balloons like an umbrella. In a crisscross pattern, it is gathered in place by diamond-shaped jewels. The white marks against the vibrant red makes me think of scars on a Donor, and I wonder if that is the angle they were going for. Reminding me and the other guests of my place in this world.

Janice does my hair in a simple up-do, twisted on the back of my head like a tornado and held in place by three red pins.

"Your mirror has been programmed for the occasion," Janice says as she places her hand on the mirror.

The reflection staring back at me twists in confusion at her words. The mirror glows around her hand, and soon the mirror glows around my face.

"I think matching red lipstick would be perfect."

The lips in my reflection automatically turn bright red the same as my dress, and my hand lifts to my mouth. Nothing is there, though the image of red moves with my reflection as if it were. Janice continues to paint my image with thick eyeliner that makes me think of Sybil, my eldest sister, and dark smoky eye shadow that makes me look older. My cheeks are flushed and vibrant looking, my eyelashes are long and dramatic.

"What do you think?" Janice says with pride.

"I don't even recognize myself."

"I'll take that as a compliment. Aston, you look beautiful."

"But only in the mirror."

"Right. Lean forward, more into the light, and close your eyes."

I do as I'm told, and the sound of a mist being sprayed hisses through the room. My face tingles like the warm bubbles of the bath, and I see red through my eyelids as a laser must be passing over me.

"There," Janice sighs proudly. "Now that is beauty."

I open my eyes, my lashes thick and heavy. They flutter

open like large butterfly wings, and through the shuttering lashes I glimpse myself, and a strange sensation forms in my chest. Only it's not myself. It's a doll version of me. Porcelain skin and accented cheeks. I turn my face to each side and blink, getting used to the feel of the makeup. My lips glisten like fresh blood, and every dark spot or freckle is hidden.

Pride. I realize this feeling is admiration. I feel pretty and with it comes a pride that makes me shameful and guilty.

Oh, I almost forgot." Janice rushes out of the bathroom and returns with a small blue hat in her hands. She talks as she pins it in front of the updo, making the hat tip forward over my forehead. "Someone has been very busy and created this special hat for you."

"Special?" I say, moving my head around to look at it in the mirror. "It looks like a blue bird flew onto my head."

Janice laughs and puts her hand to her mouth to stop herself. A warm sensation flows over my face. I put my own hand to my mouth; there's a wall of warmth surrounding my face, like an invisible shield protecting my head. The heat from it spreads over my hand as it passes through.

"This hat," says Janice proudly, "allows you to be in Recipients' presence without exposing anyone to your germs. Even if you were sick, everyone would be protected with you under that mask."

I grin, knowing that despite the fact that Marcus will probably not let me wear this around him for the sake of his terrible experiment. But now I can wear this whenever I'm around Janice if she'll let me.

"It's time, miss. You're ready," she says in a hushed voice.

Another voice, Marcus's, comes through the bathroom door and makes the beauty queen in the mirror jump.

"I will be waiting at the bottom of the stairs," he says, "whenever you are ready. Lazuli has already taken her seat, but take your time."

I cannot read anything in his voice, and suddenly my hands fidget and my knees shake underneath the blood-red umbrella of a dress. Why hasn't Gannet come yet? Before a night like tonight would have been a really good time to show up. If I even knew one thing about what the resistance was doing, I could make tonight feel useful. I want to stamp my foot. Why hasn't he come?

Janice clasps both hands around mine and looks into my eyes. Wild green eyes like nothing I've ever known.

"Shh," she says like a mother calming her baby. A mother I've never known could exist, really. "Aston, look at me."

I nod a ferocious nod that feels as though it may rip my head off my neck or at least tear those red pins out of my hair.

"You may be here as a prisoner, as the lowest class of our society, a Donor."

Is she trying to make me feel better? My stomach dips and weaves.

"But tonight, you are their guest. And don't ever forget that none of us could be here if not for you. Marcus has his faults, but he is fighting in the only way he knows how. For you."

"But he will lose. His plan is wrong."

She grabs my chin like I have a beard she could tug on and smiles. "Sometimes even the worst plans have ways of bringing us the best outcomes. Just not in the ways we predicted. You can't see the end from the beginning."

I almost hear her say 'little ash tree' the end. How did this Recipient become so wise? How does this Recipient feel so much like family? They're supposed to be the enemy.

"So, take each part of the plan for what it's worth. And remember your value. No one can demean you unless you let them."

"Okay, Janice, good pep talk, but how do I keep from shaking?" I fear my knees may bruise if they hit each other anymore.

Janice gives a good hardy laugh. "You move, miss. Now get going." She puts her hands on my shoulders and turns me around. She is right. Moving my legs does keep the shaking at bay, but my hands still fidget.

The hallway feels blinding tonight, and my simple heels click along the white marble until I step out onto the red plush carpet. I pause at the top of the steps. There was a day I paused at my own stairs, scared to tell my family the news: that I had already been tested and didn't want to donate. How differently that day unfolded than what I pictured would happen. Janice is right. She is proving to always be right. It feels good to have someone I can trust. Perhaps tonight will not go how I fear either.

At the bottom of the stairs, Marcus turns around and looks up at me. I place my hand on the shiny wood banister as I begin my descent. I peek from under my long eyelashes, and my face heats beneath his intense stare. Looking at him, for the first time I wonder what his mother looked like and if he resembles her more than his father. I find myself pitying him again. It's what he wanted, isn't it? I grip the banister tighter to drain the blood filling my cheeks.

He isn't moving a muscle and seems frozen in place as I draw nearer. The only thing moving is his head as his eyes follow my every move one step at a time, closer and closer to him. He is dressed in a black tuxedo nicer than the one at the Ambassador's Ball. A red handkerchief that matches my dress peeks out of the pocket, and his hair looks less plastic and more like the soft hair I grew to know so well.

There isn't much room between him and the last step. If I take it, I will be practically up against him, and my heart races at the thought. Instead, I stop on the step above him, and we are eye to eye.

"You look radiant," he whispers reverently.

"Thanks." I look down at my dress and clasp my hands to fidget more. "It seems a bit over the top just for dinner."

His chuckle helps me relax a little, and I let my hands drop.

"Yes, well, what can I say, we're just a bunch of sick Recipients. We don't get out much, so we have to make the most of everything. I must warn you that you might not like everything about this dinner situation."

Before I ask about what he means he extends his bent elbow. "May I escort you?"

I look at him before I accept it. There's something very purposeful in this offering. It can't go unnoticed that he asked; he allows me to choose him. I place my hand under his elbow and am impressed by how strong it is. He called himself a sick Recipient, but he is no longer the bony boy I ran into on the street corner. He is strong and healthy. Handsome and powerful. I should never forget his place and how powerful he really is. I don't know if I should be proud or frightened that I helped bring to life the master-piece pulling me forward through the mansion. I need to just do what Janice says. Take one part of the plan at a time.

We wrap around the other side of the staircase, away from the library. This hallway is wider than the other and only has a couple of doors on either side of a wide tall archway. Voices jab down the hallway along with the tinkling of glasses, yet Marcus stops at one of the doors and pulls his arm out of my hand. Curiosity turns to utter confusion when he opens the door. It opens to the large room where the sounds and voices are coming from, except it is separated by a small cage of glass.

# CHAPTER 7

Marcus puts his hand out toward me as if to usher me into the small glass room. Inside there is a tiny table and chair with food set out beautifully. So much food for such a little glass room. There are platters on pedestals ranging in height. Ones with several different shades of bread, a large platter that looks like it holds an entire chicken, pre-sliced, as well as a dark pink meat that has what I've learned are cherries and pineapples stuck into it with toothpicks. A tray of fruit is lower to the table, along with a silver platter full of green beans, potatoes, and celery all garnished with parsley like a picture from a book. I don't take time to pride myself in how I know the names of all these amazing foods now. Instead, my stomach quivers in guilt. My entire family could feast for weeks on this table set for one.

"What is this?" I ask.

The same voices and clinking glasses from around the corner come through the little room with an added buzz of recording. The sounds are most likely to make me feel that I'm actually in the same room with them. It does everything but that. It makes the hair on my arms stand and my teeth grind.

"Your dinner," Marcus says flatly.

"But I have the hat. It's supposed to keep me from spreading disease."

"This isn't about getting sick," says Marcus, biting his lip.

"Then what is it?"

"It's just an added measure of safety."

"You mean, they're worried about what I might try do to them? Do they think we'll attack them?"

Marcus bristles and peers into the dining area to see who is noticing the scene. Let them gawk, let them know how absurd they are being. "So I eat in a pen now. Like wild animals in a cage? Like I'm your pet?"

I scan the scene, looking for Lazuli. She sits in another glass box at a matching little table across the room. She doesn't move. Doesn't look my way.

I don't want to admit to Marcus how I thought this night was going to go. That I'd wished for it to be something out of a book or hoped to make an impact on the Recipients, making them join the resistance, or how I dreamed Gannet would swoop in and tell me just what the rebellion needed to know so this dinner party could be used to their advantage somehow. "Well, it isn't like you gave me a lot of time to prepare for a night like this."

"I'm sorry," he says. "But this is how we've had to live every time we visit Donor territory. It's just a way of life."

I picture the face of Adakin Malloy's son, Mr. Vincent Malloy, as he stared at me through a sheet of glass separating them from the Donors at the Ambassador's Ball. I scan the room again until I find the similar gray eyes of

Marcus's father. He looks at me over the rim of his goblet as he drinks.

"There really isn't any other way. It's too risky."

Vincent Malloy's eyes are still on me as he lowers his drink, and a shiver races down my arms. I turn to Marcus. "Just make sure the precious Recipients don't tap on the glass and bother the poor Donor creatures."

"Aston, don't..."

I ignore him as I sit and pull my chair under the table. He stands there a moment more with the door open as I unfold the napkin and drape it over my lap. I turn back to him, and his hard brow makes a knot build and unravel in my stomach.

"Go ahead, sir," I say. "Go join your people and be merry. No worries for the Donor lab rats."

One final long glare before he shuts the door with a hard thud that makes the speakers squeal.

Dinner guests indeed. I grumble my way through the salad, picking out the croutons first, and then dabble at the dessert platter in case something happens that calls me back to my prison cell early. Adakin eyes me while rubbing his chin and then I remember how I stole the serum from the machine before it could enter me. I raise my glass to him with a devious smirk. The way he squirms in his seat, gripping the ornately carved armrest of his chair, believing me more resistant to his serum than ever, makes me chuckle.

The Recipients laugh and drink as if Lazuli and I aren't here at all, though each of them takes a turn eyeing one of us skeptically. Most of them are Vincent's age except for the two men seated by Adakin Malloy and the young girl on Marcus's right. She is wearing a rich emerald gown that doesn't do well for her ashen complexion. Her mousy brown hair makes me pity her, and I have stabbing moments of guilt about my ill feelings toward her. The way she cocks her head and rests her hand on his arm when she laughs makes my eyes roll.

I give my attention to Lazuli who seems to have already finished her meal. Her face is pinched together, sour and annoyed. But her hair looks better, not the matted dreads with bits of straw and dirt like it was last I saw her. She looks well, even if furious and distraught. I wish I could talk to her. I can hear the entire conversation in the room around me, but can any of them hear me?

A Recipient speaks above all the others. "Dinner in the presence of Donors is quite convenient. It's like having fire extinguishers. Are you going to install them in all the restaurants now?"

The table laughs. My lips don't just curl in response, they open with a small grunt of disbelief. "Not if you kill them all first," I mutter.

Silence cuts through the room. All eyes look in my direction. Even those whose backs face away from me spin to see the daring, stupid Donor.

"What was that?" the Recipient who joked says with disgust and disbelief. The top of his head is bald, but a ring of brown fuzz circles the edges above his ears. Though he has a big nose, his head is small and round, making his face look squished into place.

I look at Lazuli, and though she is looking at me now as well, her face is devoid of all emotion. I look back to the table of waiting Recipients and lean forward as if there is a microphone on the table or implanted in my food somewhere.

"I just didn't appreciate the joke," I say. "That is all."

Adakin stands, which is meant to be threatening

enough to silence me, but the joking bald Recipient puts up a hand and Adakin pauses.

"No, that's quite all right. I want to hear what she has to say." He shouts next to make his voice be heard through the glass, or perhaps he thinks I am deaf or dumb or both. "Why is that, Donor? Do Donors not have senses of humor?"

A low chuckle moves around the table and some of the Recipients turn their backs again to sip their drinks.

"We enjoy a joke as much as the next," I say. "But I don't imagine many a Donor, or Recipient for that matter, that appreciates a joke at their expense. I have seen Donors die to save Recipients and to merely feed themselves. Death is not a joke to me."

"Aye, nor to me, Donor," Adakin says. "It's why we need you so badly. It's why we pay you so greatly. Death is not a joke, I agree, but it is in some cases inevitable. A way of life."

"But what choice do you give a Donor but to die? Death without a life to begin with is no life at all. And life without choice is a silent kind of death."

The silence in the room becomes suffocating. The balding Recipient stares me down with his chin tilted to his chest, making him look on the verge of pouncing. I check to see what Marcus is doing, but he only shakes his head slightly. As if to say this isn't the way to get what I want.

The duel is over when the Recipient straightens in his chair and laughs while picking up his drink. He cheerily addresses Adakin as he spins his red punch around in the glass. "Which one is this, Adakin?" he says as if I'm no longer here. He uses his goblet to point in my direction. "The high or low one?" He takes a drink as Adakin smiles.

"My dear Brutis, now why would I divulge that kind of information?"

"No? I wish I could do my own experiments on them. I bet that spunk and attitude has something to do with the numbers as well. She's the high one, isn't she? Numbers that high are like a rare jewel." The way he says "jewel" sounds nothing like a compliment. "I mean, look at that one." The entire table looks to Lazuli who sits up straight for the first time. "There's no way *she's* the one that could save us all."

Lazuli slumps even further than before as the Recipients return to their dinner. Conversation is sparse as the Recipients finish their salads and servants come to retrieve the plates in preparation for the main course.

"What I want to know," begins the sickly creature next to Marcus, who even sounds like a mouse, squeaking on every vowel like she's losing her voice, "is what the Donors do all day?" She subjects me to her soil-colored eyes as she gazes at me with pity. "Do Donors have the patience or desire for anything outside of donations? I mean, do they have interests or hobbies?"

"We are still people, you know," I say without hesitancy. "You and I are the same species, only I have an antibody you don't."

"A lot of that antibody, from what I hear," says Brutis, the bald Recipient. His eyes squint when he smiles at me and makes me want to curl my lip again.

Adakin opens his mouth to speak, seeming uncomfortable with this amount of talk, but the little mouse speaks again as if she didn't notice their leader at all. I wonder what makes these Recipients all on equal ground that they speak overtop their leader so. Perhaps they do not respect him as much as it appears on television.

"So you do? Have hobbies, that is?" sick mousling says.

"I paint." My eyes are pulled to Marcus at the confession. He is the last thing these hands portrayed on canvas. Both of his elbows are on the table in front of him, and he leans over his plate like a gorilla.

"A painting Donor!" Brutis sings with jolly surprise. "Come now, Adakin. If this experiment goes well, you must let us all have one of our own. What I wouldn't give to have a Donor that could paint for me as well as save me." He gives me a wink, and Marcus shoots to his feet.

"Speaking of hobbies," Marcus says. "We have provided an evening of entertainment for you. I'm sure these Donors are worn out from their duties today. Let us gather in the ballroom and let the Donors rest." He turns stiffly and rushes out of the room before anyone can even blink.

The other Recipients look at each other and then move. Their chairs scoot backward at different, confused paces. Some throw their napkins into their half-finished plates of food. Murmurs move about the room like a purring kitten lounging and sleepy with mischief. All of the Recipients look in my direction at least once before they exit the room, but Mouse Girl stares at me longest and is the last to leave.

It's a good thing I ate dessert when I did, since the dinner party is cut so short. I'm not invited to the entertainment; in fact, I'm completely forgotten about, and that's just fine with me. I've had all I can handle of Brutis for a lifetime. I pick at my main course of cold chicken quarter and carrots until a maid finally lets me out of my cage. I gladly follow her instructions to head to bed. The bodice of the red dress cuts into my hips as I climb the stairs, and music fills the hallways when I reach the top. The sound of string and woodwind instruments swirling around me take me back to another time. A time I danced in the arms of Marcus. I grip the banister for support as I pause to recount that night. My hand involuntarily reaches up and brushes my lips. We kissed that night. I fretted about his well-being and thought he was dead and painted his face while he traipsed through these royal halls and trespassed across Donor territory. A door shuts behind me, and I scurry along to my room.

Janice is sitting by the window, waiting for me when I return and helps me into my usual blue silk night dress.

"I heard you put on quite a show tonight, miss."

I pause to think about her words before I answer. Yes, I suppose my conversation would make the orchestra concert seem rather dull. "I only spoke my mind."

"Poor choice of audience for that I would think."

"Why?" I say as I lounge on the seat by the window. It's closed to keep out the heat of summer that is quickly approaching. I look down to try and make out the spring flowers, dying to make way for new colors to greet the warm air. "Why should I be particular in whom I share the truth of our circumstances? That menace of a man, Bruṭis, deserves a good dose of reality."

Janice shivers. "The Brutis family is dangerous, to be sure. For starters, his daughter, Amelia, is feared by most Recipients, both for fear of the virus that's strong in her veins, and her manipulative ways."

Could Janice possibly mean the mouse girl? She definitely plays the sickly part well, but manipulative? Her smiles for Marcus at dinner and well-planned chance touches make more sense now.

"But," she continues, "these Recipients are who fund the program. I would think you should be very particular in how you act around the very people keeping you alive, well-fed, and dressed."

"Funding?"

"Yes, miss. Why, the Brutis family alone pays more than half of these expenses."

"I never considered... that is to say, I never realized..." I let the sentence trail off with the drop of my gaze.

A bump from the wall behind my bed echoes through the silent room. Both of our heads turn, and then we face each other. Her face is as white as the sheets she just finished turning down for me. What comes next is the voice of the bully.

"Get back here, Lecky, or you're done for, you piece of rotten meat."

I'm on my feet at once, grateful to have a witness in the room with me. More bumping has Janice's hands shaking, and she crosses her arms as she inches to the door.

"Cats?" I fold my arms and lift an eyebrow. I wait for her to talk.

"Yes," is all she says.

Another bump and Janice dips a quick curtsy before turning to retreat. I lunge toward her.

"Wait, Janice!" But she is gone and soon I'm alone with the mute, tortured thing and its bully.

Before I can do anything about the bully, a shadow crosses my window. A trick of the eye perhaps, but something about it makes the hairs on my arms stand up. There are many night animals that fly over the garden, but something about the chill in the air has my breath hitched. I place my hand on the wall and request the lights off like I have seen Janice do so that I can see out the window better. The bully is silent or maybe has disappeared altogether. I step closer to the window, letting my hand trace along the bookshelf. There it is again. A shadow crawls across the window—meaning something or someone is on the ground, moving in front of the spotlights in the garden.

Muffled whispers squeeze my heart to a stop. That is not the young bully in my walls. Those sound like grown men. Their voices come from below my window. Then there's a strange sound like breaking sticks, or the creaking roof from back home when the wind would blow. The fear in my stomach plummets to my toes when I realize—the sounds are of the men climbing. I stumble backward and knock something over on the bookshelf. It doesn't stop the visitors. I move to reach for the wall and call out for Janice or Marcus or anyone who will hear me but stop when there are voices in the walls too. Their old whispers make even the bully sound welcome.

"What was that?" a low rumbling voice says.

I lean against the bookshelf in the dark, listening to the ghosts of my room.

"I don't know, but this is where she is."

"Are you certain it's her? We're only here for her."

My heart jumps back into my ribs at the idea that this could be the resistance. It must be them, finally come to save me. They have found the secret passages in the walls, and perhaps it's Gannet that is at my window. The goosebumps on my arms relax into sheer excitement that rustles the cake in my belly. I dash toward the bed to gather my notes. My fingers shake with glee as I flip over the covers. They will see how useful I can be. That I'm more than the leader's granddaughter or the high-numbered Donor. Oh, I'll make Papa so proud, and Grandma Bolgi will cup my chin and wrinkle her nose as she smiles at me. I wipe at the excited tears getting in the way. There are no pockets to stuff my notes into, so I fold them and tuck them under my bra strap on my shoulder. They have found me. Finally, they have come.

# CHAPTER 8

I grab the hidden bottle of serum, and it bounces against the wooden floor with a plinking sound. I don't waste a second looking at it, just swipe it back up and tuck it into the other side of my strap. I yank open the nightstand drawer and gather my stash of favorite foods, then rush around the bedpost to lock the bedroom door to keep anyone from impeding this mission. Then around the bed again, I open the bedroom window, letting the warm free air kiss my skin. Free. I'm going to be free.

With a loud click, something moves beside me. It's the bookcase. There's no line in the wall where a door would be because the bookcase was blocking it. With a grinding sound, the bookcase slides in front of the window like a sliding door. The drapes get caught behind it and the room grows darker with no moonlight. It's harder to see, but in the corner where the shelf had been flush against the wall, a dim light now glows from an opening.

The room goes completely dark as a strange figure fills the gap of the secret passageway. He merely stands there, bulky and thick-looking. Perhaps it's the darkness affecting my first impression of him, but he doesn't look like the most trustworthy fellow. He has a top-heavy muscular chest that tapers down at the waist and makes it seem like he could teeter over at any minute. His dark hair reaches his shoulders, and his matching eyebrows, thick and bushy, are the only things visible on his face. There are all types fighting for the resistance I guess.

There are no words exchanged. We're both just standing here, staring at each other in the pitch-black night.

"Is there a code or something?" I whisper. "To know you're with the resistance?" I bite my lip. That wasn't very smart. Even if there was a code, I wouldn't know if he is right or not. I wring my hands, twisting the napkin of food round and round tighter and tighter.

"Uh, yeah," the hairy ape of a man says. His voice sounds like there is an eternal frog stuck in his throat. It makes me want to clear my throat for him. "Thirteen forty-two."

It's my number. I haven't been called that in such a long time. Grandma Bolgi sent someone for me. I wish I could see Adakin Malloy's face when he hears that they have come for me, that he doesn't know Bolglarka like he thought he did. I smile as I step hesitantly closer to the man.

His smile seems to glow in the dark, and the putrid smell of his breath makes my stomach twist. Could they not have sent a more pleasant sort of person to rescue me? Is Gannet so important to the cause that he could not be spared for this operation? "I thought Gannet would come," I whisper quickly, trying to speak fast and hold my breath so as not to smell him more than I have to. "Is he with you?"

Someone pounds on my door, and we twist toward the

sound. A figure climbs in the window behind us, squeezing around the bookcase. He is shorter than the man next to me, sleeker and young-looking. Is it Gannet after all?

He pushes the bookcase, closing the passageway.

"What are you doing?" the foul giant next to me hisses. "We can't use the window now that they know we're here. The passageways are the only way out."

Another figure, short and squat with a shining head, climbs through the window with difficulty. "Of course we're not using the window, you fool." His labored breathing fills the room as more pounding on the door ensues.

The slimy sound of that voice makes my skin crawl. I know that voice but can't quite place it.

The pounding on the door intensifies, the door handle shakes violently and I whip around blindly in the dark. "Aston!" Marcus's voice is desperate and urgent through the door.

These resistance members must have done something to lock down my room.

"There's a better exit in the other corner," says the shiny-headed man. "It's hopefully more secretive than this one. Someone's clearly been in these walls lately."

*Another* secret passage? I would have thought keeping a prisoner in a place with so many ways out would have been risky.

I also wonder how these rebels know so much about these passageways. When we're safe outside of these walls, it will be one of the first things I ask them. Along with where we are going and where Gannet and my grand-mother are.

"Grab the girl," the slimy-can't-put-my-finger-on-who-it-is voice says.

"No need," says the hairy ape. "She's more than willing to come."

So many things feel wrong about this interaction, this rescue. I open my mouth to inquire after Gannet again, and my grandmother or whoever is leading this rescue mission. What is the plan? Where are we to go? But the three figures shuffle me along the floor, across the room toward the sofa and cabinet of games.

We almost make it to the far corner when the door busts through and officers storm in with lasers in hand much like they did on the day they came for me in Livonia. The lights come on, exposing me. I'm caught. The trained lasers capture me in a warm glowing bubble. Those around me are frozen into place as well. Marcus's eyes pierce mine, even brighter than the lights. They morph from worry to confusion. He looks around at my group of rescuers then stares back at me with sadness painted on his face. I copy his inspection around the room just as the ape man gets taken down by four officers and carried swiftly out.

Marcus straightens and his lip curls, making him look more angry than sad. I can't look at him. He looks betrayed, but he's the one holding me captive. He has to know I would try to escape when given the chance. This psychotic scheme of his won't work. I have to get away from Adakin.

Instead of looking at him, I turn my head toward the slimy, almost familiar voice. A gasp lodges in my throat, making it sting. Brutis stands only an arm's-length away from me, shrugging off the officers that try to grab him.

Chills shoot down my legs and make my toes tingle. Brutis? That is why the voice sounded eerily familiar. But why him? Is he part of the resistance?

"I have every right to be in here as you do." He sneers and lunges toward Marcus. "Maybe even more. This experiment needs someone more disconnected to the cause. Not a naive Donor-lover."

Another gasp escapes me, and it all comes crashing down. I'm more gullible and ignorant than I thought. My eyes ache, pulled wide with fear and shock. I recall Brutis's words from dinner. He wasn't saving me: he was trying to capture me as his pet. I teeter a little. There is no nearby wall to catch myself with, but the red orb somehow buoys me.

Marcus's eyes stay on me as if he didn't even hear Brutis. Everyone is waiting to hear what he will say. Officers waiting for orders. Me waiting for a chance to explain, but oh, what do I say? And Brutis waits for Marcus to return the insult. Impatiently, he spits on the floor.

"Get them out of here," Marcus says. He steps aside to make room in the doorway for the officers to get through. They escort the thin accomplice that came through the window. The one I thought was Gannet. Now I can tell he's a red-headed man possibly in his forties with freckles for days. They shuffle Brutis along with difficulty as some officers seem unsure if they should even touch the powerful but cocky Recipient.

When the room is clear and we are alone, it suddenly feels cold under Marcus's glare. Instead of shrinking, though, I push my shoulders down, and my chin naturally tilts up.

"I understand why he would want you." His voice is low and there are so many things hidden in the tone. Confusion, sadness, betrayal. "But…" the pause in his question feels torturous. *Please just speak, just say it, just ask.* "What I don't understand is why you looked so willing to go with them? No hands were on you, and when we came in you looked guilty at being caught more than relieved at being rescued.

Do you have any idea what he might have done to you?" Marcus points toward the door where they just took Brutis. His face is pale and ghostly. "I thought he made his presence and stance on this issue very clear at dinner. Do you dislike it here so very much? Do you dislike *me* so very much that—"

"Marcus, I didn't know it was him." I step closer but stop when he recoils from me like I have done to him.

"Who did you think it was?"

There's no way to answer him. So, I don't even try. The passing minutes feel like years. Like the fevers in the prison cell that were strung together, confusing and painful. Only I did that too. Am I really supposed to grovel at his feet and pace this room, so grateful to him that he didn't leave me in that prison cell to die? That bleeding me dry was the best solution he could come up with to keep me alive?

His voice sounds so defeated when he continues. "Aston, the security here is not just to keep you in but to keep dangers out. Do you know how many Recipients would like to have your throat? Or your arm or any piece of you really?" He stares at the ground as he whispers gruffly. "I will have Janice bring you some books to keep you busy while I'm with Lazuli."

I'm still caught in the red glowing light of the lasers. An officer stands behind me, holding it in place. I don't know if I could talk if I tried. Nor do I know if I have the courage to say what I really think. Suddenly I am outraged. Maybe it has something to do with seeing the evil Brutis again or hearing how Marcus is going to have Janice bring me books still like I'm supposed to bow down to his gracious offers even as he holds me captive and continues to force me to donate against my will. However, I think a majority of the rage and pain filling my limbs has to do with the fact that I was wrong. The resistance didn't come for me. Maybe they never will.

He looks over his shoulder as he grabs the door handle. The officer releases me from the lasers and steps around me. The absence of it makes it feel like I stepped out of a sauna. The officer leaves, but Marcus stands in the doorway staring at me.

"How did they get in here?" he asks.

I check to make sure the secret passageway is closed, and Marcus follows my gaze. I don't dare tell him about the bookshelf. Instead, I stare at the open window.

"I will send officers in the morning to secure it." His affect is flat, and something about his uncaring nature makes me realize how unusual of an appearance it is on him. My chin quivers. Even when his face was hard and menacing when speaking to Janice, there was something sad about how he looked. There was emotion in his glare like Janice hurt him personally. But right now, he looks more like an officer.

"*Stone walls do not a prison make, nor iron bars a cage,*" I say, quoting something I recently read, balling my fists by my side. "Or glass in this case."

He turns again, this time with pity in his eyes. Pity that will set me free?

"Are you quoting poetry at me?"

"It's from Charlotte Bronte," I say smugly.

"Who is quoting Richard Lovelace." I've never heard the name and feel defeated all over again. When Marcus continues I no longer know who he's quoting and it makes me feel small and invisible.

"*Peril, loneliness, and uncertain futures are not oppressive evils, so long as the frame is healthy and the faculties are employed.*" His voice starts off hushed but ends with a tone of triumph. Like he knows that my own weapon backfired against me. I've always seen him so duty-driven, believing he was doing what's right. But at this moment I don't understand him at all. He is nothing more than a captor towering over me.

The door clicks quietly behind him, and a tear slips down my cheek. I scramble for Charlotte's book, flipping the pages to find the next line. I say it out loud to the empty room. "*So long, especially as liberty lends us her wings and hope guides us by her star.*"

I hiccup a sob and stand in the bright room stupidly. I've never missed home as much as I do in this one moment. I never realized how caged I was until I dared hope to be truly free. It hurts more to discover my saviors were actually more enemies. To know Marcus technically saved me from another, worse fate. It only magnifies this awful place I'm stuck in. To boomerang back into non-existence.

Perhaps Adakin is right. I mean nothing to the resistance. I am no more an important piece to the cause than Marcus is on the right path to fighting against the virus. I don't know Grandma Bolgi at all like I thought I did.

Falling into my soft Recipient bed, I sob uncontrollably. As I slip off into sleep, calming myself from the intensity of the evening, my last thoughts bring the silver lining of the situation. At least now I know the secret passageway is in the wall. Now if I could only figure out how to open it. I can't save myself, but maybe I can save Lecky. Maybe together we can run away from here and hide in a hole that cares nothing about blood or rebellions.

# CHAPTER 9

The officers wake me with an abrupt drop of their bags full of tools. I don't recall a knock, and I push myself up on the bed, wiping the drool from my mouth as they scurry around the window. They don't speak, yet somehow move around each other as if they can read each others' minds.

The door opens again and in walks Alex. She sets up the machine on the table without speaking to me. With a flip of her hair, she occasionally puts her nose in the air like she's angry or too good for this position.

"I haven't eaten breakfast," I inform her.

Everyone knows donating on an empty stomach isn't very smart. I look down at myself, realizing my disheveled appearance. I fell asleep on top of the covers, and my hair is plaited in a wave of tangles along the side of my head. Did Janice try to come and couldn't wake me?

"Yes, well, it will have to do today. I don't have time to wait since I have two Donors to treat today."

Treat? Perhaps it is the stress that takes my sanity and sends me into a giggle. What funny terms they use. "Treat" makes it sound like a special occasion. Makes me think of potato candy on my birthday. Alex eyes me with a stern glare, and I lower my smile to the floor. What an odd time to find humor. "Why am I donating, anyway? I thought it was Lazuli's month now. Was she not donating this past month?"

Alex doesn't stop her work as she answers. "The other Donor was not well enough to donate right away."

Rolling out of bed, I step toward her, invested in this information. "Lazuli is sick?"

Alex nods. "Or rather, was. We feared she wouldn't even be able to participate at all. Scars knows she didn't help the situation. I can see why Master Marcus was so fascinated by you," she says, but not in a complimenting way. "After meeting you, I myself wondered if I was wrong about Donors. Then I tried to test the other one and—" Alex clicks her tongue and shakes her head as she flips the cover off the needle. "Donors are just as dumb and unreasonable as I imagined." She stands, and, for once, seems to realize what she's saying. "Except for you of course, Donor."

Her smile is pinched and forced. Her next words come through her teeth and seem hard for her to say. "I can see why Master Marcus likes you so much." She puts her hand out toward the chair. "President Malloy has asked for your blood to also be drawn during her donation. I imagine it's to create a storage of sorts. Too precious not to. I'm only following orders, but I have exactly forty minutes to do it, so please have a seat and let's get started."

As Alex gets to work on my arm, the officers leave as mutely as they entered. Nothing looks so different about the glass they replaced. Maybe a slight blue hue to it.

Once the needle is in and the machine is whirring Alex stands. I have no way to check the machine for serum. I watch her every move. If Adakin Malloy wants me to donate even when it's not my turn, that can only mean one thing.

Alex stands in front of me with her arms folded and taps her foot almost in time with the whirring machine. The gears stop and then shift making a soft *click click* sound. The whirring picks up again with more of a whining tone.

There it is. Making my returning blood more purple than red, the blue serum sparkles in the tube. I lift my head to Alex. Her eyes are already on me. She knew. She had to have. Her stare makes it very clear she won't do anything about it if I protest. So I don't. I stare at her the duration of the donation until my arm turns cold and a smile creeps slowly upon my face. Inside I tell myself I mean to smile, that I am smiling at Alex to let her know she hasn't won yet and that if it's up to me she never will. I will always be of more use than a sick Recipient like she will. I'm more important than she will ever be. It took breaking me in Recipient territory to see that now. Just like Janice said. They need me.

She rushes when the machine beeps. So quickly in fact, that a few drops of blood fall onto my blue dress and the table. She doesn't even attempt to wipe it. Without a word, she is out the door, and I am left smiling at the back of it.

Inside I want to cry again. But I smile nonetheless. I may be more useful, but that doesn't make being used any easier to bear.

The afternoon sun brightens my room. I haven't moved from the seat for hours. Something feels different about this serum. My limbs are sunken into the wooden chair, weak and flimsy like the yellow, limp spring plants dying in the garden. Maybe it's just because I haven't had food or water in hours. Where is Janice? I stare at the bed longingly but can't move. I need food. I need water. What ironic fate the heavens bestow on me to actually be begging for water like I once tried to do to escape my blood test day. Here I am at the complete mercy of my captors. Hungry, fatigued, and dehydrated. Evidently, I'm not as important to the Resistance or the Recipients as I originally thought.

Though I hear the door open and see it out of the corner of my eyes, I don't have the energy to move my head. There's just my smile. My thoughts swim lazily about, shifting into a more pleasant way of thinking. I notice the colors of the light beaming through the room and the happy shadows dancing on the floor from the leaves blowing in the wind. Such vibrant colors. Such an array of shades.

Adakin Malloy's voice steals across the room. "Sorry to keep you waiting, but I had to make certain this concoction was more effective. After last night's charade I thought it better to take extra measures with this meeting."

# CHAPTER 10

I can't open my mouth, and just the thought of it makes me realize how dry and crusted my lips are.

Adakin makes a movement I can't completely see from the way my head has slumped down onto my chest. I assume he is using his hand on the wall to call someone in the way I still don't understand.

"I imagine you think yourself very smart for replying to Brutis at dinner last night. That you consider yourself brave for standing up to a Recipient bully."

His steps echo with a *clunk-tap*. First the heel then the toe of his shoes *clunk-tap clunk-tap*. How can I be this weak already?

I try to pull my head forward as he draws closer. Instead it rolls over my shoulder until it falls backwards. At least now I can look at him under my lowered eyelids. He's wearing a dark suit with a navy tie, but nothing can hide his belly that protrudes with a matching waistcoat.

Watching my head dance around amuses him. His laugh seems to catch him off guard as he takes a break from his well-crafted speech. "I'm glad something works against you." He laughs again and puts a hand on his belly with pure satisfaction as he licks his pasty lips. "I may not be able to make you conform like a regular Donor, but docile is a good start."

I want to spit in his face and tell him I have no idea what he's talking about, but I can't even blink. I'm so drained and helpless.

"I hope you learned your lesson about what egging on a Recipient can do. I hope it was worth it to you, because you won't be getting as much freedom now."

My walk to the library and back? So. Much. Freedom.

"I assure you, Abner Brutis would not be as generous as we are here. He may fund most of the procedures, but he does not make the decisions. And it is essential that I have you here, dear Donor Aston. I know how important names are to you. Does it trouble you so much to still be called a Donor?"

I grunt, and he laughs merrily. The scent of honey wafts over to me, and I smile deeper. My face is burning from overuse, and my neck begins to ache, but the red on his face is so beautifully mesmerizing. His laugh is pleasant, isn't it?

The door opens again, and Janice enters. I spy the glass of water on her tray, and it tinkles on the metal as her arms begin to shake once she spots me. She stands by Adakin, staring at me.

"Stop gawking and put it on the table," he barks at her.

Janice does as she's told, and I can't even tell her thank you. Adakin tells her to give me water, and I smile at her as she lifts it to my lips. Am I dying? Is this how I will die?

The cold water feels heavenly, and my neck gains strength enough to lift as water dribbles down it less and goes into me more. I'm soon gulping at it, and Janice's soft hand is on the back of my head to help me. Adakin orders

Janice to feed me. She does so with as much gentle care as a mother bird, while Adakin waits patiently, watching. When I have enough strength to place the fruit in my own mouth, he dismisses Janice.

Adakin walks to the window and taps at the new glass. It pings a funny *twang* sort of sound, like rocks hitting an electric cable, and he smiles. I lean forward, thinking I will stand, but my legs are still weak and untrained after sitting for so long. They don't budge. After trying to move the two giant slugs with my arms, I fall back into the chair, out of breath.

The sounds of my effort make Adakin turn around.

"Don't overexert yourself. There's no use trying, you see. You fought through the last serum a bit more easily than I imagined so I had to take more precautions this time."

He is near me again. His aged lips are white with saliva hidden in the edges and crevices of his mouth. His see-through skin is as thin as Recipient paper, and I very likely could overpower him if I wanted to, if I had strength to. If I were stupid enough to try. The word "leader" in conjunction with this sorry piece of flesh before me makes me even more ill. "Sick," I croak out, hoping he knows I mean him.

"Maybe, but I'm desperate to find your grandmother."

"Why?" The more I talk, the more my voice remembers how. I clear my throat as I try to shift into a more comfortable position. My strength is returning by the minute.

"Well, to cure us of course."

His words don't make any sense. "Liar," I say with blinking eyes weary from the length of the smile that never leaves my face.

"Oh Aston, there is so much you don't understand." He

paces the floor for a moment. Listening again to the *clunk-tap* of his shoes makes my face relax slightly, and I feel more myself than I have all morning. My mind races, and for some reason floats across memories of Torrin and a day so long ago when we sat at the kitchen table. Questions—they surge forward in my mind, pressing against my thoughts to be answered and heard.

"Why do you still need Donors after all this time?" I fight and scream in my head against the fog that tries to take over. I growl with the next words. "Why haven't you found a cure yourselves yet? With the number of scientists you have working here it should be easy. What makes you think my grandmother knows anything about it?" The sentences exhaust me. I fall back limp in my seat, breathing heavily yet smiling again. The white in his bright yellow beard is bleach white, and I appreciate how clean and perfect it is. Such a nice beard really.

He eyes me skeptically. "Curious," he mutters. "Perhaps I shouldn't have fed you at all." He picks up his pacing again. "It's true I have many scientists working on this, but most don't survive through the trials, and I have to retrain new scientists every week. No one knows quite as much as Bolglarka, I fear, and the only ones who I get to obey me perfectly are the officers. But the problem is the creation of officers reverses the necessary skills needed for a good scientist. So you see my dilemma."

He, of course, speaks of how drained of all emotion and independent thought officers are made to be.

"To solve such intricate problems as the virus, a mind must think very outside of the box, very free range. Which can also be a dangerous and risky thing to let loose.

But I fear the virus attached to our DNA is more sophisticated than any of us can decipher. You have an antibody we do not, and there's no way we can determine how to get it."

"Why not," I grunt again as my thoughts are broken up with a smile in between. My next words come out giddy and small like a child asking her papa about sweet rolls from the store. "What about inter—" I can't finish the sentence.

"Mating? Donors and Recipients? In theory it makes sense. A next generation product of Recipient and Donor should have a fifty-fifty chance of having the antibody so that even if they're born with the virus in their genetic makeup, their chance of survival would be greater and even more greater if they then procreated with another Donor. But theories are rarely correct no matter how much we want them to be." Adakin rubs his bearded chin. "How best to explain this. You haven't heard of tarantulas, have you? Many, I'm sure, are grateful they did not survive the wars, but they're a fascinating breed of spider. The female eats the love of her life in order to make the next generation strong. Is that what you would have happen then? It's true that a next generation would have a fifty-fifty chance getting the immunity gene, but no Recipient would survive that contact. And even those with immunity in their blood would have the virus too. Have you heard of cancer? It's been eradicated for centuries, but it is technically the same idea. Even if this wasn't enough, we've tried test-tube babies, genetically engineering the fetuses to have the highest chances of survival. Yet every case was exactly the same. The added antibody somehow eats at the virus-infected fetus before it even has a chance." A gloss falls over Adakin Malloy's gaze as if he is on the serum instead of me. This evil creature can't have a soul, can he? What does he see now that makes him pause in such a way?

He sighs and smiles at me. "So you see, it is crucial that we find Bolglarka."

"No, I don't see." A bubbling hatred fills my chest, and suddenly his hair doesn't look quite so bright, and the light in the room is dull and infuriating.

Adakin frowns and fumbles for his pocket. "Preparation is the key for success, Aston. Preparation and the upper hand."

My face smiles and then falters, and he mutters something under his breath.

"Preparation?" I ask.

"Yes. You, for instance. You fail because you are impulsive and too trusting of others. Perhaps if you were more leery of situations, thought the worst of others and more about yourself, you would be further along in this New World."

He finds whatever he was looking for and walks over to the other chair at the table. Falling heavily into it, he places a small vial of yellow liquid on the table only a few feet away from me. He sighs and pats his forehead with the top of his forearm.

"Take the sodium potassium pump for instance. It's our body's best invention, I dare say. No need look far for the best inspiration in technological advances. Our own nervous system is the key to all of our greatest inventions."

He pulls up the very sleeve he just doused in his own sweat and exposes a delicately thin arm covered in brown spots. "When our skin is touched there is an intricate way of sending a message to the brain through the releasing and accepting of ions. But once the message is sent, what does our body do?" He pauses for effect. "It expends even more energy to accept back those same ions. Why would our bodies put forth so much effort just for the purpose of being prepared?" He slaps the table and I jump. "To cut reaction time. Old America had this already figured out. Used the same ideas and principles with technology and droids. But how much time is wasted having to pass a message or input a command into a droid? What would happen if the droid's interface was directly connected to a person's brainwaves?" He slams the table again; my wide eyes and processing foggy brain keep me rooted in place. "No more reaction time. The connection between human and droid is now quick and seamless." He snaps his fingers. "Every moment spent making decisions is time wasted. It's as if they share the same brain: soldiers and droids. Chauffeurs and maglevs. And in some rare cases, Recipient and maid."

Bile rises in my throat. My mind rests on the image of Janice. She can't be controlled like some droid, can she?

"Only, in order to keep out interferences or the confusion of human desire to dream or wish for things we don't really mean, a soldier's emotions had to be adjusted. Otherwise, an emotional thought could make a droid turn on them and lead to an innocent person's death."

*Yes, you sound so concerned for innocent lives.* My smile loosens and my face relaxes. "So you decided to use the same interference on Donors?" I say, thinking of the serum and my own struggle to control my emotions and thoughts.

"Not exactly, no. But yes, I guess it's the same idea. With Donors, however, I wanted it to evolve with their blood. Still affect them years after donating. But yes, to have the same idea of control, emotions needed to be tampered with—leveled out."

"What robots, then, is our blood connected to?"

Adakin's chuckle, like a dead engine revving, sends prickly briars across my skin.

"Not a robot, though tempting and terrifying at the

same time. I had much more intricate plans in mind for the Donor blood. It was never meant to link them to a specific device, but to evolve to where they would react of their own will to certain things. To work much like their epigenomes are already working, affected by outside sources or exposures. It's like brainwashing without the months of torture. A Donor's blood obeys the command of their leader without knowing what or why they're doing it, and the best part is—they love it! They think they're rich and powerful."

Anger rolls through me, and I move so quick to the front of my chair that my head spins. My lip is curled, free of the serum, and my eyes narrow at him. Adakin jumps, grabbing the yellow serum bottle. I look down at the little vial; his knuckles are white from how tight he holds it.

His chuckle makes my head swirl again, and my stomach flips as though I may hurl. He brings up his vial and shakes it lovingly before his face.

"Remind me to show you my hives next time. I had no idea you were this inquisitive about how everything works, and I'm very used to training new apprentices since they never last long here anyway. You know, without a queen bee, under certain circumstances an entire community of bees can die off completely. But that's also why there are beekeepers." He taps his head like he's tapping the rim of an invisible hat as he stands slowly. "Queen bees are the beekeeper's essential tool for control. We mark them. We track them. We fear and worry when we lose them. Now tell me where Bolglarka is." His stare is hard and steely.

We sit like this, staring at each other, for several minutes. I can't tell if he's really thinking I will soon tell him all about my grandmother or if he's looking into my eyes to find results to an experiment with the serum.

"When a queen is born it quickly kills its sisters because

there can only be one queen at a time. You could have your own colony, Aston. In fact, I encourage it, but I need to know where she is. Her rule is over. Now don't make me take drastic measures to get the information out of you."

The waning of the serum makes a sadness come crashing down on me. I lean forward, determined to try and stand again. The possible truth that this Bolglarka is not the person I thought I knew my whole life weighs on my shoulders, pushing me down, trying to knock me over. Yet I push through it with a growl and soon my feet are under me, and I am eye level with the great Recipient king, Adakin Malloy.

His terrified look gives me strength. "I'm no queen. And I'm not a bee either. I'm a person. And I demand freedom and justice for everyone. Especially those you seek to surely destroy." I wobble, but my eyes stay firmly affixed on his decrepit face.

His face contorts in disappointment and the thin flaps of skin under his neck begin to quiver. "You stupid, foolish child," he sneers. He steps so close to me the smell of honey makes my stomach churn and my vision blurs. "I know how these donors worship you. They think your blood makes you different, full of greatness that will save them." He leans close to my ear and his whispering tickles in a way that makes me shake. "But I know the truth about you, Aston, and you deserve no such attention. You will regret this silence."

His meaning is lost on me as perspiration floods my face and nausea takes over my whole being. Is he threatening my life or something else? I swallow, thinking of all those I love who he could hurt.

The King leaves my room with fear in his smile. And as soon as the door closes, I collapse on the floor. I think I weep or maybe I just sleep, I can't tell, but I don't move the entire day. I fall into a restless sort of sleep full of nightmares about bees, and this time I'm not stung to death like in my odd recurring dream as a new Donor. This time they fill me until they are running through my veins, and my blood drips golden as honey, golden as the vial Adakin held. Every drip stings, and I cry out in pain. I'm aware of someone, Janice maybe, entering with food and trying to wake me, but the nightmare courses on. I shout again when smiling Alex comes to take some of my golden blood away, only, when she retrieves it and faces me, it's not Alex. It is Grandma Bolgi.

I gasp awake and sit up in bed. The room is dark again and the bump behind my wall returns. I gulp the air and wish I could open my window to feel some sense of freedom no matter how false it is.

"I am no bird and no net ensnares me. I am a free human being with an independent will." Whispering into the empty room hurts my throat, but I don't care. What would dear Charlotte think of our world now when more ensnares us than just station and poverty like I originally thought?

The knocking comes again, and I twist to the side of my bed, letting my legs dangle.

"Lecky, you disgusting rat, what did I tell you? This is the last time."

I don't wait for this bully to finish. I jump to my feet and make my way to the bookshelf. I will save someone tonight.

# CHAPTER 11

Prying my fingers in-between the wall and the bookshelf, I pull with all my weight, but my arms are sore and weak.

"Get over here butt-face!" the voice in the wall says, and new bumps sound through the room.

I brush my hand up and down along the bookcase and then flip my hand, doing the same on the wall. Nothing. No line or button. There's nothing that would indicate how to open this secret passageway.

I fumble with the books on the shelf, pulling them out several at a time. Nothing seems to do the trick here either. Leaning around the other bookcase, I notice lines on the back of it where it is meant to slide over the window. But how in the world do I get it moving? I stand in front of the books, looking at each one critically.

"Take that, you scum bucket."

I step closer to the shelves. There has to be something here. But I've moved and pulled every single book and nothing's happened. My attention is drawn to the book-ends, picture frames, and odd trinkets. One is a portrait of our leader, the stock photo that hangs in all the classrooms. I move the black framed portrait out of the way, making a track of dust on the shelf. Another frame has a picture of Mason Cross, the first Donor, shaking hands with the King. Ew. Adakin really is that old. The little picture frame moves easily and falls face-first on the shelf. I leave it, and I touch a bronze bookend in the shape of a beehive and a shiver runs up my arm. The line of books falls over when I move it out of the way, and still the bookcase is in place.

Frustrated, I lean both hands on the shelf and as my head falls back, I spot a shiny gold sculpture in the shape of our New World Emblem on the top shelf. It looks as if two arms sprout out of the wood of the shelf like a tulip. In the hands rests a dark-red ruby, cut carefully and placed upside down like a red droplet.

What was it Brutis had said at dinner that night? "She's the high one, isn't she? A rare jewel in our land." I recall how his eyes formed slits at the thought, and a different sort of shiver runs over my arms as I remember his presence in this room.

This room that Marcus and Adakin both said was funded by Brutis. That's how he and his accomplices made it in here so easily. Brutis wrote up the plans for this addition to the Malloy house and paid for it. Brutis must have made the passageways as a way for him to have access to the Donors, and the dinner party narrowed it down for him which one to kidnap. My eyes never leave the statue, and I reach up on my tiptoes for it. Instead of coming free in my hand it tilts forward with a loud, winding *click*.

Whirs and snapping sounds make me step back, and the bumping in the wall stops. *That's right, Lecky. I'm coming for you.* The bookshelf slides over the window perfectly, revealing the opening in my wall.

A short laugh escapes me, and the genuine smile that spreads across my face hurts my sore mouth.

I stop to put on the ridiculous-looking bird hat, so I can protect Lecky from any of my germs, and then I peek into the opening.

Light shines from it, and when I step closer, I can hear the breathing of Lecky's tormentor. I place a hand on the edge of the wall and lean my head in. Directly in front of me is a tiny metal staircase. I turn my head toward the source of the light, the part of the wall that is behind my bed. The space is bigger than I imagined it would be. On the other end of this long hallway is a boy aiming a flashlight in my eyes. I shield my face, trying to get a better look at him and ready to give him a talking to. The boy looks slightly younger than Torrin, and his black hair pokes out over his ears and down across his eyes. Surely this isn't the bully. His skin is olive toned with spots along his arm and face that are lighter colored. As if he has some sort of dry skin condition. The torch shakes and bounces as he points it at me.

"Lecky?" I say, wondering if this is the poor boy being tortured. Right, the poor mute boy isn't going to respond. I step through the small entryway wondering how in the world the gorilla guy made it through.

I take another step and Lecky shuffles backward against the corner, pulling something large against him. "You can't take him from me, he's mine."

I freeze. So Lecky does talk. "I'm not going to take anything from you. I just wanted to help."

"Then how did you know my rotten cat's name?" Just as he says it, the object in his hands wriggles free and jumps from his arms with a small meow.

"Lecky? Is the *cat's* name? Well then who..." The light

reflects in his dark eyes peering between a lock of hair. "*You're* the bully."

"Please just let us go. I was only trying to get him back. He likes to come here at night for some reason, and I can't ever get him to stay away. Just please don't tell—"

"Lecky's the cat?" I say again, unable to keep from smiling no matter how much it hurts. I can't help it now. I slap my knee as I bend over and a laugh bubbles up my chest. My head rocks forward with the motion. Janice was right after all. It was a cat. It feels so good to laugh it soon intensifies, and I put an elbow on the wall and lean on it for support. "This whole time I was trying to save—" Before long, I'm wiping at the tears that are being squished out of my eyes. "A cat?"

"Please don't tell. Especially not Juice. Don't tell Juice, miss."

The boy's frightened voice quickly sobers me, and I wipe my face as I sigh loud, moaning sighs to stop the laughing. "Juice? Who would I tell, boy? I'm probably in as much trouble as you for finding this door. They'd move me out of this room faster than a heartbeat of blood if they knew about this."

He seems to think about this for a minute and then slowly stands. "So you won't tell Juice?"

I faintly recall Janice introducing herself to me. "*My friends call me Juice... but that's a story for another time.*"

"You mean Janice?" I say.

The boy giggles, and the giant cat winds between his legs. "Yeah, Janice."

"How did you find this place?" I stand up straight now that I've recovered from my fit of laughing.

"Lecky found it. Those stairs connect right to our room in the attic."

"The attic? What are you doing up there?"

"It's where we live." He says it so matter-of-factly that I don't know how to question him next.

The wood creaks above us and the boy shifts uneasily, stepping toward me, then thinking better of it.

"That's Juice, I mean Janice. I have to make it back before she notices I'm gone."

"Wait, Janice is checking in on you? Is she your maid too?"

The boy squinches his face. "No bloody way. Now move, I gotta go."

He pushes me out of the way, but I have to move back into my room in order for him to get by. He slinks past my room with his cat. In the opposite direction is another set of stairs leading up. He is two steps up into the shadows of the small stairway when I call out to him.

"What is your name?"

"Trip," he says hesitantly and then is gone.

I stare at the empty stairs now almost blue without the torch. A faint click of a door echoes through this little hallway, and I know he has made it back safely. Trip. My little bully in the walls. I chuckle again as I step to the bookshelf and push the statue of hands holding blood back into place. The book case slides effortlessly and silently back into place as well. So quietly I'm sure I would not be able to hear it at night. Not a pleasant thought, but not enough to ruin my victory. I wonder who else knows about this passageway?

My walls shimmer with a rippling white light like they did when I tried to call Janice but got Marcus instead. When I turn around it happens again. It starts in the center of the wall right above the desk opposite my bed. It looks like a stone thrown into water with bright-white waves that vibrate away from the center.

"Aston," an electronic voice hisses into my room as the wall ripples brightly again. "Are you there? Aston?"

"Who's there?" I step to the shelf and grab the statue firmly in case I need to make a quick getaway.

"Aston, it's me." I recognize the voice as it sounds less electronic this time. But last time I recognized a figure; thought I knew a voice... I shiver. The sound of this voice does something strange to my insides, though. It's like warm lava melting everything within me. Then the next words hiss over the lava, and I'm chilled ice cold just like his hands.

"It's me, Gannet."

# CHAPTER 12

My hand relaxes then slips off the ruby droplet. "Gannet?" I whisper in disbelief.

I stride across the room, staring at the now dark wall, wondering if I'm dreaming or if I imagined that bright white epicenter completely. But then it's back again, and I can hear it. I hear him, wonderful, never-failing Gannet.

"We're testing our tech to see how to infiltrate the walls. Seems there's more than wood or drywall holding you in that room."

All I can do is giggle. I can't believe my ears.

"How are you?" he asks, and I close my eyes to the sound of his caring voice. Always caring. "Are you okay? What are they doing to you? Have they hurt you?"

"Yes. I mean no." I grunt and roll my eyes. "Yes, I'm okay. No, they haven't hurt me. Not really. They're only doing what Recipients do best—bleeding me. What tech? How are you doing this? Are you in Bloomfield?"

*Please be here! Please come and take me away tonight.* A funny knot forms in my stomach as I remember the last "rescue." *Make sure to set up a code first. I have to be more careful this time.*

"No. Actually, I can't tell you where I am... or how I'm doing it either. We have to make sure this doesn't get picked up first. It's our first attempt to break through at all, and I convinced them to risk trying to call you."

The lava leaks through the chilled cracks of my heart. He's not here. But he's fighting for me.

"Thanks," I say stupidly.

"I'm sorry, Aston."

I close my eyes again, trying to picture his warm, hazel puppy eyes and his soft tan face. His apology causes emotion to strangle my chest. "What for, Gannet? You were the best technician I ever had."

His laugh is like the caramel color of his eyes—warm, thick, and sweet.

"I was the *only* technician you had. And I could have done better at protecting you."

"I was pretty stubborn. I didn't know it was the resistance... I should have let you tell me about them that day."

"Your grandmother said you were stubborn. She only laughed when I told her about trying to inform you. But I've wondered since then. What was it you thought I was going to tell you that day?"

My hands quickly rescue my burning cheeks, and I'm glad it's dark and he can't see me. I don't want to think about my mistake. I don't want him to know how I thought he was trying to confess his love for me and propose marriage. I don't want to think about how I misread his friends' words when they said they were glad Gannet found me, that the whole New World was. I thought they were referencing what a nice match Gannet had found in me.

A muffled voice in the background makes smaller ripples across the walls.

"Did we lose service?" someone in the background says.

"I don't know. Aston? You there?"

"I'm here." I throw my head back and look at the ceiling. I didn't know others were listening.

"Good."

The muffled voice in the background tells Gannet something else, and I wait, wringing my hands, thankful for the subject change.

"Okay," Gannet says to the people with him. "Aston, we need to know about your cell."

"My... cell?"

"Yes. We were able to decipher the code of your compass address to infiltrate the intercom system, but we have no idea where exactly the prison is located. Did you say you're somewhere in Bloomfield? You're in Recipient territory? Do you know if you are underground? Or how high up? Do you know anything about your surroundings that could give us a clue?"

How was Gannet able to get me that sketch if he didn't already know where I was? Did they have Donor spies hidden within these Recipient walls?

"I'm in no dungeon," I say slowly. "I'm in the palace. The Malloy house."

A long pause rings through the air, making me wonder now if the connection is lost.

"Did you say... you're in the Malloy cell?"

"No. Not in a cell. In their very house. Mansion really." Once I start, I can't seem to stop the information. I tell them about Brutis, his money that funded this room and his attempt to kidnap me. I tell them about the library with the secret office that I can't enter and how the window is now

120

locked shut. I tell them about Lazuli and the technician and the scientific study with false hopes.

There's a long, strained sigh on the other end when I finish. Hopelessness fills the room from their silence.

A voice in the background says in a hushed tone, "Scars galore. The palace?"

"Aston, I need you to do something for me," Gannet says firmly.

"Yes." I step forward, leaning even closer to the wall, trying to get as close to Gannet's voice as I possibly can. Others may have given up hope, but not Gannet. Not faithful Gannet. I wish I had known all along that he wasn't the drugged technician I thought he was but that he was sincere and genuine. How different things might have been then.

"What is it?" I say.

"We need to know about their tech."

"Their tech?"

"Yes. It took us three weeks to break this circuit code just for audio. But we're going to need to know more in order to complete our tasks."

Their tasks? Am I not their task, then? My cheeks warm. I'm grateful Gannet doesn't know my thoughts or how self-centered they are. It makes me think again of my misinterpretation of Gannet's motivation. It's never love. Gannet has always cared about the rebellion first. I somehow became a part of that loyalty, but not anything more.

"Aston?"

"Yeah, of course. I don't know much. I know they use lasers instead of water, and their mirrors have power to replicate the reflection onto your skin." I sigh and slump my shoulders. I've been waiting for them to come for weeks, determined to show them how important and useful I can be. I doubt knowledge about bubble baths and makeup mirrors is going to help my case. "And their walls are blood activated."

"What do you mean, 'blood activated'?"

I stand up straighter. "It can read my blood through my skin like all of our portable scanners."

"Any part of the wall?"

"I think so. I haven't tested it out too much. I'm not very good at it. It can read minds too and I—"

"Read your thoughts? How in scars..." He trails off.

I don't say anything as I can almost hear their discouraged minds thinking.

"We need you to find out everything you can about the walls. And about the hallways and any rooms surrounding you as well. We're hoping to have a live connection with the screens in your walls in two weeks. We'll give you a sign of some sort to know when. Be ready. But Aston—" His voice is deeper now, and my throat closes over. Hearing his voice brings back so many memories. Of home and family and everything I knew. He is there with them. He is on the other side of the wall. Exactly where I want to be. Exactly where I tried not to be for sixteen years, and now I wish for nowhere else.

"Yeah?" My voice falls so flat and small in the giant room that I'm not even sure it's broadcast across the miles to Gannet.

"Be safe."

Two words. Those two words say so much more. I don't know if it's my imagination or if it's what he really means, but just like I read the lines on that sketch of the bird, I read the meaning in his words right now. Words he spoke to me as a technician, as a friend. Be safe. Be safe when I cannot keep you that way.

"I will. Gannet?"

"Hm?"

"Do you have any news about my family?"

The pause is torturous. And for a moment the way he mumbles with the other people in the room makes me wonder if he is ignoring my inquiry.

"Safe but in hiding. Look for the sign. See you in two weeks."

The audio starts to crackle, and I step again closer to the wall. "Torrin!" I shout.

The audio is clear again for a second. "What?"

"Get Torrin. My brother. He can help with the tech."

I hear a chuckle. And an uncertain "okay" that sounds like they won't look for Torrin at all. Then Gannet is on again, his voice hissing with a whisper as the crackling intensifies over it. "Take care, Aston. Don't worry, it won't be much longer. I—" It cuts out before he can finish, and my room is doused in silence.

I step forward and place my hand against the cool wall. The bright-white light outlines my hand instantly. *Steady your thoughts, Aston.* Figure out the tech, the walls, the halls and rooms. I add another one to the list. Figure out a way into Adakin's office. My hand zings at the memory of touching the door, and as a click echoes through the room, I realize I forgot to focus my thoughts.

# CHAPTER 13

I release my held breath. "Janice?" I say into the empty dark room. Too many visitors in one night.

"Miss Aston? It's four in the morning. What are you doing up already?"

"I..." Did I call her? I'm so excited to get it right, to have contacted the person I was wanting to without even saying anything, and with distracted thoughts. I don't know what to do next. "I need you, Janice. Is it too early to call on breakfast? I received my meals so differently yesterday that... " My hands automatically rub at my arms, remembering Adakin in this room. How glad I am that it didn't reach out to him. How does that work anyway? Do I have access to whoever I think about? That's what I need to figure out.

Janice yawns loudly before answering. "Right away, miss."

I notice how the light dims around my hand indicating the lost connection before lighting up again waiting for my next command. Swiftly I remove my hand before it can make a mistake.

Quicker than I thought possible, my door opens, and Janice enters in her regular white uniform with a tray in hand. Has she not slept all night?

"Janice, forgive me for waking you so early. How inconsiderate of me."

"Never mind me, miss. I don't know how you're still standing after what the president put you through yesterday. I brought as many meats and cheeses as possible."

"Cheese?" It's all my weary distracted mind can register. Janice laughs as she sets the tray on the table. "Thank you, Janice. Now I hope you can get some more sleep until your regular duties wake you."

"No use now," she says as I stuff my mouth with several cubes of smooth orange cheddar. "Once awake there's no going back." She yawns again and sits at the table. "Hope you don't mind if I join you?"

"Please," I say, stretching out my hand over the food.

We sit in silence for a little while until Janice lets out a sigh. I wonder how much she knows about the tech behind these walls. Or that I know about Trip.

"How do these walls work, Janice?" I've always been known for my tact.

"I'm not the best one to ask. I just know how to work them for what I need. I've never questioned how they do it."

"But they read our minds?"

"Only to a degree. And they're not foolproof. Mistakes happen all the time. A kink I think the system will have worked out before too long. Once I accidentally called my Great Aunt Bea when I was cleaning and didn't even realize my mother was talking about her in the other room."

I laugh at the blunder and think of my own mistake.

"So, it will call whoever or wherever you're thinking about whether you're wanting to or not?"

"Within your access, yes." She reaches out and grabs a link of sausage.

"What do you mean?"

"Well, everyone's blood has a range of access, authority, if you will. The only person who's able to access anyone anywhere, I would think, is the president. The higher your position, the more access you would have. And family members can block access. Great Aunt Bea, for instance, we couldn't contact her through the walls for a good two years after that fiasco. It took the death of my Uncle Paisley for her to let us have access again."

"But it seems so faulty. It's so sensitive and susceptible to mistakes. One thought and you're connected. What if your thoughts wander?"

Janice laughs a staccato type "ha" as she sips the orange juice she has poured for herself. "Better learn to school your thoughts around here, missy."

I think about what Adakin Malloy said when he was in my room. My memories are tainted with leftover fog from the serum, yet I can still hear his words. "To cut reaction time" he had said. Was it the serum that also affects our ability to, as Janice says, school our thoughts enough for these walls to read our minds? Or does the use of this wall tech have nothing to do with the serum at all? If this wall communication was linked to the serum that would mean these Recipients would have to be on it as well. Wouldn't it?

"What about outside sources?" I say. "How does one house contact another down the street or even farther?"

"We are full of questions this morning, aren't we? No wonder you couldn't sleep." Janice sits up and I grab a handful of cheese to hide my intense curiosity.

"Like I said, I'm not exactly sure how it all works. But I think it works similarly to computer servers. Your blood is given a server address to know how to communicate to other servers. The walls are made completely out of blood-activated touch screens and run underground as well. They act as the wire that connects the two servers. How the screen reads the mind is the part I'm unsure about, though."

I already know the answer though, don't I? Adakin Malloy, yesterday in this very room, told me about the officers with nanobots in their blood connecting them to droids and in the process, having their emotions completely stripped from them. But Donors have serum running through them—what do Recipients have in their system? I slowly nibble at my cheese as I think over the possibilities. But Marcus seems so free of anything. Could he really be drugged with something?

I put my hand to my head. I shut my eyes tight for a moment. Maybe when I open them, I will be more awake and able to think through this fog. Slowly recalling all the events of the night, I open my eyes and stare at Janice. "How are you connected to the boy in the wall?"

She chokes on her cheese and bugs her eyes. "I don't know what you mean, miss," she says after recovering. When she tries to turn away, I grab her arm.

"I mean the boy called 'Trip' with a giant mangy cat, Janice."

It does something strange within my soul to see a person look at me the way Janice does. I have to force myself to remember she is the Recipient, and I am the Donor. A Recipient looking at me with their face contorted with fear makes my hand retract like a spring and my heart drops with confused panic.

"Don't tell anyone, miss. I could be in so much trouble if anyone found out. Trip's my boy, miss. He doesn't mean to get into so much trouble. He doesn't know what they could do to him, what they could do to me if they knew he was hiding here." Her voice squeaks with terror, and I grab both of her elbows to keep her from falling.

"Of course not. Shh. Of course not, Janice."

She grabs onto my arms and we hold each other. Staring into each other's eyes in that moment, we become blood sisters in a sense. We exchange the look that we realize connects us. Fear. Fear for more than just ourselves but for someone we love. How can this sweet, dear woman be a Recipient? How can I feel such a closeness to someone who uses my people so egregiously?

"I have a brother very close to Trip's age," I say. "I know what it's like to be afraid for their life. Your secret's safe with me. Don't worry."

I hadn't noticed the room filling with light until a bright ray of sun cracks into the room, hitting Janice right in the face. Her wet eyes glisten for the first time, and she catches the falling tear before it travels far.

"Thank you, miss. I knew from the beginning you were different from all the rest. You are smart and brave and free." She squeezes my shoulder in a way that makes me wish she was my family. That I could be loved by my family the way she loves and accepts me.

The door plows open, hitting the wall behind it. For a moment I almost think my wish is true and Torrin is bounding into the room, but it's only Alex. Janice and I step quickly away from each other.

"Oh, you've eaten," Alex says, not as a question but in a dissatisfied statement.

"I was given no orders not to," Janice replies stiffly.

Alex starts my donation and messes with the little black box with her back turned to me. She glares at me before she leaves. It must have been part of the plans to have me unfed and weak before donations again.

This donation, though early, is uneventful. No serum as far as I can tell. No Adakin. When it is over, I'm left completely alone. This is Lazuli's month, after all, and now I don't even have access to the library. I play chess with myself for hours and take a nap since I got no sleep.

Standing by the window, admiring the flowers, I notice someone going out to the garden. Two of them. They move out from under the thick shade of the ash tree I stood by. Marcus, with his hands behind his back, strolls slowly with Lazuli by his side. Though she keeps her distance from him, she cuts her eyes up to his face curiously. I'm happy to see her so well, but seeing her also makes me grip the windowsill until the wood bruises my palms. She looks better than I've seen her in a while. Finally, some color to her face and her hair is growing back healthy and shiny again. Black like a raven's wing. So black it's almost purple.

Their lips move but I can't tell what they're saying. I try to open my window but know it's useless. I am more caged-in than ever since the break in. My hand starts to sweat against the glass as I stare. Marcus stops walking and puts a hand on Lazuli's shoulder. My hand on the window turns to a fist as something squeezes tight within my chest. *Stay away from her*, I want to say. He points across the garden to something, and though Lazuli looks in that direction I can tell from here how her eyes dart to his hand on her.

She walks closer to him from then on. Around the pond full of rainbow-colored hybrid koi fish. Their elbows almost touch. Near the hydrangea lilies where Marcus and I argued, he pauses and looks at her. I never thought about

Lazuli being taller than me, but they are more eye-level than Marcus and me. Their lips are still, and I can't read what's being said through their eyes.

I slam my fist on the window. A low pong reverberates through the glass. Marcus looks up in my direction, and I spin out of sight, planting myself against the bookshelf.

I squeeze my eyes shut. Why does it bother me so much to see Lazuli with Marcus? I knew this was going to happen. But he took Lazuli to the garden on her first day. I didn't get that kind of freedom until a whole month of donating to him.

I push off the shelf with a grunt. I need to think of something else. Someone else. Like Gannet. I shake my head. No. Like Torrin. Think about what Torrin would do if he were stuck in here. How would he find out about their tech?

I feel certain my answers are in that office in the library, but how do I get there now that I have no access? I reach out to touch the doorknob. My fingertips tingle from the electricity before I even make contact.

I turn away with an angry sigh and throw my hands up in the air. What am I to do? I plop onto the velvet sofa and spot the book Marcus gave me on the history of the germ wars. It's large and cumbersome, like our own history textbooks. I can already tell, though, that their pictures are not altered or photoshopped like ours. Thumbing through the pages, I land on a random picture of the virus through a microscope. It's giant in comparison to the other cells in the picture, a large blob with spikes and peaks of different lengths. Underneath the picture it reads, *A masterpiece in its own way, the HIVE-19 virus has spikes to bind with the host cell and captures human proteins on its lipid surface. Its aim is the guardian of our defense, the white blood cell. And it carries a companion bacteria, which piggybacks on the virus.*

I flip the pages looking for something I don't already know. A picture of the deadliest bacteria ever known comes into view. It's the second-largest killer and starts with a common cold, leaving the body prepped perfectly for this awful detonator. The black and white image of circles layered on top of each other resemble a flower. Hence the name "Triantacoccus." Trianta—Greek for rose. Under this image reads, *Triantacoccus sp. is a mutant bacteria from the Staphylococcus family with nectar-inhabiting microbes. It was the first of its kind as a virus-bacterial complex capable of infecting humans, insects, and plants residing in soil for long periods of time. Once the complex virus is in the bloodstream, attaching itself to most of the host's blood cells, it could then reach the host's DNA. Having access to the sperm and egg cells then made it a vertical transfer virus and a dangerous STI. The bacterial part of the complex virus can be found in the mucus membranes of the GI system, the respiratory system, as well as certain organs like the liver and kidneys. It first presents itself in the form of NF (necrotizing fasciitis, or flesh eating disease) on the inside organs and STSS (strep toxic shock syndrome). Symptoms include: lowered blood pressure, loss of appetite, shock, severe abdominal pain, purple discoloration of the skin, fever, vomiting, and eventual internal bleeding.*

A chill runs up my spine and I flip through the pages again. I stop at a page that is titled: "The Creator" and find there is a page missing. My fingers run along the ragged edges in the center of the fold. My gaze rolls over images of the old world. Children with distended, naked bellies and flies in the cracks of their eyes, women making mud pies and handing them to children who eat them like cookies, different shapes of wood or fabric thrown together in a lopsided hut with holes and gaps. These were their homes? I read the caption under one of the images.

"Before the development of WWC (world wide consecration), hunger was the leading cause of death. When the WWC banned a corporation's ability to outsource overseas for cheap labor and created a third world country tax, a balance was underway."

I turn the page and glance over images of homes being built. There are smiling faces and families shaking hands while taking boxes of what looks like food. The caption: *Triumphantly, the WWC ended world hunger, and with the medical and technological advances, the eradication of cancer and HIV2 was an added victory. It was a great time to be alive.*

I stare at two small contradicting images. The happy, "it's-a-great-time-to-be-alive" photo, and an image next to it of people with their mouths open mid-shout, carrying posters that read, *We have a right to independent corporations. End the consecration tax.*

The caption underneath reads, *Though many rejoiced over the benefit to the countries, others were not supportive of the invasion of privacy in the corporate world. Thus began the Corporate Wars that we now call the Germ Wars and the introduction of the IPC.*

IPC? I've heard that before. I read on and stop when the name "Adakin Malloy" pops up on the page.

*A firm believer in the IPC and a corporation's right to the private use of their funds, this programmer from Great Britain formed a union with a team of mathematicians, statisticians, programmers, and some of the best scientists in the world.*

The next page mentions the woman Marcus mentioned. *With the help of her team of scientists, Eva Tabor created the first virus for the first germ war. An oil dispute between her native country of Hungary and the world's top oil producer,*

*India, was taken to the next level of combat. It's unclear if anyone then knew exactly what Tabor was capable of or if Tabor herself knew what she was doing.*

I stop reading and turn the pages one by one as the history of the Germ Wars relays in picture form. Images of people's skin deteriorating from the bacteria. Hospital beds lined with those infected and dying of simple colds and dehydration. Children with dark circles under their eyes, much like Marcus's when I first met him. The elderly lying helpless on the streets, shriveled and purple. It makes me think of Janice's husband and how she couldn't bear watching him suffer. Lastly, it makes me soberly consider Marcus's mother. I often underestimate what he and other Recipients have had to go through. If I had seen all this, would I form a nation of Donors to save them?

*Tabor and her team of scientists worked at a feverish pace through the next four years, creating viruses and vaccines for different countries and becoming rich with their own corporate success. The goal of the IPC was soon lost in the frenzy of power and money.*

My mouth purses together in a straight line. This Eva is a monster. I hope she died quickly with the Recipient virus. Though I know the general timeline of this history, I have never had so many specifics, and I have definitely never heard of this Eva Tabor. This horrible excuse of a human being that killed innocent people for the sake of corporations. Yes, Adakin may have been the leader of this organization that eventually backfired on him, but this woman was clearly the one holding the murder weapon.

This bit of information makes me want to get into that office even more. Perhaps there's something in there about this Eva. About this group. And about how to get me out of here and with the resistance to fight against people like Eva and Adakin.

I sit on the sofa staring out into the room; the setting sun goes unnoticed as my mind reels and different images cross my vision. How do I get in? How do I get to the library?

A thump behind the wall floats through the room.

# CHAPTER 14

The walls! I slam the book closed and throw it onto the sofa as I make my way across the room. I pull on the golden idol of hands and blood and watch the bookshelf slide effortlessly and silently out of the way.

"Amazing," I whisper.

I put only my head in where Lecky the gray cat is twitching his tail as he steps around the small hallway. His green eyes reflect back at me and soon he is purring his way to me. Mute Lecky. I smile again at my little victim.

"Come here, kitty," I say.

I bring the soft, happy creature into the room with me and sit on the floor, leaning against my bed. The boy Trip comes down the stairs and freezes in place when he sees the door open. He peaks around the corner until he sees me with a purring Lecky in my arms.

"You old scumbag traitor," he grumbles to the cat. He stops in the secret doorway and leans against the frame, unsure about entering.

"Have a seat." I point to the floor and scramble to find the stupid bird hat.

He creeps in, eyeing me suspiciously, and takes a seat under the bookshelf directly across from me. "You don't need a fancy hat for the likes of me," he says circling his hand around his head. "That dumb virus don't scare Juice and it don't scare me."

I hesitate with the hat. It is rather silly and cumbersome and Lecky swats at a piece of ribbon that is dangling off the side. Trip's complaint sounds exactly like something Torrin would say and a twinge of sadness makes me put the hat on anyway. "Better safe than sorry. Now, we need to figure out exactly what we're going to do about our mutual friend here." Lecky continues to reach for the dangling ribbon that is now close to my face and it makes me laugh.

"What do you mean 'do'? What is there to do with her? You ain't going to get rid of her, are ya? You ain't going to turn us in?"

"No, no. I only meant... Well, I have some questions. How do you feed her, for instance?"

"The kitchen," he snaps at me with a shrug.

"These walls go to the kitchen?"

He nods once while tracing the wooden floor with his finger. His black hair is dirty and knotted. I wonder if I could help give this boy a proper bath and maybe some clothes that don't expose his knees and elbows.

"Where else do these walls go, Trip?"

"I haven't gone in all of them. I only have the night to go through them and some of these passageways go too close to other rooms. I don't risk being heard, especially not now that..." He flicks his gaze up at me. Especially not now that he knows he can be discovered so easily.

My hands stop on Lecky's back as my mind is thinking of the risks and the possibilities too. The gray fuzz-bucket leaves my lap and slinks to her owner who smiles at her return.

This boy's innocent joy makes my nose sting with emotion. I picture Torrin, who loved his questions and his Papa and his port screen games. Trip has perfect teeth like Marcus and signs of well treatment in his childhood. But now he is so unkempt and unpresentable. Is it from his father, Janice's sick husband, dying that made him become so forgotten?

"Janice is your mother, then?"

His smile fades when he looks at me and he gives his attention back to the cat when he speaks. "Somethin' like that."

"You *are* a Recipient, correct?"

He laughs and looks at me like I'm the stupid Donor everyone assumes we are. "You think me a Donor?"

"Were you and Janice rich before?" I don't know how to say "before your father died." Before Janice was convicted of his murder. Before they were forced into this life of slavery. How did Janice bring him here to hide out in the attic? Is it illegal for a convicted Recipient to keep their children?

"I was richer than Juice. She came to our house as a maid, like she is here. My mother hated Juice. Said she smelled funny and had a distrustful stare and sticky hands. The kind of sticky that made things disappear in the rooms." He puts his hands in the air and wriggles his fingers. Lecky stops purring and opens his eyes to protest.

"Juice was your maid?"

"Yeah, once. I was little. My father was..." he lowers his head even further before his low gruff voice returns. "Was not a very forgiving man. Heavy hands, I think is what Juice called it."

"Heavy-handed?" I ask.

He shrugs again.

"Juice had a way of getting me out of messes. Out from under his... hands. She's who I learned how to snoop from. It's how I found these walls." His shoulders lift with pride.

"But how did you get here? Did Janice... kidnap you?"

He contemplates this. As if he had never thought about it before. He looks me square in the eyes, and it's the first time I notice the flecks of green in the brown. "No, miss." He refers to me in the way Janice insists upon. "Juice *saved* me."

These two odd creatures, Janice and Trip, feel like kin. I lean back against my bed and smile at him.

"I know what you mean, Trip." I clasp my hands and put them on top of my head as I watch the boy and his cat. I always pictured Recipients harsh and selfish. Greedy like Adakin and Brutis. But these two show a different side of the Recipients that I hadn't ever considered. It seems there are Recipients suffering from this regime just as much as Donors are. Is it possible that there are just as many Recipients suffering on this side of the wall, like this young boy adopted into Janice's loving arms, as there are Donors suffering on the other side?

The moon shines bright into my face through the window. "I need to get somewhere in this house, Trip. Do you know where the library is?"

"Of course. It's right above the kitchen. Quietest walls of the whole place. And the first place I discovered. But there's someone that goes there at night."

His eyes narrow with warning. I bet I know exactly who is going there at night and exactly where they are going.

"Can you take me there?"

He frowns as he considers it, then picks up Lecky. He stands and sighs. "Sure. But if I hear someone coming, it's your own bloody butt that will be caught 'cause I'll bolt faster than Lecky chasing a mouse. I won't hang around for no one, not even a Donor who Juice likes."

I smile to hear Janice has talked about me and that she likes me. Trip seems so independent and sure of himself. Like a little adult. Like Torrin.

"Deal," I say, putting out my hand.

Trip looks at it and then bunches his face to one side in a small grimace like he's saying "I don't think so." He turns away from me instead. "Come on," he grumbles. Something about that grumble doesn't sound annoyed. It somehow sounds sweet and caring. He leads the way through the dim hallway and up the stairs. At the top is another small hallway.

We stop in the attic where he drops off Lecky. Through the small doorway, I spy a pile of blankets on the floor with a tray of food by it. Is that where he sleeps? My heart aches for what this little Recipient boy, who talks rough and doesn't make eye contact, has been through. He shimmies back down the hallway and turns. The space is small and confining and our breaths bounce around each other. My hands hold onto the walls for support as the floor tilts forward slightly.

"How are these walls not blood-activated like mine?"

"These walls are not screens like all the other walls. This is like the back of the screen. Whoever designed them made sure there was no detection of what went through them."

Curious. Is it really possible that Brutis has control over this whole space? It makes sense that he would have created passages to the Donor rooms for later escape, but what use would he have for access to the kitchen or the library?

"Here," Trip says and starts to descend down a narrow ladder of sorts. "It's not as thick as the staircase to your room so be careful."

Of course. The staircases were meant for kidnapping. This staircase possibly was only meant for one person. I wonder what the library has that is so important to a Recipient like Brutis? Just as important as a Donor.

We climb down for what seems like ages and then I reach the last step.

"Down that way is another ladder to the kitchens, but this here is the library," he whispers now with cautious excitement.

A small black circle hangs randomly in the middle of the wall. He slides it up and out of the way and two smaller circles flood our hallway with light. He pushes his eyes against the circles. "Come see," he says and moves out of the way.

I put my eyes over the holes and can see the library perfectly. They are aimed at the very office I need to get into.

"Whoa," I gasp. My heart hammers and my stomach flips. I can't believe we made it here. But now what?

Just then the door to the office opens. I pull away when the King steps from the room.

"Is someone there?" Trip hisses. "You need to have your eyes there or it will be an eyeless portrait. Quick."

I push my face back in place and watch without breathing as Adakin runs his hand across the frame of the door and a crisscross of red lasers hum into place. He shuts the door behind him and leaves his palm on the door handle as more locks click loudly.

"There's no way we'll be able to get in there," I whisper.

Thankfully Adakin walks in the opposite direction. I fall back and let the black circle fall over the eye holes.

"The room I need to get into has blood recognition locks and a laser grid."

"Blood recognition could be tricky." Trip pauses for a moment, thinking. "But maybe with a tech scrambler we could do it? And the lasers should be a cinch, you just need a mirror." He digs one out of his pocket. "It's how I get in the fridge for Lecky."

"That's it?" I say, confused and shocked. "And what about a scrambler?"

"I could probably make one. Just hang tight, you desperate Donor." He squeezes past me and disappears, like a cat himself, up the ladder. Again, there's something about his name-calling that feels endearing.

With the dim light of Trip's torch, I stand alone in the hidden hallway when I hear someone else come into the library.

"Thanks for showing me all of this." It's Lazuli's voice like I've never heard it before. There's something more that makes it sound different, more than just the scratched scars from her year of torture. There's something wistful in her voice. Like she is a dream version of herself.

"No problem. It's the least we can do for the best Donors in the New World." Marcus's voice, dripping with compliments, makes me roll my eyes, and I stick my tongue out at the wall.

Lazuli giggles and my stomach churns. "I'm not the *best* Donor. My numbers are so low. I'm a traitor Donor. I lied about my numbers."

"And sold out your best friend and that very Recipient who you caught in his lies!" I hiss into the darkness. How could Marcus be so forgiving of Lazuli the little snitch so easily?

Marcus says, "I'm hoping it can prove a new way of life for both of us."

"I applaud your valiant cause. I never knew Recipients could care so much about our people."

Oh gag! Who are these two? I want to pound on this wall and shout that I can hear them! I want to tear down this wall and tell Lazuli the truth—that this plan is ludicrous and will never bring peace to anyone. That it is as delusional as the serum makes Donors. It's a lie. And what is this about the "best Donor"? Believe me, I'm not competing to be Marcus's favorite in anything. I stomp my foot a little too loudly and their conversation pauses. The next words deflate me into a cold, mucky puddle.

"You know, you're nothing like Aston," Marcus says.

What is that supposed to mean?

"Aston always was the dramatic one," Lazuli says. "Had such drastic views of how things should be. I always agreed with her that things were unfair. But, your way makes so much more sense. Why break all the rules and get into trouble? It only hurts the cause worse and puts our families in jeopardy."

I ball my fist as I watch them casually stroll in a circle. Lazuli never really liked books. The door shuts behind them as they leave, and I pound my fist on the wall. "I put them in jeopardy for you, Laz!" I hiss. "You're the one that lost your family! I was only trying to fix things!"

"Shut up or you'll get us caught," Trip whispers down the ladder.

I shake my hands to ease the tension building in my shoulders and tug my stupid hat down further. I don't need Marcus or Lazuli. I just need to get in this office, find out about the tech—maybe from Trip who seems more like Torrin by the minute—and get out of here.

Trip lands next to me, catching his breath before he talks. In his hands is a heap of wires that looks like he gutted an officer's handheld scanner.

"Have you done this before?" I ask.

"Only on the blood-activated walls around my attic, but how different can the lock be?"

I sigh and push down what Lazuli said about me. I am not the dramatic one. "Only one way to find out, I guess." I try to laugh, but who am I kidding? I don't want to think about what the king will do if he catches me. Or Trip.

With that, Trip shows how a kick with his bare foot opens the portrait like a doorway into the library.

# CHAPTER 15

I stand looking at the large open doorway. "With as high tech as these walls are I would think this would set off an alarm or something."

Trip only shushes me as he tiptoes along the floor with his wires trailing behind him. He places a black sticky pad over the doorknob, careful not to touch the metal. The humming of the lasers makes the hair of my scalp tingle.

With metal clips, he attaches wires of different colors to the black pad, and soon the miniport screen from his pocket lights up.

A door shuts in the distance and we jump, our heads spinning in unison toward the sound. He shuts off the miniport, plunging the room into darkness again. A shadow creeps toward us as if it also came from the portrait hole. I grab Trip's hand, and he silently retrieves the wires and the miniport, leaving the black sticky strip on the door. We slip against the wall, plastered to it like portraits, hoping to be invisible in the dark. Slowly we edge our way down the wall and away from the door.

The shadow passes us silently, never noticing us, and

stops at the door as well. In a matter of minutes, he has made his way through the door and the lasers, but his stealth proves him to be an intruder like us. He opens drawers and throws papers all around. Trip turns his face up at me, but I only shake my head. I don't know who this is or what they're looking for. But now I know more than ever that we must get in that office and find it before they do.

The sound of thumbing through pages flits through the library and the pages flip faster as the intruder loses patience. He throws them out the door where they land with a loud echoing thud.

"We have to get out of here," Trip says, and we scoot farther away, inching toward the portrait.

"Wait," I say as we're about to step through. "I don't want this person getting away with whatever they're after. It may be the very thing I'm looking for." I make it sound like I know more about what I'm looking for than I actually do. Something about this person feels familiar, though, and the unwarranted need for revenge fills my belly. Maybe it's just leftover weird feelings from seeing and hearing Lazuli with Marcus. Maybe it's all the cheese I ate; whatever it is, I want this person caught and I want what they find.

Trip sighs and then retrieves another black sticker. "I can keep them from getting away. But we'll have to come back another time to get your stuff." He puts the sticker on the wall and attaches the wires. His miniport lights up and he quickly taps away at it. "And we'll have to be quick." Seconds later an alarm sounds, and the walls flash bright red.

He rips the sticker from the wall and steps through the portrait door. He waves his arm for me to follow him. I hesitate for a moment, looking back at the open office. I wish

Trip had talked about his plan instead of just sounding the alarm. Sounds like another impulsive person I know. I smile at him. He reminds me a little of me. "Quick!" he says above the alarm and we shut the portrait door just in time to see Brutis's confused face lit up by the flashing red lights. Looks like he went free after kidnapping me.

I'm laughing as we run up the ladder and shimmy down the hallway. "Did you see his face?"

Trip shushes me.

"I wonder what Brutis was looking for." I sober at the thought.

"Be quiet. They'll hear us and we could get caught."

"Nonsense." I grab Trip's arm and stop him. "Hear that?" We listen to the stomping, thumping sound of officer feet on the other side of the wall. "That, my friend, is justice. Whatever you did to the wall is getting Brutis what he deserves."

Trip looks at me funny. "I..." He looks at the shaking walls as if the drumming of officer feet is a familiar, unwelcome sound to him. "I electronically transferred someone into the room," he mutters.

We look at each other and I'm hoping my face conveys the complete and utter confusion I'm feeling.

"I put a digital fingerprint in the library of someone who has never entered these walls and probably never will." He stares off solemnly and then shrugs.

I laugh before asking. "Who?"

"My father." There's no more laughing or discussion as we make it back to his room in the attic.

With his hand on the tiny doorknob, he looks back at me. "Did you mean what you said back there?"

I tilt my head questioningly instead of answering.

"When you called me your friend?"

I don't remember calling him my friend but the way his eyes sparkle even in the dim glow of his miniport, so hopeful, so longing for friendship and connection, makes me smile. I put my hand on his shoulder. "Yeah, kid."

"Never thought I'd be friends with a Donor," he says as he opens the door, a pleased tone to his voice. Lecky is curled up on the scrambled heap of blankets on the floor. Janice stands, her foot tapping on the edge of one of the blankets, with her hands on her hips. Trip and I don't move. Even our mouths are sealed shut as the three of us take turns staring from one to the other in shock.

Janice speaks first in exasperated unfinished sentences. "Mongrel here but no Trip. When I heard... I knew but I didn't think... because why on... What on bloody New Earth were you thinking?" She walks briskly toward Trip and firmly takes him in her arms and gives me a confused yet stern look.

"It was me, Janice. I talked him into taking me to the library. And then—"

"Never mind that right now, miss. Yours will be one of the first rooms they check and if you're not there..."

We all understand her meaning before she's finished and as shouts continue to ring out through the house. The alarm still blares in the distance as we move swiftly down the stairs and into my room. Janice comes with me and turns back to Trip as I hold my ready hand on the jeweled droplet.

"Get back to your room, Trip, and keep that bloody cat in there with you!"

Trip takes off and Janice nods at me. The boots of officers come down my hallway as I push the droplet back in place and the shelves move.

"Janice, how do we explain you being here?"

"I don't know, miss, but come up with something quick. I thought it best you have a witness of you being in bed this whole time."

I nod and my door starts to open. I look to the bookshelf that is not yet closed and panic stabs at my chest. I rush around the bed with Janice in hand, and we hastily greet the officers just as they step through the doorway. The click of the shelf draws their attention to the corner, and they step closer. I step in front of them, pulling Janice with me, which makes her yelp, and the officers give me a stern look.

"What's going on, officers?" I try to sound worried. "Why all the alarms?"

Marcus enters behind the group of officers and they begin to do a sweep of the room. "There's been another break-in, have you heard anything in here?" He walks right past me, straight for the window, and peers out.

"No," I say weakly.

He turns toward us finally but looks as if he can't bear to look at me. His eyes study Janice instead.

"What is your maid doing here?"

I notice the absence of her name and his insistence on referring to her by her station yet again. It makes my chin lift defiantly into the air.

"I had a nightmare and called on Janice."

"A nightmare?" He sneers. "You?"

"I heard the sirens and was then doubly glad she could be with me for this stampede of officers. I hope you caught the intruder?"

Nodding, Marcus grumbles something inaudible.

An officer approaches him. "There is no sign of breach on the walls, sir."

Without another look in my direction, Marcus leaves

and his officers follow. When the door shuts behind them, I sigh and slump and then give a puny stomp of my foot.

"Now do you mind telling me what you were doing sneaking around this house, putting Trip and yourself in danger? And who it was exactly that they caught?" Janice places her hands on her hips like any good, concerned mother would.

"Janice, I don't know exactly how to explain it to you but believe me when I say I *need* to get into Adakin's office."

"What for?" she asks without moving a muscle in her stern face.

"I don't know exactly. But if it's that guarded and Brutis is after it—"

"Brutis again?"

"Yes, Brutis is who they caught tonight snooping in there before we could. And if he is after whatever is in there, then we need to get it first." I make a pathetic smile with my shoulders scrunched up to my ears in the most pleading way I possibly can.

"You want to get into the Recipient ruler's secret, heavily guarded office to search for something you have no clue what it is, just that someone else wants it? And not just any someone else but a nasty perverted rich Recipient who has tried to kidnap you? That is how you are going to argue your case to me?"

"Well, when you put it like that—"

Janice sighs and lets her hands fall from her hips as she turns her back to me.

"Janice, listen—"

"No, you listen, Aston." She spins closer to me and her face is so close I can see the faded lipstick darker in the cracks of her lips and smell her floral scent and dish soap hands. "You may risk your own life and that of your family's, but when it comes to Trip, he is not yours to risk. Do you understand me?"

My eyes freeze in shock and my breath is stuck in my chest for a moment. "Okay," I whisper, close to tears.

Janice sighs again, more defeated than angry. She rubs her brow as she shakes her head and puts one hand on the back of her hip. She whispers, "What is it you think is in that office? What are you hoping it will do for you?"

I bite my bottom lip to keep my chin from quivering. What do I tell her? The only person here that reminds me of home. The only person that keeps me, in a way, connected to family. Can I trust her with my life?

I take a deep breath. "I need some information to help the resistance when they come." My words drip with emotion, but I hold my head up as high as I can.

Janice just stares at me, calculating and serious. I don't know what I'm expecting her to say or do. She just told me I could risk my and my family's lives but to never touch Trip. How do I tell her she feels more like family than anyone I've met here? Right now, I realize I may have told her the truth so readily as a way to test her. To see if she sees me the same way I am beginning to see her, or if I'm nothing more than a poor stupid Donor, good for one thing.

"And you're certain what's in that office can help you?"

"No," I say since we're being honest here. "But I have a hunch." I shrug one shoulder and look at the floor. Why does everything sound so idiotic when I say it? Sure, if you stop and think about any of these ideas they sound awful. But feelings aren't meant to be mulled over, they're meant to be acted upon.

The ticking clock on the wall marches forward throughout the room. I bounce my knee impatiently every now and then. Janice is not one to act without thinking, but how much time does she need? I open and close my mouth so many times, almost saying something, but determined to be patient if it means Janice will be on my side.

Finally, she moves to the chair by the table and says, "I think it's time I told you why my friends call me Juice."

# CHAPTER 16

For three whole boring days I've been cooped up in my room with nothing to do. In comparison to hidden passageways and plans for breaking and entering, playing cards and checkers by myself is rather boring. All I can think about is Gannet as we draw closer to the two-week mark of his return. Trip and Lecky, who really is a sneaky fuzzbucket, come to visit me. Lecky finds the stash of food in my drawer without any difficulty, and I have no choice but to feed her bits of my stolen goods. Especially when she plays with the strings hanging off the curtain so adorably.

Janice says she has a plan, but we must wait for the noise of Brutis's break-in to die down first. The story of her name is yet to be proven. Evidently, she can slip through any lock as if she were made of liquid, and Trip's mom was right about her having sticky hands—which I'm not quite sure how I feel about. Murderer she is not, but a thief? Is that any better? If Juice is correct, then she should have no trouble getting me into the office and her hands on whatever it is that I need to help the resistance without anyone knowing it's missing. I just hope I find out what that something is in time.

Some days my breakfast comes late and some days not at all. I've told Janice about the little stash in my drawer and to not worry about me. Most mornings the first thing I do is eat something from my drawer before I even get out of bed. Either a cracker or banana to help tide me over until breakfast comes or before the unpredictable Alex with her even more unpredictable donations comes. I never want to be caught in that weak state in front of Adakin Malloy again.

I grab an apple from my drawer, and as I near the window I spot Lazuli and Marcus strolling through the garden yet again for another morning walk. They have been amongst the flowers almost every day this week, and I would like to say I'm used to them now but I'm not.

I take another big, hard bite of the apple, making the skin of it cut sharply against my gums. One arm is around the front of my waist, holding up the elbow that holds the apple dramatically out to the side while I chew. Marcus and Lazuli walk so close they could be holding hands. And when she laughs at whatever he said just now she touches his arm.

I grunt and bite the apple again. Marcus bends and retrieves a dark blue flower that resembles a daisy but with a dark navy center. He hands it to her, and when she retrieves it, her fingers linger on it.

I throw the apple as hard as I can at the window, wishing it could shatter. A few weeks ago he was proposing to me, and now he's sharing flowers and long walks in the garden with my best friend. The apple bounces back, making a loud bong ring through the room as Alex enters.

She makes her way to the table, and I kick the apple core under the bed.

"I haven't eaten breakfast yet again," I say, since she doesn't know about my stash. "You know this is dangerous; why do you do this to me?"

"I only follow orders. And you shouldn't worry yourself so much about it. You're too precious to everyone here to let you get too close to death."

Her words are anything but reassuring. She says them with disgust and jealousy, and I'm shocked to hear how similar it sounds to things I'm thinking about Lazuli. Am I really that jealous of her time with Marcus?

My donation goes quite the same way. Except this time my blood returns to me, purple and sparkling. I'm smiling before I know it, yet not as strongly this time. The small amount of food this morning must have given me enough strength to at least still hold up my own head. Or the serum isn't quite as strong as before. Something feels different.

It does seem to affect my judgment of time, so I don't know exactly how long I'm sitting in the empty room before Adakin Malloy enters. When he sees my beaming face, he turns smug underneath his wrinkles.

"Well, that's more like it." Adakin claps his hands and rubs them together. "My father always taught me to school my emotions. It's about the only advice of his I truly took to heart." He smiles at his joke.

Something about what he says strikes a chord with me. School my emotions? Exactly what I'm trying to prove to the resistance that I can do. That I am reliable and consistent. That I am an asset and worth saving.

"We're taking a field trip today, you and I. My own little experiment."

"Outside?" I say.

"You might say that." His smile makes his skin stretch and sag in unnatural sorts of ways. His hand is on the wall, and his stare never leaves me. I can't look at him long, however, for the room slowly shifts into a different room. The walls go all white, and I squint my eyes, and then it portrays something else. Somehow the furniture disappears, and it looks as if we're outside. Yet the corners of the room are still somewhat visible where the images blur together.

"It's a..." I don't know how to describe it. "A projector? Like a movie? Virtual reality is old tech." The sound of hundreds, maybe thousands, of bees buzzing makes a sinister hum fill my room. I am still in my room, aren't I?

Adakin laughs as he walks away from the wall, but the image remains. "Yes, but this isn't virtual. Virtual reality puts images in front of your vision for you to process as semi-real. This is called perceived reality. Your mind is seeing what I want it to. My computers are communicating with what I put into your blood. It's reading your electrodes and actually altering your brain waves. Right now, you're seeing my beehives in real time as if you were there. And because our brains can send messages so real, you can touch and feel everything as if you were there as well. See, look," he points to my face excitedly and steps closer. "You're sweating! Your mind is also connected to this setting to react based on its interaction with you. Your mind is relaying all needed information as if you really were under the sun in my garden."

I wipe the perspiration on my brow. I look down at my wet hand and then to the sky. Not only do I squint at the bright light, I feel the heat of it bearing down on me.

"Touch something," he says like a child getting a treat.

"Excuse me?"

"Touch something. Anything. The grass, the trees, anything. Touch it and see how real it feels. I want to know how much effect this has on you since... well, since you don't always react to the drugs like I expect. Simply touch something." The last words come out as an impatient command. I'm sure he isn't used to having to tell someone twice to do something.

I'm too afraid to step anywhere. Instead, I squat down and first stare at how real the grass beneath my feet looks. It's greener than any grass I've ever seen. My fingers brush the top of the long, haphazard blades and it tickles my palm. I push my hand flat against it. It's cool and spongy. There's no indication that there's a hard wooden floor underneath. It looks, feels, and smells like real grass.

From my squat on the floor, I look up at three large boxes on platforms. The hum of the bees sends a chill up my arms. "If everything feels like I'm here, can they sting me?"

Adakin's revving laugh only makes more waves of chill bumps, and I stand.

"Only if I program them to see us. Don't worry, I have as much control over them as I have of you right now." He steps closer to the box on the end and puts a hand on top of it. Several small bees buzz out of an opening on the bottom and circle the box before taking off.

"You know, I was so frustrated after our last visit. Like I said, you, for some reason, don't seem as affected by the serum as most Donors. And we can't just have you running around like that, especially not in Recipient territory. I bet if your little technician had known that the serum doesn't work well on you, he wouldn't have risked so much to keep it from you."

I hug my middle as it churns from his words. He knows

everything. Then why did he let it go on for so long? Did he know about Marcus traipsing through Donor land this whole time too?

"And then I visited my bees." He taps the top of the wooden crate-looking box and gazes at it lovingly. "And that's when it came to me to try this instead. You know bee larvae are fed different things based on what their roles are as well. Queens are given a royal jelly and worker larvae are given a bee bread with a certain chemical in it that makes them sterile. It only makes sense that you should be given something different as well."

"So bees make the honey that helps you make different serums?"

"Oh, Aston, I don't think you could even begin to fathom the role bees have played in our history. They were the driving force of the virus you know."

"Eva Tabor created the virus. I've read about her. She was an awful woman."

Adakin steps away from the beehive and bees swarm around him as he walks closer to me. His laugh is different now. A deranged, low cackle with a hint of pity mixed in it. "Poor Aston. If you only knew." He sighs and tilts his head with a dramatic frown. He looks back at his swarm as if they are his only family. "Yes, Eva Tabor was the creator of the virus. And the cure too. She held all the answers and never shared them with anyone. I was the tech, Eva was the science, and Balto was the environment. Together we discovered the best way for it to spread." The king pauses and looks at me. "Bees. At first the powder was on their legs, placed in the nectar in flowers." Adakin holds up his arm as the bees gather and crawl in bunches across his shirt. "Bees travel up to thirteen miles from their hive. Yet with a bit of tweaking and engineering and brain tricks, bees can travel over fifty-five-thousand miles looking for their hive and infect a whole continent." He smiles as the clumps of bees move to his bare hand and he twists his arm slowly marveling at their caressing movements.

Their buzzing feels louder and my heart feels pressed against my ribs.

"What was not planned was for the host virus to live on in plants and the ground. It did not work as most viruses do, and it caught us all off guard." He chuckles again. "Or perhaps it all worked exactly according to Eva Tabor's plan. Perhaps she wanted half of the population gone. She was a very power-hungry person."

He gives a wrinkled wink that makes a rock lodge itself in my stomach. "Come over, Aston." He gently shakes the bees from his arm and removes a lid to the box he is near. He slides a long, skinny wooden piece that looks like a filter out with the tips of his fingers and rests the bottom corner on the other wooden slats that are lined in there like rows of files.

I step closer reluctantly. Soon I am only inches away from him and the smell of honey is so strong I feel like I should be smiling, but maybe this is just honey and not the serum. He had said the serum doesn't work the same way on me. How can that be? I smile and can't control my face when I'm under the serum. But I am still able to fight through it if I try hard enough. Do other Donors not even have that? I shudder at the thought and grab my arms.

"There," he says, pointing with his wide giant finger. "See the large one with a yellow dot on its back? There she is. The queen of this hive."

She is bigger than the others, and I study how she moves across the wax. "Besides the laying of eggs, the queen's other main purpose is to create a sense of nationalism or unity within the hive. Their goal in life is to ensure that things run smoothly." He looks at me with a sly grin.

I hadn't realized how close we were, and I step away.

Adakin slides the file of bees back into place and bunches them all closer together. The hum of their buzzing intensifies, and I take another step back, eyeing the bees that swarm around us.

"Ah, listen to them, Aston. The beehive is a composite being that functions as an integrated whole. It's where I got my ideas for the perceived reality and most of my serums you know." He carefully places the lid back on. "One-point-five kilograms of bees in a honeybee swarm, just like one-point-five kilograms of neurons in a human brain, achieve their collective wisdom by organizing themselves in such a way that even though each individual has limited information and limited intelligence the group as a whole makes first-rate collective decisions. It's where the term hive-mind came from."

There's a blur and a ripple through the tree to our right and Adakin frowns when we look there. He steps over to the tree and it's as if he can see both worlds, the perceived one and the actual one. But how?

He talks with someone, and I can barely hear him above the humming of the bees. "How could that have happened? No, I can't leave now. I had this whole hour scheduled. I have something to do."

There is a rumble of something that I can only assume is the voice in the actual reality of my room speaking to Adakin, but I can't tell who it is or what they're saying. My head starts to hurt, and the sun seems exceptionally bright. I shield my eyes and grab my forehead.

With a growl, Adakin is towering over me; his shadow feels cool against my skin.

"You ask too many questions and now our time is wasted." He is angry and impatient.

"Tell me where Bolglarka is if you don't want these bees to sting you."

I stare at him as best I can with the sun shining above his head. Is he telling the truth? He said they couldn't harm me, right? Wasn't that what he said? No, only if he programs them to. How real will a sting from perceived reality feel? Am I willing to risk finding out?

I can't betray my grandmother. The resistance is working to rescue me, and I will prove I'm trustworthy. I try to shake my head but I'm so stiff with fear it comes across slow and robotic.

Adakin growls again as he swipes at the sky, or maybe the wall, like a giant lion paw attacking its prey with its claws.

As soon as his growl dies off, the sound is replaced with the increased humming of the bees. The King turns his back on me and vanishes into the air like a magician. I back away from the growing noise as tiny black and yellow bees make designs in the air. It's worse than my nightmares. Louder and more real no matter how much I try to tell myself they're not.

They rush forward, encompassing me. Their chorus of buzzing is deafening now as they circle around me. Something ripples against the tree again. I hold my breath and tense as they descend on me, crawling over my arms with less delicacy that they showed their master. There is nowhere to run. I try to brush them off and through my shoulder. They move up my face and my other shoulder; dozens crawl all over me stinging as they go. I fall to my knees and tiny bombs go off one at a time all over my legs. I scream and swat blindly now as everywhere hurts.

There's so much pain I don't know where to move or what to do. I bring my hands up to my face and wipe at clumps of bees.

I collapse to the ground and the humming disappears completely. The fall is harder than it should be. There is no cool grass beneath me, only my hard wooden floor, and I don't register at first how much cooler it is in the safeness of my shaded room. All I can feel are the throbbing red lumps of stings where the bees attacked me.

Someone kneels over me and touches my arm. I flinch and shake and shout.

"Get them off me! Get the stingers out! Get them off me!"

The voice shushes me, and I know from her touch on my forehead it's Janice. "There are no bees in here, miss," she says in a cooing way. "Just you and me."

I open my eyes and look at my arm that pounds with pain. There is nothing there at all. Not even a red mark. Pain my body at every angle, every inch, like there are tiny nails wrenching into my skin. Breathing heavily, I look up at Janice, her face contorted with concern.

What do I even ask of her? Tell her? How would she treat sores and stings that don't really exist?

"Adaki—" A sharp hot razor stabs my gut. I double over, hitting my forehead against the floor. It passes and I try again. "He's trying—" A roll of nausea has me bent over again and the stings along my leg flare with new vengeance. Why can't I speak?

"I don't know why the president wants you so badly, miss. But if this is how he cares for the highest blood in the nation I think we need to help the resistance sooner than I thought."

I fall limp onto the cool, hard floor.

"Brutis has escaped the officers and his trial. That should be enough distraction to move tonight."

Tonight? "Janice, I can't," I say through labored, painful breaths.

"I'm sorry, miss, but I'm not sure if we have much choice."

# CHAPTER 17

She flicks her eyes to the food and says, "Be careful, the soup is especially hot."

After she shuts the door behind her I lift the hot ceramic bowl and see a folded piece of paper underneath. I retrieve it and unfold it carefully close to my face. It is another sketch of a gannet. This time it is upside down and its feet face the sun. Its feet. There are three of them. Three A.M.?

So Janice is how I'm getting notes from Gannet. I knew I was right to trust her.

I crumple the note and throw it into the small bowl of Jello until the poorly made paper begins to dissolve and the sketch is blurred. Tonight? Tonight, Gannet? Of all nights tonight is when he expects to have a report on the Recipient tech that holds me prisoner.

I shove a spoonful of soup into my mouth and burn my tongue. I grab the glass of ice water and gulp and then stand and start pacing my room. Near my door I hear voices and put my ear up against it.

"So this is Aston's room?" Lazuli's voice seems to squeak on the mention of my name.

"On the complete opposite side of the building," Marcus says.

"Is her room much like mine?" she asks in a flirtatious, teasing way that makes my stomach roll.

"Not exactly." The stiff way Marcus replies makes me smile for some reason. It pinches one of the invisible bee stings on my cheek.

"Which room is larger?"

I hear Marcus sigh before he answers. "They're the same size. Only different colors and arrangements based on your needs."

"Needs?"

"It was my grandfather's doing. I don't know much about the particulars or why they're so different, only that he insisted upon them. Her walls have more access."

Their voices trail off, and I begin pacing again with a little more umph in my step this time. I want to stomp against the floor. My hands are in fists. I've been caged in this room for almost two weeks now. I am covered in bruises no one can see and am being tortured by someone who can move about like a ghost in the walls. Meanwhile Lazuli and Marcus go on a string of dates full of long glances and hidden touches and late night walks around the castle.

I kick my bedpost and then grunt when pain shoots up from my poor big toe. Stupid bed. Stupid room. Stupid Recipients.

"Stupid! Stupid! Stupid!" I yell. No one hears. No one cares.

I pace at the window, expecting to see the lovely couple

walk through the grounds again, but instead I watch the sunset in silence. Alone.

I lie in bed, throwing an apple in the air and catching it like a toy ball. Waiting for the bump against the wall. I want to help the resistance more than ever now. A vengeful sort of hate bubbles in my chest as I hope that Lazuli is not also contacting the resistance. This is *my* mission. I'm getting out of here and then she and Marcus can have each other.

My hand slips off the apple when it comes down, and it falls hard against my throat, making me cough and sit up. Instead of a random bump on my wall I hear Trip's special three knocks. I'm off my bed in an instant and pulling the droplet of blood. When the bookshelf moves out of the way and Trip peeks his head through, I stifle a laugh. He is dressed all in black with a black headdress covering half of his face.

"What?" he says defensively. "We can't take any chances." He looks so self-conscious all of a sudden. I have the sudden urge to tousle his hair like I would Torrin's, which stings my eyes for a second.

"You look very stealthy. Where's Juice? What's the plan?"

"Same plan as mine," he says defensively. "Just with no interruptions this time. We'll get you in, get what you need, and get out. Nothing fancy and no getting sidetracked."

"Right, of course not."

He raises an eyebrow that looks so like Janice I would have sworn they were blood relatives.

"What?"

He doesn't answer me, he only turns and silently moves up the stairs. We move quicker this time though a little shakier. I hear Janice whispering to Trip as we gather around the two holes that look out into the library.

"We will have around ten minutes before the default alarm goes off. That's all I can get us. You know you two are lucky someone else went in before you because that would have been your fate. If you had gone in there and tripped the default alarm that can't be turned off..." Janice trails off and I can picture her shaking her head.

Though I can't see Trip's face, I feel like I can hear his eyes rolling.

"No distractions. In and out, okay?"

I feel their eyes on me in the dark. Why does everyone keep looking at me when they say that? I wring my hands instead of putting them on my hips for I may just yell right now, my nerves are dancing so. What would I possibly be distracted by? After listening to Marcus and Lazuli tonight I have never been more focused on the goal. Well, at least as focused on the goal as one can be without seeing it, because I still have no idea what I'm looking for.

"Janice, maybe this was a bad idea." Doors close in the library and I jump. All of a sudden, this doesn't seem like what Gannet meant. "I still don't know what I'm doing." Gannet said to find out about their tech, not break into the supreme leader's secret office and risk everything.

"Well, you'll have ten minutes to figure out what it is."

"But what if we get caught? Is it worth it when we don't even know if there's something in there we need?"

Trip swivels in the dark and his hot breath beats on my crossed arms in front of me. "You choose *now* to realize the stupidity of this mission? *Now* you're scared?"

Janice shushes him before he can say anything more. "Aston, I trust you. There are a lot of people who trust you. You know, I first saw you on a secret screen channel. Leaked security cameras showed you saving a girl on the streets. You stood up to officers twice your size and won, not because you knew what you were doing but because you followed your heart. I'm a planning woman. George and I thought about what to do for months before we actually did anything. But right there, when I saw you save someone not because there was a plan but because you knew it was the right thing to do, I knew I had to do something to save Trip. I knew I also had to stand up to those who were wrong. There are Donors and Recipients alike who have followed you this past year. You have inspired people of both nations and given them hope. Now, if you feel there is something in there that you need, I say we follow your instincts. Just don't. Get. Distracted."

I scowl at her reminder to not get distracted. Trip places his homemade device onto the door handle and the locks shift out of the way. Janice places what appears to be a glowing red mirror shard under the door.

Trip gives a dark nod and opens the door slightly, careful not to touch any part of the doorknob around his device. Once cracked open, Janice uses several other jagged pieces of the same glowing mirror to deactivate every angle of the lasers. She tapes some to the door frame at certain angles, and after several tense breaths and two sweat wipes, they open the door completely.

It's pitch black and Janice hands me a pair of glasses. When on, they make the room glow red in the dark, and I can make out the furniture and the shelves. I move through the room quietly, heart pounding, wondering what for scars sake I'm even looking for.

"Ten minutes," she whispers. "Check the drawers and I'll check the file cabinet. Look for anything in the room that seems new or shiny. If Adakin was worried about

Brutis finding something, he may have updated his security after the break-in, and perhaps the thing Brutis wants is what you want as well."

The mention of Brutis and I having commonalities makes me shiver, and I step quietly toward the desk. The drawer glides open and several vials of liquid roll forward and clink against each other. The smell of honey floats up to me, and the invisible stings on my arms and legs ache on command. I rub the pain on my elbow.

"Find something?" Trip whispers.

I shake my head and shut the drawer. Another drawer has blank paper, soft and smooth, stacked neatly in a tall pile. What am I bloody doing here? I sigh.

The bottom drawer doesn't come free, and my heart clunks along with the lock that bumps when I try again to open it. Could this drawer hold what I need?

"This one's locked," I say a little too loudly. I kneel down as close to the lock as I can, and through the night vision glasses can see the finger scan lock. "Looks like a new blood-activated lock."

"Not very original of Adakin to just put it in a drawer, but okay." Janice moves away from the file cabinet, and quicker than I thought possible, has the drawer opened.

"I found something too," Trip says. The only thing visible of him in the night vision glasses are his eyes and nose peeking through the black fabric. "I think it's a key of some sort." He holds up a golden statue that matches the one in my room, the mark of the nation with two hands holding up a ruby droplet.

"I have one of those in my room," I say. "It's how I open the door to the walls."

"What makes you think it's a key, Trip?" Janice asks. She leaves me to my drawer and steps closer to him.

"Engraved on the bottom it says, 'the key.'"

"That's a good indicator," I say sarcastically, and Trip chuckles. "It's probably just some cheesy sentimental gift or something. I don't think it means it's a literal key."

I give my attention back to the drawer and see there are only files and papers here. Most files now are electronic, and though Recipients can print on beautiful paper, they rarely do if they can help it. What is so important in these files that they risked printing them for anyone to find? Perhaps they hold information not found anywhere else, things Adakin didn't want anyone hacking into a database to find. I pull a file out and let it flop open on the desk.

It's a report of some sort. A questionnaire that sounds familiar.

> **As a child, when my friend was in trouble, I was:**
> *a. Concerned, empathetic, and loyal—regardless of the problem*
> *b. Supportive, patient, and a good listener*
> *c. Nonjudgmental, optimistic, and downplaying of the seriousness of the situation*
> *d. Protective, resourceful, and recommending of solutions*

I know this questionnaire. I took this test once. My eyes scan the top of the page, and the name typed across the top makes my heart stop: Sybil Vazeto #1151. I grab another file and read the same questions with different answers and the name Shannon Vazeto #1198. I get tunnel vision when I see the red stamp across her name. "Not viable." Viable? What does that mean? What are these records?

Some of the files have names I don't recognize, but they

all have a configuration across the bottom that is different for each person.

"Janice, I don't know what these are, but is there a way to take them? There's a lot of them."

She moves like an owl in the night and soon has a mini-port hovering over the papers without question. "There's nothing important in the cabinets," she says. "I'll make copies, you check those shelves. We have two minutes and then we need to get out of here."

I move to the shelves and use my finger to guide my eyes along the rows of books and trinkets. I look at my hand and then rub the dust off onto my dress. "Not a very clean office," I whisper. And then there is a shelf that is pristine. I can tell the wooden shelf is spotless even in the dark. I take my time now, looking over the books, and pull out one that is titled simply "The IPC." My heart hammers a warning. A giant pounding signal. This must be it. This has got to be the answer I knew was in here. After putting the book under my arm, I pick up a picture frame that sits on a stack of books. It's a group of people in their mid-twenties maybe. I spot a young, carefree Adakin Malloy and am shocked by how much Marcus looks like him. Brutis is on the other side of the group and looks almost exactly the same. Even in his twenties, his hair is missing. It's when my eyes roam to the second row in the group that all time seems to stop. Two women, front and center, have their arms around each other, and their heads are slanted and bumped up against one another. I suddenly recall a similar pose with Lazuli and me, our heads together, our bare arms slung over each other on a summer day after playing in a broken fire hydrant. But there is more than just the pose of these women that makes me think of my childhood memory.

Trip steps up to me. "Find something?" he says. Not even his gasp takes my eyes away from this picture. "Bloody... is that you?"

"No." My voice is strained and awkward, like I've forgotten how to breathe. "It's my grandmother."

# CHAPTER 18

The eyes of the woman I thought I knew so well stare back at me. Friends with the Recipient King. And the woman she embraces? Could this be the evil Eva Tabor?

"Aston," Janice says urgently. "I warned you about getting distracted.

I spin around in a panic and shove the picture under my arm with the book. Janice is still taking pictures. I think of the files and how she's creating an electronic version of them. Something that can be hacked. Something the Resistance can retrieve? I don't know what I'm talking about or if it's even anything they want. Oh, scars galore, what the bloody hell do I need?

"Tech. I need to find info about their tech. And that key. Trip, bring that with us just in case."

"How about this electronic manual?" Trip holds out two small metal bars side-by-side with a ball on the end. He opens the bars like a book, and a screen is projected above it. "All it says is 'the walls that connect us.'"

"Trip!" I want to shout but try to keep it in. I almost laugh out loud. How fitting. The walls that divide us are literally the technology that will connect us. Programmers can be a little geeky sometimes. "If that's what I think it is, yes! Bring it."

He closes it and shrugs then slips it into his pocket.

"Thirty seconds," Janice says. "Wrap this up. I'm almost done. I found an index of sorts that looks like it has the information of all of these files. Are you sure this is what you needed?"

"No, but anything helps." Her miniport gives a strange glow to the room that makes my glasses not work correctly. I bump into an end table and knock over a small cigar box. "Scars," I hiss and bend over to gather the contents. A vial of blue sparkly liquid rolls on the floor. I catch it and slip it into my pocket without thinking. There's also a red ruby keychain and a yellow piece of candy that smells like honey. When the scent hits my nose, I smile, then shut the box quickly, but it's already too late. For some reason my body is reacting to the smell of that small yellow candy. But I'm not supposed to react to it. Adakin said so himself that they don't affect me the same way, right? Suddenly there are bees everywhere. Tiny shadows that swirl in the corners of the room.

"Janice," I say louder than I know I should. She seems to read all the hidden messages in that one call for help. My red vision becomes crystal clear as she turns off the miniport and scoots around the desk. Behind her, the small black shadows hum through the air and my invisible welts start to ache.

"Time's up," Janice says. She hooks her arm under mine and pulls me. I stumble backward, unable to take my eyes off the swarming bees. Are they really here? My heart is plummeting, and my breath is tight and labored. They're not real, are they? They're not real.

When they follow us through the doorway, I unlink arms with Janice and dash toward the portrait hole in the wall. I turn to see Janice and Trip running toward me with the black dots of tiny bees moving behind them.

"Quick!" I yell, pumping my free hand toward them.

"They'll get you," I hiss, recalling again their sting and a dull pain rips down my shin. "Hurry," I whisper frantically, getting my hand ready on the portrait for when they jump through the hole. Once they're in, I yank the door closed, but several bees make it in. They buzz around Trip's head, and I swat at them and groan. Swatting only makes them multiply. For every one I hit, three more appear. I drop down in a crouch and put the book and picture frame above my head, whimpering pathetically.

Their hum drones on and they sound like they're hitting the wall behind me, banging on it to get through. I hum to myself to drown out their sound as frightened tears run over my cheeks. Janice's arms wrap around me. "Aston. There's nothing here, Aston. Do you hear me? Your mind is distracting you from what's real. It's playing tricks on you, miss. There's nothing here."

"But I can hear them," I say with my eyes squinted shut. "Even when I cover my ears, I can hear them."

She releases one of my shoulders, and soon there's a bitter sort of smell that fills my dripping nose. I open my eyes, and Janice has a miniature brown envelope held just above my top lip. Slowly, the humming dims and morphs into my own pathetic hums. I stop. It's silent, and I'm overcome with embarrassment.

"What is that?" I point to the envelope and wipe my face.

"Dried St. John's wort."

I know the flower. It's the very flower in the home of a resistance base I visited without knowing it, and in the office of my lawyer, and the very flower that Gannet said they used to overpower the serum.

"A small patch of the flower has been growing in the garden as of just a few months ago. There are a few Recipients trickling in to the resistance. Because of you, Recipients are seeing the truth of our system." She folds the paper and puts it away.

I look up to Trip who has removed his headdress and stares wide-eyed at me. I must have scared the poor boy, and my face warms to know that he had to see me that way. With a heavy, long sigh, I pull the book and frame back to my chest and stand slowly. I'll always be an emotional nutcase.

"Thank you," I whisper to them both. Nothing is said as we trek back to our rooms. When we make it to my trap door, Trip hands over the "key" and the device we hope is the manual for the blood-activated walls. Both Janice and Trip decline meeting Gannet tonight or talking with any of the resistance. Janice even asks not to be mentioned at all.

"This was you, miss. You did very well tonight." She puts a hand on my shoulder and then slides it down to my hand where she gives it a squeeze.

I thank them and say goodnight. Trip doesn't make eye contact. With his head tilted toward the floor he mumbles, "I know what it's like to see things." He wraps his hand around one of his fingers, wringing it like he will twist it right off.

Saying nice things doesn't come easy to him. He'd probably rather call me a fuzzbucket or blithering dunderhead. Name calling, like he does with Lecky, is somehow his way of expressing affection. So his effort to be understanding and make me feel better touches my heart so deeply I want to wrap him right up in my arms.

"Things they want you to see," he says. "Things that ain't there."

The realization that he means his parents, that his parents did these things to him, makes all the terror of my fake bees dim.

He looks at me then, and that glimpse speaks more than his words could. He understands. In the next, instant he flies up the stairs without looking back.

Janice and I stand in silence. His confession has sobered us both. In this silence we share our own bond and understanding. I understand why she had to save Trip, and she now understands why I need to save myself.

"If you—" Janice starts then twists her face with contemplation. "*That* serum doesn't go away, miss." She looks at me long and sympathetically. "It lasts and lasts and keeps you... silent."

I think of the time I tried to tell her about the bees. The roll of nausea that forced my lips closed.

"It's a serum that keeps court cases... clean." Her face speaks of experience with this serum. That she's tried to speak through it like I have. "It also makes you... a watcher."

I look at her questioningly. I don't understand.

Janice removes a piece of paper from her pocket. The paper is soft Recipient paper, but it is old and worn. Carefully preserved but read over and over and possibly passed on from one hand to another.

I read the words quickly as Janice waits. A scribbled note explaining a new serum that contains microscopic nano-bots that run through one's bloodstream while also communicating with other, surrounding tech. Officers. Bald and emotionless. I know this already. How do I tell Janice the president already told me all this when I can't seem to mention his name without getting sick?

Then I come across something I haven't heard before. A variation of this serum that can "seal the tongue." A serum that can be programmed to keep a secret. The serum that Adakin finally got to work on me is a variation of the officers' serum. He gave up on trying to control my emotions and make me compliant and compromised with the ability to keep my mouth shut.

I read faster now, placing my finger on the page to help me. Being a variation of the officer serum means... I scan several sentences over and over again. A bunch of tech mumbo jumbo that I don't understand.

Janice looks at where my finger is. I look up into her face.

"Human surveillance," she whispers.

We are now like human surveillance cameras reporting everything to the enemy. My hand drops and Janice grabs the paper, folding it and putting it away.

"Janice," I choose my words carefully to avoid anything that could set my stomach on fire and legs burning with stings again. "How do I move forward? Knowing he is—" a sharp burning stab shoots through my gut. I wince, and Janice touches my elbow for support. "How do I help the resistance now? How do I even talk with them?"

"Everyone sees what you want them to see. Hears what you want them to hear." She speaks each word like it's a special code, well-rehearsed. A code that doesn't make any sense to me.

I roll my eyes. What she said is bogus. Especially if what

this note says is true! What was the point of this mission tonight if we literally broadcast everything to him?

Janice speaks more firmly this time. "School your thoughts." She looks deeply into my eyes. "But never your emotions." More code. She looks at me like what she says should make total sense.

I sigh in exasperation. "Yeah, I'm an emotional person, I get it. I'm working on it, okay?"

Janice grabs my arms, shocking me into silence. "Yes emotions. It's your best quality."

I try to shrug out of her grasp, and Lazuli's words in the library echo through my mind. *"Aston's so dramatic."*

Janice jerks me back in place like we are running out of time. "Something you've been free to practice with, unlike others' personal prisons. Intense feelings alter—" Janice gasps and grabs her stomach. "Be *free*," she says simply, "take advantage of being free, and they hear what you want them to hear and see what you want them to see."

There's a strange feeling in my stomach that resonates up into my chest. Emotion. Moved by Janice's words. Maybe these are not code, just simply charted words that maneuver around the serum. What is Janice trying to tell me? That emotions will magically break the barriers of the human surveillance?

"Because often"—Janice sighs between words, like she is exhausted—"what we wish for is closer to the truth than we think." She looks at me long and hard. Her words still don't make a lot of sense. How will my emotions affect Adakin's eavesdropping?

Janice smiles. "How do you think I keep Trip here with me?" She drops her hands away from me and puts them in the air. "I am emotionally bound to him as if he was my own boy. Secrets are still possible, Aston." She says it with a smile before slipping through the secret door without a sound. A smile teases my own lips to hear her say my name instead of "miss." Slippery and sticky like juice.

We leave each other knowing there are still many unanswered questions. Everything except the manual was placed within the wall for safe keeping. Now I pace in the dark, twisting the small metal sticks in my hands, thinking about how to be open with my feelings and keep things secret from Adakin. I'm too distracted, however, by the metal sticks in my hand to control anything. Nervousness and excitement bubble through my chest as if I'm still sneaking through Adakin's office. Maybe I should open it and read it. See if it's really what I think it is. I can't make myself do it, though, and my mind jumps from one thing to the next like a rambling child with a short attention span. The bees, the picture of Grandma Bolgi hugging an evil scientist, Trip and Janice's words, secrets and how to keep them, the resistance and what they will think of my findings—my mind bounces from one to the next and back again; always lingering on the photo of my grandmother. What if Adakin is right? What if I don't know her at all? She seems to have kept even more from me than I realized.

Fifteen minutes after three, my walls ripple white again. I stand statue-still, waiting to hear Gannet's voice. Instead, it's a different voice that comes echoing through my room.

"Aston?" It's deep with questioning but gruff with emotion, and my heart feels as though it may explode.

"Papa!"

# CHAPTER 19

"Ash tree." His voice is like a floodgate. So many emotions in his words, so many emotions in me. Relief, sadness, guilt—I hear it all in his few words that fill my room. Is this what Janice meant? Is this what will keep my secrets from Adakin? For a moment it feels easy, if only this is all it took.

Another voice comes through, hard, raspy, and demanding. "What have you discovered?" I don't recognize the deep male voice, nor do I appreciate his impatient and inconsiderate tone.

I wipe at an unnoticed tear and stammer, "I... I..." There is commotion and criticism in the background as if a whole group of people are arguing. Janice's words and note make me panic. Human surveillance? Be free? I don't have time to think about what this all means. What if this conversation compromises their safety? I recognize Gannet's voice grumbling and complaining to the raspy one.

"Careful, Dustin, you're beginning to sound like the Recipients. Maybe you've spent a little too much time studying them." I've never heard Gannet so angry.

"You heard Bolgi, without this information we can't get anywhere, and she's the only one who can get it." The voice sounds slimy and menacing, and I hug myself in my cold empty room. Where is Papa? Is he there anymore? To hear the sound of my childhood protector makes me want to crumble at his feet and have him stroke my hair like he used to at night. I want him to have the answers, not the other way around. And then of course, the fear of if I'll even be able to share my information, or have enough emotion to keep this meeting secret, seizes me.

Papa isn't here to protect me, though. It is my turn to try and protect others. I straighten my back and step closer to the wall as if I am approaching a podium. I think of Papa so fiercely I'm on the brink of tears and hope this emotion is strong enough to hide behind.

"This isn't a good night to have contact." I gain confidence by how strong my voice sounds considering everything going on inside me. "So we must be brief. I just barely broke into the president's secret office in the library this evening. If it is ever discovered, this room will be one of the first places they look. If this conversation can ever be tracked..."

"It's secure," Gannet and Dustin say in unison.

"Good." My sudden strength and confidence surprises me. I feel like I am in another perceived reality and perhaps my own body and voice are just more mind tricks. Maybe in reality I am standing in a cell after all and hallucinating these conversations. Perhaps I am talking to no one. "First, I want to know about my family."

There is disagreement from the other end where Dustin starts to yell that there isn't any time.

I'm starting to really dislike this Dustin creature. Little does this man know, I have had years of training and the best teacher when it comes to yelling and getting your way. I put on as much of a Mam voice as I can. "I have risked my life and the life of my family for the freedom of a nation of Donors. I believe it is within my rights to ask at least one thing of the resistance." I take the silence as a green light and softly whisper into the dark, "Papa? How is Torrin? How is Mam?"

There is such a long pause I begin to wonder if I will trust the words that will come out of his mouth. "We are all surviving, Aston. We are fine."

I don't believe it, but I will make myself repeat those words and this lie in order to make it through. It's what papas are for. To tell their families whatever they need to know to get through difficult times.

Wiping another tear from my face, I pace with my hands behind my back like Marcus. I tell them the little I do know about how the calls through the walls work. I stop walking when I'm met with frustration from the raspy, rude Dustin, who is angry that I don't know the IP addresses of people's blood. My limbs shake when he yells at me for not knowing anything about how the perceived reality works or about the different kinds of serums that seem to affect me differently, or how Adakin Malloy manipulates the PR. I keep the information about the droplet statue and picture to myself and am thankful they cannot see me holding back tears.

"Stop it, Dustin. Have you not heard anything she's said? This information can help us." Gannet is shouting and has his own sort of rasp that's more like a growl. If he were in the room, I would feel the need to run to his side. "Scars sake, she's been through more than any of us in this room put together and you can't stop to give her an ounce of respect and gratitude for what she sacrificed tonight? You really are as bad as the Recipients!"

There's a scuffle and it sounds like furniture is being thrown around. Papa shouts something inaudible, and I fidget with the metal bars, now sweaty in my hands.

The manual. Oh my scars, how could I have forgotten? But what if it's not what I think it is? With a shaking voice and hands, I try to speak above their arguing.

"I have—" I clear my throat and try again. This Dustin person will be so very upset if it's not what I think it is. "That is, I think I've found something that could hopefully tell you everything you need to know." A last few scuffles and then silence. "I'm hoping it is a manual for how the tech in these walls works and how they are programmed. It's in a strange device that doesn't have a screen but a small projector of information."

My fumbling hands open the little metal bar and up pops the projected words again. "It's titled *The Walls That Connect Us: A Guide to Activated Walls*." I frantically try to scroll to the next page but am uncertain how. I push on the little bars at the base of the projection and finally, when waving my hand across it, the image slides out of sight and a new image appears. It seems to be a 3D projected model of a building. I recognize certain bushes and plants that are at the bottom of my window, and then excitedly exclaim without taking my eyes off the revolving image, "I think... I think this is a model of the Malloy house. The house I'm in." I swipe again and again excitedly. It is what I think it is. It has to be. "These must be the blueprints of the house. I wonder if this is what Brutis was after. This was probably his and perhaps has all the hidden passageways of the house in it. Here, it explains the places of the house where the walls are not connected and how they transfer information."

"Great job, Aston." Gannet's milky, somber voice makes pride melt my hesitancy away. I beam into the room.

"Yeah, great," Dustin says sarcastically. "It's on a little device. How are we supposed to get that information? Spend a whole week on here broadcasting that information while she reads it to us? That's not going to work."

As much as I hate to admit it, I think he's right.

"Hold on," I say, and I'm already across the room.

"Aston, what?" Gannet says.

"I'll be right back." I quickly open up the secret door behind the bookcase.

"Aston, no."

"Don't be stupid."

Gannet and Dustin speak at the same time.

"It's okay, just be quiet." I dash up the stairs to the attic and swing open the little door. Lecky jumps up and hisses at me.

"Bloody varmint!" Trip shouts sleepily.

"Trip, I need you again. The resistance needs you."

He rubs his eyes and yawns. "Uh-uh. I'm no Donor lover. I just was doing Juice a favor. Since she likes you and all."

I grab his sleeve and yank gently. "Come on, Trip. Just help me one more time."

He shoves his blankets off his lap with a sarcastic, "What is it?"

After giving a simplified version of what we need to do, and right before I start to worry it is too simplified to understand, Trip stands and moves to the corner of his room.

"I used to use this when I was younger and wanted to

get information to Juice without my parents finding out." With loud clunks and bumps, he takes wires, black boxes, and silver clips out of a bag in the corner and has them spread over the ground like a groundhog making piles of dirt as he digs. "It should be in here somewhere. Aha." He dangles something in the air that I can't make out. "It's similar to the device Juice used tonight, except this doesn't just store information; it can transfer it pretty easily too." When he stands and moves toward me, I turn for the stairs.

We make our way clumsily down to my room, and for a moment I worry they have already left, because the vulnerable, risky position I left them in was too great.

"Gannet," I shout a little too loudly. Before he speaks, I pause and scan the darkness. There's nothing except an eerie breeze that hits my skin. It gives me a sense of déjà vu, but I shake my head when Gannet answers. "This is Trip. He helped me tonight. He thinks he has a way to get you the information."

"You'll need a miniport to receive it, but it has to be logged out of the ID," Trip says.

I recall Torrin helping me with hacking into the medical records site without realizing it and stand by as Trip gives them similar instructions on how to access the compass anonymously. Something ripples across the window, a blur like rain beating waves down the windowpane. I step closer to it, and irrational terror seizes my breast. Trip drones on in the background, but I'm immobilized with fear. Like a mirage getting clearer with every step, Adakin Malloy appears in the room before me.

I open my mouth to scream. To shout for them to stop talking, to stop letting this president see what we are doing, but no sound comes out. My mouth opens and closes over and over again yet I am suddenly a mute, crying silent tears as the two behind me continue on with their illegal actions. Adakin floats in the air, his body made of smoke and his face translucent like a ghost.

"Are you talking to someone?" He looks around the room, coming closer to Trip as if he cannot hear anyone else. "Ah. Found yourself a rat I see." Adakin watches Trip speak to the resistance but then looks out at the wall with confusion. He can't hear the resistance. He can't hear Gannet. A small, cool relief washes over my insides.

Trip begins telling Gannet about logging out of ID's and Adakin listens studiously.

I open my mouth to tell Trip to shut it, but nothing comes out.

"Don't worry, Aston. They can't hear or see me." His voice sounds like an echoing stutter, the connection is weak yet strong enough to still control my voice and the setting. "I just thought I would check on you. Seems like you've been busy tonight. Your little rat scurrying down from the attic is quite devoted, I see. All experiments mean sacrifices, I suppose. And to get the results I want, it's only natural that I would have to give up a little myself. It's a risk." He is soon right in my face, and his presence feels like a cool mist on my skin. "So before you rejoice over your smart little rebel party, just know this. You are programmed to never be able to tell them that I know about this breach of security, so I would suggest you not try unless you want to experiment on the consequences. And if you waste my time again, there will be more than just a few bee stings. I need to know where Bolglarka is, and I need to know now." He starts to dissipate as he leans backward. "Now please get your rest, Donor." His form is no longer seen but his voice is still heard. "We wouldn't want our top Donor dying of exhaustion."

The room returns to full volume, and I grab my head with one hand and the bookcase with the other. I spin on my heels, and Trip is standing and wrapping cords around his device like a technician finishing up his work with pride.

He turns and beams at me as the room is soon full of clapping and happy mumbles of excitement. I step quickly to them and open my mouth. A burning wave of nausea hits my stomach, and I remember Adakin's words and the conversation with Janice. I am physically unable to speak about it. How do I tell the resistance I've been compromised? Adakin knows this is happening, yet I can't tell them anything. How long did it take Janice to figure out the right words that would not betray her bondage?

There's also a selfish part of me that doesn't want to tell them anything, because I so badly want to be a part of the rebellion. If I tell them this emotional girl they already don't want is now a walking megaphone for Adakin, I don't stand a chance. Adakin knew this about me. That I am impulsive and irrational. Yet when I have time to actually think about the consequences and risks... I am very much a coward.

"What is it, Aston?" Trip asks.

"Aston, you did it. With this information we know everything about their tech. Everything." Gannet sounds so happy.

"Yeah, but—" A voice grumbles in the background.

"What do you mean 'yeah, but'? Dustin, you're such a cynic."

"But we don't know what any of this information means. It's just a bunch of code mumbo jumbo. And so unless this boy—"

"Hey!" Trip shouts out. A protest that is ignored as Dustin continues.

"—is going to help us through every single step, we're still not getting anywhere."

There's more arguing, and Trip leaves to go back to bed. I roll the words of Adakin and Janice and the note over and over again in my mind. Toy with the consequences? How sick could I possibly get if I pushed through it and told them?

Dustin grows impatient and leaves the room. It is only Gannet and me. His voice grows soft and reassuring, but I don't hear any of it. I only hear Janice saying *let my emotions free* and see the blur on the window that I know means Adakin can hear everything! Gannet speaks of times when the only thing between us was a needle. My stomach does a warm flip at the memory and the window clears for a second.

Wait. "Gannet, what did you just say?"

"Checkers?"

My stomach flips again just at the word, and the window is clear glass again. No blur of surveillance.

"Remember when we played that game?"

"I do," I whisper, and the more I wrap myself in the memory, the longer the window stays clear. Emotions. Adakin said to school my emotions, but Janice said to school my thoughts and let my emotions soar. That my emotions are my best quality. Emotions must block the communication or broadcast between the serum and the tech!

Gannet and I whisper about the day we first met in front of the facility. He tells me about how long he stood on the street staring at my terrified face.

"I'd never wanted to save someone from the donations

so badly before," he explains. "I was faced with either giving up my cover as technician: sworn and blood-oathed into retrieving the blood of every willing Donor, or letting you sacrifice the love of life present in every part of you. The way you walked, the way you looked at things, the way you breathed even, was full of hope."

"Torrin," I whisper with my eye still on the window. Clear.

"What's that?" Gannet says, sounding closer to me than he has in months.

I can't save them. I can only condemn them further. But perhaps Torrin would know what to do to help me. Will he know enough about the prison walls of my mind? Or does his talent stop at the wires and ports alone? Gannet calls for my Papa and Dustin comes unwillingly and loud.

"You need to get my brother, Torrin. He will know." My voice sounds completely defeated. Please protect Torrin from Adakin. From everything.

"She's right," Papa says. "If we could get him out—"

"It's too risky," Dustin grumbles.

"Risky? Out? What's going on? Where's Torrin?"

"Look what you did." Dustin sneers.

"She should know about what's going on," Gannet pleads. Since when does Gannet beg? He's a resistance leader. A professional at keeping things secret.

"Fine," Dustin growls. "Things have changed here a little bit since you've been gone, princess." I hug myself again at the way he calls me royalty as I stand in my castle room. "Donations aren't nearly as calm as they used to be. And since your show at the bloodbath ball, and then your dramatic televised public pardon by the president, we may have more followers of the resistance than ever, but it lost its order."

"Partly from your men—" Gannet tries to interject but Dustin continues.

"Some Donors started to make their own protests, and things got a little messy. More public executions and increased donations. School has turned into boarding schools and donation facilities are being built into them. Kids don't come home at night anymore."

I gasp and my fingertips find my lips. A voice I haven't ever heard before shouts from the back, informing everyone of the time.

"Scars, cut it off. Aston, we'll be in touch."

There's a jumbled sound of Gannet and Papa talking over each other. Thanking me and telling me to be safe and not to worry.

Adakin's words haunt me as my legs wobble, and the room shifts into a gray haze from the oncoming sun. "We don't want our Donor dying of exhaustion. Dying of exhaustion." It echoes in my mind as I lower myself to the floor. Torrin. Papa. What about my sisters and baby Pip? I welcome the cold, hard floor as my cheek presses up against it. What is going on out there? What have I done?

# CHAPTER 20

For two days, I am like a mute zombie. I even begin to wonder if President Malloy programmed me to not talk at all. Trip and Lecky come by, but I only stare at them playing on the floor or watch Trip analyze the two droplet statues, finding all their similarities and differences.

When I look at Trip, I picture Torrin. Is he locked up in an attic too? His talents hidden? Or is he finding ways to help the resistance inside his prison just like Trip is? I stare out the window, feeling defeated and cowardly for not even trying to see what would happen if I told them about Adakin Malloy knowing that they have the manual. It's as if he knew we would break in. As if he planned it and made it possible. But why?

Does he know everything I took? I pull onto my lap the book I stole from his office. "The secrets of the IPC." Does he know I have this too?

I open randomly to a page and read the first thing my eyes fall on.

*Most knew the IPC (International Population Control) as*

*the radical movement to free the independent corporations, but in reality, it was an internationally funded program that was necessary after the eradication of world hunger. IPC was founded by two individuals. Adakin Malloy, a young entrepreneur when it came to technology, and Eva Tabor, the top scientist of her time.*

I pull out the picture frame from beneath the sofa cushions and look at the woman next to my grandmother. Another wave of nausea rolls through me as I look into this woman's eyes and consider what I just read. Population control? Could it really be possible that these germ wars were merely for the sake of condensing a growing population?

Grandma Bolgi's hair is yellow like mine and sticks out in all the wrong places. Her smile is the same. Infectious and broad. Did she know? She clearly was a member of this group, but was she a part of it from the beginning? How much did she help them kill innocent people?

I look over my room and study the window shining with the setting sun and Trip pulling a string along the floor for Lecky to chase. Nothing has really changed. The events of history are still the same; it's just my understanding of their motivations that has changed. Does it really make it worse to kill someone because things are too crowded than to murder people because of an argument over oil?

The door opens, and I scramble to hide the book and picture frame while I watch Trip lunge for Lecky and dodge under the bed.

"It's just me," Janice says, and I relax a little. "Though I can't say I approve of you both just lying around so carelessly."

"No one ever comes here anymore," Trip says nonchalantly. He sets Lecky back on the ground, and the mute cat runs to the table and wraps her tail around the chair leg as Janice sets down a tray of food. Trip's words are true. No one comes by this room anymore. For some reason, even the donations have stopped for a time. This week has been quiet except for our own escapades. Perhaps that is why. Maybe President Malloy ordered we be left alone to help us feel a sense of false victory. A chill runs down my arms, and I give a small shiver. Or perhaps he means to torture me with plenty of time left to my own devices before telling me this is all a set up.

"All right, miss?" Janice asks.

I nod and make my way to the table. "What have we got tonight? It smells delicious."

Janice removes a silver lid, and steam swirls and dances into the air. "An Old World favorite. Spaghetti. I had this meal the night my Gavin died."

"I thought your husband's name was George," I say, filling my mouth with red noodles before I even sit down.

"Gavin was our little boy." Janice just smiles sadly at my plate as she places a roll on it. "Spaghetti was his favorite. We knew it would be soon, so we made it special for him. He passed away only a few hours later. I didn't even clean the stain of the tomato sauce from around his face. I could imagine him just sleeping with a full happy belly that way."

There's a moment of silence as we three stare at the large plate of noodles that wind around like twisted veins and the lumpy red sauce as bright as my blood. We think of those lost and those we wish we could share this food with. I think of children who can't sleep because of empty bellies. Either way, children are dying on both sides of the walls. One from hunger, one from disease. Is there no wall that can actually connect us?

I finally break the silence, hoping to sound more chipper than I feel. "There's enough food here to feed a Donor family for a week. Won't you two join me?"

I'm pleasantly surprised they both agree, and soon forks are clinking against empty plates, and napkins are getting stained red like evidence in a crime. For the first time I feel completely comfortable with these people. They no longer just remind me of home, they are home. I want the resistance to save me, tonight if they could, but for the first time I think about the effects of me leaving. Adakin must know about this little rascal, Trip. Why does he let him just stay here and help me? Or maybe that's exactly what Adakin wants, for Trip to help me escape so he can follow me to Bolgi. Perhaps I should make this new home my forever home. Would that save more people than trying to go back into the arms of the resistance? Lecky purrs at my feet. I smile as I lift her onto my lap, stroking her soft gray fur.

When dinner is over, Janice piles our dishes onto the tray and orders Trip up to bed. I stand by the trap door, watching him slowly climb the stairs, when he pauses. Lecky rushes up to the attic, but Trip turns and runs to me so quickly I don't have time to prepare for the hug he wraps around my waist. My arms are frozen in the air until they rest on his back and squeeze him close.

"I'm glad you're here, you dingy Donor." And then he leaves as fast as he came. I'm stuck stunned at the bookshelf with a smile on my face.

Yes, how in the world am I going to leave this new family behind?

Exhaustion takes over quickly. There are no dreams in the kind of drowning sleep I enter. I hear something though. It is someone I know, and my bogged-down brain clumsily tries to register it. A cold hand brushes across my brow, and my lazy heart skips at the touch.

"Aston." The voice calls to me from above the water of sleep.

My eyes flutter heavily until they open, and I am staring into the smooth, soft face of Gannet. It must be a dream. A perfect dream in the deepest of sleep. So deep it feels real. Or a perception. Please don't tell me Malloy can use Gannet to torture me like the bees. I won't be able to handle it.

He smiles when our eyes lock. His warm brown eyes boil me inside-out. My bed shifts under his weight, and I know it's not a dream. I bolt up, all of a sudden conscious of our precarious situation. I hold the blanket up to my chest.

"Gannet, what are you... how are you here?"

"With the manual you found, and you were right, Torrin was just the one to decipher it. He figured it out in no time. He even discovered how to manipulate the perceived reality." He shows this again by moving my long hair off my shoulder this time, and the way the tips of his fingers brush the skin of my collarbone sends a new wave of chills that I don't mind at all. Or maybe a little. This is my technician. My Romeo, yes, but the Romeo I gave up on. I wilt a little from his touch, and he stands and steps away from the bed while clearing his throat.

"You got Torrin?" I ask.

"Not exactly. We were able to contact him, and he helped us. He is still in school."

I move out of the bed and stand next to him. "What's the plan then? Are we escaping tonight?"

"Not yet." Gannet runs a hand through his hair. It's then that I notice the difference. Gannet is skinnier than normal, and his face isn't flush with color like I remember it being. "We may know how to manipulate the reality, but we don't know how to actually transfer something from one reality to another. We tried a couple of Torrin's ideas, and they were beyond unsuccessful. They were disastrous. There's nothing in the manual about PR, really. Torrin just used the knowledge of it to figure all of this out. And with the blueprints he was able to create different replicas for us to study the best routes and escape plans. He really is amazing."

Gannet grins at me and though the sparkle of serum is over his eyes I know it's not real, only an act he puts on to fool others. He is pure and free from the effects. It warms my heart to see him admire Torrin. To appreciate and see the talent in someone I've loved my whole life. I nod and smile back.

"So the plan is put on hold. I snuck out and tested this here to make sure it works at this distance. Aston, it's amazing. It looks and smells"—he steps closer to me with each word—"and feels just as if I were here." He puts a hand on mine and squeezes it.

"I know," I say wistfully. Remembering how real the perceived reality can feel though, I dip my head.

"What is it?"

I want so badly to tell him about President Malloy knowing all of this. About the danger we are all in. About how a PR can feel so real it can take your reality and shift it into anything he wants it to be. I stare into his concerned eyes, and my lips begin to ache with determination to tell him when my body physically refuses to. Adakin finally found a serum that works on me. I am no longer a person moved on the whims of emotion but of forced order and logic.

Gannet misunderstands my efforts and pulls me closer to him and shushes me. "It's okay, Aston. We'll figure this out. With Torrin having proved himself now, I'm sure it won't be long before we break him out of there and have him up and running with a plan. Don't you worry."

His chest is surprisingly warm for one with hands so cold. I know he isn't really here. It is my mind sending a message of how firm and welcoming his embrace is. It is my mind telling me his hand is tickling up my back, soothing me in a way no red bubbles ever could. But mind trick or not, it feels good to have someone hold me again. Someone I realize I can trust to tell me it will be okay. There isn't a place in my heart that believes him, but there's enough of my mind that wants to live a lie for just a little while longer.

I open my mouth to tell him. I have to push through whatever curse Adakin put on me. I hope Gannet will understand the sacrifice I make. I pull back to look into his eyes one last time and hope he can somehow save me from whatever the consequences of telling the truth will be. Nausea rolls through me again.

At the warning of pain in my stomach, the window ripples with an incoming Adakin. I won't let him steal this moment; I must overcome this control he has over me. Emotions. Let my emotions soar. I look around the room and consider what to do. I could cry. Nowadays it would not take much to let myself cry. Adakin's face begins to materialize into the room with a wide grin showing itself first. I squeeze Gannet's hand tight. Strong emotions break the connection. With fear spurring my heels forward, I lean up on my toes and kiss Gannet quickly. Pulling away with a gasp, we stare into each other's eyes. Strong emotions indeed. I'm sure my eyes hold all the fear and regret and confusion I feel. What must he think of me to be so forceful and presumptuous? If only I could tell him that kiss was for his own protection. I look at the window when I can't look at him anymore. At least it worked. The window is clear and there is no more risk of Adakin.

Gannet hooks his finger under my chin and pulls my face to his. There is something in his eyes as well. A truth he seems to have held in for far too long, yet instead of both confessing, we inch forward, never taking our eyes off each other until they are closed. Our lips touch in the slowest and softest of ways. Not because we have to, or out of fear, or to save the other, but because there is connection. I don't even think about this being a perception anymore, he is in every way touching me, holding me, and kissing me. Smooth-faced, soft-eyed Gannet, my technician, my friend, is kissing me in my bedroom in Bloomfield.

He lets go of my hand and slides his hands down my shoulders, pulling me closer to him. His smell and warmth are better than anything I could have imagined on my own. He can't be in my head.

It ends as slowly as it began, and for a moment we rest with our foreheads touching and our eyes still closed.

"I didn't know how much I wanted you until you were taken away from me." His hot breath kisses my chin. It seems to seal my lips shut. How can I tell him now? Did I really only kiss him to protect him? Or was there more to my release of emotions as well?

I am stranded in between both worlds. I am no longer just a Donor, nor will I ever be a Recipient, yet I love bits and pieces of both worlds.

A thud hits the wall, yet not where they usually come from. Gannet pulls away from me and looks over my shoulder toward the bathroom on the other side of the room.

"What was that?"

"It's—" I'm about to say it's Lecky, but another thump

interrupts me and this time I'm certain it did not come from behind my bed. "I don't know what that is. If it's over there..."

I trail off as I move closer to the bathroom. I suddenly recall when Brutis was here he wanted to escape through a different passageway. One from the opposite side of the room. With Gannet in the room with me, so to speak, I know it's not him coming in to rescue me. Someone else is making their way toward my room. Someone else is on their way to kidnap me. I spin to tell Gannet to leave, but before I can say anything the wall beside the bathroom slides out of the way like the sliding doors of the facility.

They've found me.

# CHAPTER 21

Gannet reaches for me instead of disappearing to save himself and wraps his arms around me. I guess we will find out just how real the perception of him is if he tries to defend and protect me. I picture in my mind the ape-like man, large and bulky. The perception of Gannet doesn't stand a chance against him.

We stare at the black passageway as a thin waif of a girl steps through the doorway. Her hair is the color of russet potatoes, brown and muddy, and her skin is as white as the inside of one, pasty and chalk-like. Her brown beady eyes cinch up with her skeletal smile.

Behind her, three men with arms the size of the cantaloupes I detest duck out of the hole in the wall. No sirens go off, no flashing lights or running officers. No one knows they're here, and I wonder what they will do with me once they have me. There is no way perception Gannet could take on these three. I'm not sure real Gannet could even take on these three.

The girl finally speaks, and her English is broken up and strained. "I am Sofie," she says. "I have come to rescue you."

Her smile is so broad her lip seems to fall behind her top gums and get lost under her nose. At first, I think she is mocking me. Then, I think about how easily I thought Brutis's men were my rescuers instead of captors.

Gannet and I both repeat in unison. "Rescue?"

We release each other from our defensive embrace and listen. They are an independent band of resistance amongst the Recipients. Gannet relaxes but steps in front of me as he listens. After about five minutes of explaining their rescue mission, Gannet deems them faulty.

"It'll never work. You don't understand the grid of security put on her blood. We've read the manual. There's no way her blood will pass through these walls undetected."

"And you don't understand exactly who I am. How do I expect a simple Donor to know our ways? I have wealth and power. I can stand on my own if things go awry." The muddy-haired girl sounds as whiny and proud as I've always known Recipients to be.

"But can she?" Gannet says roughly with a thumb thrown over his shoulder to me. "If you get caught, what happens to her? And where will you take her? Home to be your slave instead of theirs? What makes you think President Malloy would be okay with that?"

"I said rescue, not kidnap."

"Where will you take her? Waltz right over to Livonia and hope holding hands with a Donor will save you?"

The face Sofie makes with her nose wrinkling and her brow pulled together makes me wonder just how many times someone has stood up to her. Probably never. I bet she always gets her way. I don't give her a chance to respond. I speak up right after Gannet finishes. "Are you rich and powerful like Brutis?"

Her mouth closes and her face falls.

Gannet looks at me and steps aside as he sees I am having more effect on her than he.

I saunter forward as I speak. "Brutis has little say in this matter; in fact, I believe he's had restrictions placed on his spending and wall access, and he is proprietor. Believe us when we say I am not a Donor Adakin Malloy is willing to give up so easily. Nor without severe punishment to those accountable for trying."

I don't know if my words are exactly correct, since he seems to be allowing a lot more to slip through these "secure" walls lately. Perhaps Adakin couldn't care less who takes me as long as he can still manipulate and harass me about Grandma Bolgi.

Gannet speaks more calmly this time. "The only way she is getting out of here is through the PR."

Sofie flinches at the term, and I wonder for a moment what realities she has experienced that haunt her night-mares as do mine. And then it hits me. She is standing here wanting to help the Donors, or at least this Donor—me—while in the presence of one of the resistance leaders.

"Sofie," I say enthusiastically, and I step closer to Gannet and grasp his elbow. He looks down at me, but I keep my face toward Sofie. "You know about the perceived reality, don't you? You want to help? Then join the resis-tance itself." I wave my hand in front of Gannet. "Help them save not just me but everyone. Donor and Recipient alike."

Gannet shifts his weight under their scrutiny. Sofie studies my face and wrinkles her brow. She turns to Gannet as she contemplates my words. Their group seems genuinely excited to find out he is from the real rebellion. They have a sort of committee meeting right here in my bedroom, joining alliances. Soon they are all agreeing on how to contact each other and ways she and her fellow Recipients can help.

As her large bodyguards duck back into the walls, she turns to me. "I have seen many things in my life, but the sight of you is unparalleled. I wish more Recipients could see that Donors are not what we've been told they are." She looks at Gannet as much as me as she speaks. "That they can be smart, and kind, and diplomatic. Perhaps Master Marcus is on to something. Together we could do more good than isolated from one another. You inspire many, Aston." She bows as she finishes, like I am royalty. It makes me feel something. I don't know how to describe it. Am I uncomfortable because of the bowing?

Gannet reaches for my hand and gives it a squeeze as we both watch Sofie disappear in the wall and the secret door close. I'm not sure that woman—yes, I say woman and not Recipient—may ever understand what her words did to me. I realize now what I'm feeling is a consequence of being respected and valued for something other than my blood. To be recognized for something I can and did control—my choices and kindness—and have it vocalized makes me feel alive in a way I never have before. I am more than just a Donor. I always knew it, but now I feel it.

# CHAPTER 22

My month alone is over. Marcus should arrive any minute, but the only thing I'm looking forward to is how much more pleasant Alex should be with Marcus around. I was so nervous about the donation today, I wasn't able to eat much breakfast. Instead, I let Lecky have some of my cheese and stashed away a banana and pancakes wrapped in a napkin.

As I pace the room waiting for the door to open, I regret the full glass of orange juice I guzzled. It sloshes and burns alone in my empty, nervous stomach.

I shouldn't feel guilty about kissing Gannet. Marcus and I are through. I have made it very clear there is no way I could ever forgive him, and he has made it very clear he cares more about this program than anything else. Not to mention the friendship he has found in Lazuli. I should be happy about their alliance.

Staring at my bedside table where Gannet and I kissed makes a smile wash over me, a pleasant change to have it voluntary. I wrap my arms around myself thinking about how different a pair of cool soft lips can feel and how real his hands were on my back. There is a sinister part of me that wants to see Marcus's face when I tell him how wonderful my night with Gannet was. I would never put Gannet or the resistance in danger like that though.

The door swings open, and I twist with a startled jump. A quiet Marcus walks in followed by a nervous Alex.

"What is it?" I ask, worried that something's been discovered. Does he know about my secret passageways or my nighttime conversations with the resistance? Does he know about Gannet already?

"Nothing," he grumbles. He pulls out the chair at the table and slumps in it in two fluid motions. "Let's just do this."

Alex shifts the needle as she tapes it to my arm and the needle runs over a tendon. It sends an electrical shock of pain up my arm which makes me flinch and yelp. It gains no reaction from Alex and only gets an eye from Marcus.

Marcus coughs, a short and slow sputter then wipes his nose with the side of his hand.

"Are you sick?" I try to say casually, wondering if Lazuli's exposure might have impacted him more than I realized.

"Yes, your presence is killing me." He gives me an evil grin that tells me he is perfectly fine. "Recipients get things stuck in their throats too, you know. We *are* human."

"Did Lazuli enjoy the gardens?" I say.

"I thought I saw you spying on us."

It feels more embarrassing to hear the truth on his lips. "It's hard not to spy when you were walking right under my window."

I sigh, and then spend the next few minutes staring at the wall to ignore him.

Marcus speaks finally, sounding bored and hopeless. "Should we play a game?"

"I'm not in the mood for a game," I say, which is true.

"I could... get you a book?"

"That's all I've been doing the past few weeks is reading." I look over my shoulder and reply with a dramatic and sarcastic, "So thank you but, no."

Alex awkwardly removes the needles in silence, packs up, and with a tiny curtsey, sneaks out of the room. The two of us sit in silence for a few moments longer. I rub my new bandage, smoothing out the wrinkle the tape has made over my skin.

"Aston, what do you want me to do? I practically rewrote Recipient law to have you saved and bargained all of my inheritance to have this home built for you and your friend until we can come up with a better plan, but all you do is argue and condemn me."

My mouth opens as I think about how to best defend myself, but he stands up and keeps going with hands waving in the air. "You've challenged one of the most influential, powerful, and craziest Recipients there is. You practically assisted in his kidnapping of you. You've done nothing but make it perfectly clear what you think of Recipients. You have secret meetings with the King, pleading your own case with him, no doubt."

I try to protest, but he doesn't stop. "You sneak around the house as you please and insult me in front of my staff. I've lost all funding and support for this project. How on New Earth are we to come up with a new plan now while fighting all these obstacles? It doesn't seem to matter what I do, or how much I try, it's never good enough and it leaves me stuck between you and my superiors, making it completely impossible for me to help you out of this situation. You are a caged bird because you have flown into it."

His eyes are more pleading than angry, and I don't know how to answer him. He has listed off only the bare minimum of what I have done. There would be no Recipient in Bloomfield that could save me from condemnation if they learned of my snooping and my own little research party. Helping Recipient resistance groups gain access to the Donor rebellion, secret meetings with the resistance leaders, and handing over key information about their technology and defense systems? Adakin probably knows. But Marcus doesn't.

"I don't consult with your grandfather behind your back. I have no choice in the matter."

"What do you mean, you have no choice? Just simply don't talk to him. It's what I do when I'm done with him. He can be persistent, I know, but he eventually leaves you alone."

I tilt my head and study his face. How could he not know what his grandfather is really doing? What he is really like? "You saw what happened to me when Alex first left the serum in the machine, didn't you?"

"It was an accident, Aston. I wish you would learn to forgive and not hold on to such grudges. We Recipients are not all bad as much as you would like to believe."

Another scoff escapes me. I can't believe what I'm hearing. Could Marcus truly be so innocent to what his ruling society does to my people? "Marcus, it was no accident. And I'm not really allergic to the serum. I'm somewhat immune to it, actually. What you saw was the reaction all Donors have to that poison. Only, it is meant to strip Donors of their ability to feel or think clearly as well. I'm able to push through it for some reason. I can still think, and it doesn't last on me as long as it does on others."

"That's nonsense. A syrup that makes people—"

"Happy."

He laughs.

"A strange donor who doesn't smile?" I use his own words against him, which makes my cheeks burn, thinking of Gannet. "You noticed it yourself. Donors are always happy." Marcus sobers and stares at me.

"I've escaped the drugs since my first donation, and it's ultimately what drew me to you." I look at the floor admitting that, yes, I once fell for this lanky golden-haired boy. I pace to ease the awkwardness. "I thought you were free of the drugs as well. Your grandfather," I say the title slowly, anticipating the nausea. Somehow these topics are not blocked. Or maybe it's the words I choose, navigating around the issue as Janice had. "Has found another serum that works on me, though. He has left me without food or water before a donation to keep me weak and allow the serum to take more effect. He has used me as his own test subject on new drugs. He has tortured me with his perceived reality." I speak louder and faster with each word, wondering why I'm able to say them. Perhaps my emotions allow me access here as well, or perhaps it's who I'm speaking with that makes the difference.

With the mention of PR his face goes whiter than when I thought he was a sick Donor. "He showed you the bees." It's not a question, but a terrified statement and I swear Marcus just shivered.

He knows.

My voice trembles and tears threaten their way loose. "Choice, Marcus. Choice is all I've ever wanted. It's a foreign thing to every single Donor. When they are drugged into submission, how could they possibly see clearly enough to ever choose again?"

My vision blurs, yet I square my shoulders. I lift my chin as a silent tear runs down my cheek.

"He is not who you think he is, Marcus, and he is not honoring this experiment the way you think he is either. He knows this test of yours will fail; in fact, he hopes it does."

"But the virus—" Marcus doesn't finish his sentence. He sounds so young and inexperienced.

I step closer to him. "The virus was created by your grandfather and an evil, heartless scientist named Eva Tabor."

"My grandfather wasn't a part of it, he—"

"He was a member of the ICP with Eva. He was their tech specialist. Eva created the poison and Adakin invented the distributors. And you know why? IPC stands for international population control. These killers invented a weapon to destroy innocent lives, because it was getting too crowded. And his bees were the way he did it. Now he has manufactured serums to control and manipulate every part of the human mind. It's the ultimate power. He owns our blood and controls our minds." I'm so close to him now I can smell him, and I put a pointed finger firmly on his chest for emphasis. "The virus that kills you is thriving in your body because of your grandfather."

Our eyes are again locked, and the awkward tension has been blown away by our heated conversation. He doesn't look away. I can't tell if he is letting it all sink in or combating the facts. He looks at every facet of my face, surely realizing he has no reason to think me a liar. He has to know this is true. There has to be something he's noticed in his grandfather, even the slightest hint of the decrepit deceiver Adakin is, that helps him see that I am right.

He spins away without a word and marches to the door.

"Marcus!"

He doesn't stop. With a firm grip, he opens the door and slams it behind him. I stare at it long and hard before I move a muscle. What will he do with this information?

I sigh and pick up a book to read.

My eyes lift when Marcus slips back into the door, a piece of paper crumpled in his fingers. He stares at it like he could make it disappear if he grips it tight enough.

He gently grasps my hand and places the note into my palm.

"Here," he says, and wraps his hand around mine as he closes my hand into a fist. "I thought I was going to be doing all the enlightening today. But you've given me much to think about."

His hands are smooth and warm. I haven't been this close to Marcus in a long time, and I open my mouth to protest.

"Just read it." He turns abruptly and slips out of the room.

*I have spent most of my life in the limelight of both Recipient and Donor territory and was taught at a young age to not heed the false reports made about our family. I was told that trying to argue a truth was never worth the effort and accomplished very little. But on at least two accounts I feel the need to defend myself and that is the accusation you made of my connection to the Power*

*Plant Bombing, and the attack on the bee farms.*

*First the assumption that I had anything to do with the attacks on Donor Bee farms.*

Assumption indeed. I harumph into the empty room and then continue reading.

*I was just a boy when the hives were relocated to royal grounds. Donors knew we were coming. Notice and funds were provided for the families to move inland because the bees were dying and we had technology the Donors didn't.*

I scoff out loud as I pace. Technology Donors didn't have, ha, that's an understatement. They stole the bees to enact control on us not save the bees.

*When we arrived in the new Dakotas not only were the hives already set on fire by the Donors but there were traps in place meant to compromise our security. I remember the chaos, my first real introduction to officers as they moved in to protect us.*

I stop in my tracks and look around my room as I take in his words. This isn't right. Gannet said the Recipients set fire to his home, that the death of his family was his motivation to join the resistance for revenge, but did Gannet's rebellion start long before coming to New Livonia?

And in confession, I also remember Gannet. I had found a place to hide and when I saw another boy, scared and running, I pulled him under the bushes with me. I didn't realize he was a Donor at the time and I never put it together that he was your Gannet until you told me what he accuses me of. Because when we came up from our hiding place to smoke and a flattened, desolate town, in the light he knew exactly who I was and quickly blamed me for everything he had lost.

In the end, it was my Mother who begged for his relocation and position, a technician, a way to start another life. Though I've thought a great deal about that Donor boy since that day, I care very little about what he thinks of me now. All I care about is that you know the truth: that I had nothing to do with that so-called attack on Donors.

Secondly, my dealings with the power plant bombing. It is true that I needed you to donate, and, when at a loss, I consulted with a cousin who originally helped me set up the secret blood tests.

I shiver remembering the technician at my door but quickly read on.

My cousin said they had a connection with someone from New Chicago, who had access to homemade bombs. I'm ashamed to admit I was not as involved in the plans as I should have been. I had grown too accustomed to things being done for me, plans being made around me, speeches being written, and all I needed to do was follow instructions.

The only part of the plan I was aware of was that this would put your family out of work for a time, making things slightly tighter for you and put the pressure on you to donate.

I was told to deliver a package that would give the Donors a big firework show.

I thought it would be impossible for me to walk through Donor territory. I thought there was no way others would not recognize me, but no one even looked at me. No one noticed the ill Recipient who marched right into the power plant and tucked a bomb right in the middle of their town. I was given precise instructions. Detailed plans that made me trust the informant completely. Orders so perfect, what would ever give me reason to question them? I was never led astray before. However, they were missing one vital and horrifying bit of information. Workers.

I have played that day over and over in

my head. The routes I was given allowed me to go unseen. Under no uncertain terms, I was told and believed the plant to be empty. However, as I replayed the directions in my mind, I realized it was always implied but never actually stated. The instructions never mentioned the workers, but it was a fact I was positive had been looked into and taken care of.

It is no excuse for the pain my misguided actions have caused, but I swear to you, Aston, that I had no idea there were people in that Power plant when I delivered that bomb.

My cousin slapped me on the back in congratulation and told me it was either their lives or mine. Aston, you have to understand this is how we were raised. Donor lives were the solution to our problems, dispensable, a commodity. But the more I came to know donors, to know you, the more this secret has weighed on me.

Thirteen dead, the reports came in the next day. Thirteen fathers and brothers and sons gone because of me. I have carried with me many burdensome titles, but murderer was never one I was prepared to hold. It is something I will live with for the rest of my life.

The way you looked at me that day when

you discovered what I had done will forever haunt me. It was unbearable, but I heard my mother's warnings about nothing good coming from trying to convince someone you're innocent. I was taught you can never convince someone through arguing. It will only condemn you more. So I don't expect forgiveness from you. It is merely something I felt you had the right to know the full truth about.

Yes, I am a murderer but I am trying to let that fact change me, not torture me. It is the only silver lining I've been able to find. This tragedy was what first awakened me to my naivety and blind trust of both sides of the wall. It made me realize just how flawed our system is. That there is no more "us and them," because we are all deceived. The system is flawed and I still firmly believe we can fix it. No matter what you may think of me, I hope you know how sorry I am and how important you are. Not just to me but the whole new world, and not just because of your blood, but because of what you have taught me, about Donors, about life, and about love.

# CHAPTER 23

I yawn when the door opens, but when it's Marcus carrying the tray of breakfast and not Janice, I pull the covers up to my chest as if he hasn't already seen more of me exposed.

The words of his letter kept me up most of the night, but I'm still unsure how I feel about them; about him.

Marcus doesn't even look at me and sounds much too chipper for the early hour. "If what you say is true about my grandfather, you're no more safe in the house than out of it."

I nod slowly, without taking my eyes off of him. "I suppose that's true. What are you getting at?" I move out of the bed as he talks.

"I've agreed to have you on strict lockdown for your protection. I'm finding out now, under orders of the very people who wish to harm you." He sets the tray on the table and moves to me with ease. An ease I haven't quite replicated yet. There's no way to move away from my bed, though. "Grandfather didn't like my ideas of letting you roam to the library in the first place, yet never objected to

Laz's movement around the whole house. It makes sense now."

The use of a nickname is not lost on me, like he and Lazuli are old chums. I fold my arms over the blankets. "So?"

"So where to first?" He walks back to the table with a happy stroll. "The library? Or the gardens? Or somewhere new?" He gestures to the table, and we both sit to eat even though I'm moving much more slowly than he is. His smile is so wide I worry for a moment about him being drugged. Did he go to Adakin and this is how his grandfather dealt with the problem?

"Lazuli enjoyed the music room. Is that something that interests you as well?"

"Music room?" How much time did they spend together? It seems their time has been much more enjoyable than I have given Marcus. Our time together is spent arguing and accusing.

"Yes, the music room. Do you play anything? Or sing?"

"No," I say and grab another grape. "No, Lazuli was always the musically talented one. I only painted." I stare at the purple grape in hand and squish it, watching the clear insides come out like a tube of paint.

Marcus slams the table and I jump, squirting the grape all over my night dress. "That settles it," he says. "I don't know why I didn't think of it before." He pops some cheese into his mouth and stands. He points at me when he talks, and his voice is muffled from being full of food. "I'll ring your maid. Be ready in fifteen minutes because we're"—he stands excitedly with his hand twisting in the air above his head—"going to the market to buy paints!"

"Market?" I stand and watch him run across the room. "Are you mad?"

Marcus just winks as he rushes out the door.

"Market?" I repeat to myself. Surely he doesn't mean the Recipient market? But to go back home to New Livonia's market is too much to dream for. I pace the floor, wringing my hands and looking at my thin night dress. Oh, why can't there be a decent pair of pants somewhere in this mansion?

Being out of this building and through the gates is what I've wanted isn't it? But something about the possibility of roaming free through Recipient territory is exceptionally terrifying too. Especially after meeting Brutis and his men. What if there are more that do not like me or what Marcus is doing? What if there are those who wish to have me for their own like Brutis had? And let's not forget how well the "dinner party" went. I was not their guest, after all, I was a caged animal for the diners' entertainment. Who's to say I won't be caged again and pulled down the street like an animal in a street circus this time?

After I've paced and worried about every possibility, Janice opens the door slowly. When she finally makes her way through, I can see why she's so slow. Her arms are full of billowing blue lace and ruffles like she's been attacked by a giant lace squid. I rush to help her.

"Not that anyone will listen to me, but I will have it known nonetheless that I do *not* approve of this plan."

I take some of the material from her, freeing her from the monster fabric. "I don't even truly know what the plan is, and I already don't approve of it," I say.

"Glad to hear it." Janice puffs with exertion. "Maybe you can talk him out of it where I cannot."

"Did you actually try to?" I can't believe Janice would talk back to Marcus. I want to know what he would say if she did.

Janice cinches her lips to one side in a funny smirk.

"No," she says sharply, clearly not liking being called out on the subject.

It makes me laugh a little, and we dump the fabric on my bed. "Will it really be as bad as you think to go to the market? And what is all this?"

Janice sighs and puts her hands on her hips. "This, dear miss, is your dress. And yes, it could be worse than either of you care to acknowledge."

"No," I groan. "Aren't the dresses I wear each day enough? Not another giant frock. Why do Recipients dress like this?"

"Our clothes should represent something about us. Have more purpose than just protection." Janice starts to move the blue tulle and lace dress around so as to find the top. I undress and soon it is going over my head.

My head is stuck in the middle of the layers of scratchy tulle. As I swim and swat my way to the top, I question her further. "Worse how, Janice? Will there be more like Brutis who want a Donor pet?"

Janice doesn't answer right away. In fact, I find my way out of the dress and slip my arms through the long, thin sleeves before she finds her voice again. She smiles a sad smile.

"There are lots of Recipients who do not like Donors, Aston."

"But we're their saviors. We keep them alive." I say it a bit too flippantly and sarcastic. My cheeks warm, as I remember that I'm talking to a Recipient right now.

She puts her hands on my shoulders, but then looks like she can't find the right words to explain. A corner of her mouth pushes up like she pities me. "I think there are just so many that are jealous. They've suffered for so long. They don't just want your blood, they want the cure. Many

Recipients are growing impatient with Adakin to supply one."

I recall how Brutis interrupted Adakin and how out of control Adakin seemed that whole night. If the resistance can come in right as there is a Recipient coup, maybe we actually have a chance of gaining the upper hand. More information to help me be useful.

Janice seems disturbed by how her words make me smile.

"Thanks for your concern, Janice." I place my hand on her shoulder. "I promise to be safe."

She pats my arm and looks down at my dress. "Let's get you ready."

Janice helps me back to the bathroom and when I look in the mirror I laugh. "I look like a giant blue flower."

"I think that might be what the designer was going for," Janice says.

The dress is off-the-shoulder with a zig-zagged band running across my chest, around my arms, and across my back. Draped and hanging in all different directions from the band are hundreds of small blue lace flowers making it look like wisteria climbing across my chest. On random ends of flowers are embedded tiny pearls. The sleeves are giant and puffy but made of see-through tulle. It gives the sleeves a dreamy look, like if you squint your eyes you wouldn't be able to tell it was there. From the stripe of flowers across the front the layers and layers of tulle just fall in one frumpy heap.

"It's a bit big," I say. "I don't think it fits."

Janice comes up from behind me and her closeness makes me realize how much I've come to trust her.

"We're not done yet," she says.

She hugs me around the waist and pulls up a diamond

belt. I help her position the center of the belt, like an eye of jewels, directly over my belly button while she ties the ribbons behind me. I work on bunching the fabric evenly so it makes little lines from my bodice to my waist. There's something therapeutic about running my hands over fabric so methodically. It helps calm my nerves. Janice steps back to admire me. I swoosh the skirts, noticing a high slit in the front that comes up past my knee.

Janice comes around and inspects me. "Makeup should be a bit more subtle this time, I should think." She doesn't put much on my face, just light peach-colored rouge, light pink lips, and the dark trim around my eyes that makes the blue in them stand out. It's all done in an instant, since she merely places her hand on the mirror, and her vision comes to life on my face with a warm, red scan.

I think we're done until she starts to do my hair. She puts a product on it that smells like glue and makes my scalp sting. While I watch her in the mirror, she sticks her tongue out as she works, and my hair transforms into a hard, shiny up-do. Just like the Recipients.

Seeing it makes my stomach twist. "Are we trying to make me blend into the crowd?"

"No. They're going to know exactly who you are by association alone," she says through grunts as she pulls and tugs at my hair.

"Then why try so hard to make me look like a Recipient?"

"Because Recipients are proud creatures who value hospitality and respectability above most anything else. They'll not touch you because of who you are with, but they'll respect you or at least not think as ill of you, I hope, because of how you honor their way of living."

Janice takes a deep breath and slaps her hands down by

her side as she inspects her work. I give a weak smile. Her face turns somber. "Please be careful, miss."

I don't try to smile anymore. Janice means it. Why does it feel like there's something she's not telling me? What else does she know that I don't? My chest tightens as I realize she cares about me more than my blood or my position or value to the resistance.

"I will, Janice." Her eyes look so pleading, so sincere. "I promise," I say.

She places my "special" hat on my head and squinches her face at its condition. It's gotten so much use since that dinner so many nights ago, and she lifts a piece of ribbon out of my face and tucks it back up.

Marcus knocks on the door and calls out. I step hesitantly out of the bathroom. He is dressed just as formally as the night of the dinner party. The memory makes me fidget with my bandage. I can't feel it or reach it through the long sleeves. My face feels warm, and I put a hand to my cheeks to cool it. I still haven't said anything about his letter or his confession. He's still a Recipient. He still lied to me about who he was. But I also have no doubt that his words in that letter were sincere. Can Recipients truly feel remorse? My denial of this fact is met with something he said in his letter, "This is how we were raised." Are my conceptions of who he is as a Recipient merely the product of how I was raised to view him as well? An inconsiderate leech who only values power and possession? What if I'm as wrong about him as he was about us? Again, I remember his letter. All the things I judged him for that weren't fully true.

WHEN WE REACH the bottom of the stairs, instead of turning around and going under them toward the library, we walk straight across the large marble entryway. I strain my neck to look up at the chandelier overhead. Thousands of bright glimmering crystals.

Straight ahead are two wooden double doors. As we step up to them, they open without anyone touching them, as if they read our mind. Walls that can talk and doors that can mind read. I shiver as we step through them to another entryway. This one is much smaller but has three sets of clear double doors.

Marcus had offered me his arm earlier, but I refused it. Now I fear I may need it just to keep from falling over. I take another deep breath. We step close to the doors as they also open for us. I take another breath and feel lightheaded.

"Are you okay?"

"Fine," I say. At the bottom of the mansion stairs is the largest maglev I've ever seen. Which I know doesn't say much since I've only ever seen one in my whole life. I want to take everything in. I want to look over at the garden wall that lies under my window as physical proof I'm more free than I've ever been here. I want to take in the sky so large and open, the water fountain in front of the mansion, the lake that stretches out beyond the fountain, reflecting the clouds and thick, surrounding woodland. But all I can look at is the elongated silver maglev, shiny and sleek. Like a mirage, the door to the maglev disappears and lets us enter. Inside, it's like a room with sofas and tables and everything you could possibly want.

The ride is silent. I know he is watching me, but I don't care. Every tree that goes by is astounding, such a thick forest around the mansion. Growing up in crumbled-down Livonia where it's a miracle to get Papa's garden going at all makes seeing this many trees and bushes and plants growing wildly feel rather miraculous.

Once we enter the main road, there are homes right away. Larger than the ambassador's mansion but not quite the level of the palace, of course. They stretch out so far apart from one another. Some with gardens and some with large wide lawns. None with rubble or broken anything.

The maglev goes by so fast that even though the homes are far apart, I count them quickly. More than twenty homes and then they start to clump together. Still not on top of each other like in Livonia. Every home still has a yard and maglevs to boot.

I grow dizzy trying to count them all. I had no idea how many Recipients there really were. I try again but fail to pick at my bandage. Instead, I just let my finger rest over the lump of scars. What will Recipients do to me in the marketplace?

# CHAPTER 24

I'd like to say the Recipient marketplace is much like the Donor's. But it's not. Sure, there are shops and crowds and carts placed outside full of wares, but the smells here are so strong and unpleasant. The Recipient marketplace smells like the glue that's in my hair. It fills the air like smoke that scratches its way into my lungs, and I cover my nose with my hand. It's nothing like the burnt sugar scents of the bakery back home; it's more factory made, like the little bottles of perfume I saw in the first shop on the street. Manufactured is the word that comes to mind.

The difference that stands out most of all, however, is how clean it is. The roads are as white as the inside of a facility, their carts are painted white, and their buildings are white brick. Nothing is out of place. Every building down to the signs and streetlamps, everything is symmetrical and pleasing. But the sight of it makes me uneasy. So much precision makes my head spin. And lastly, there are no beggars or men lying in the gutters, no officers or droids. Everyone here is trusted. Everyone has money. It's easier to stay rich when you already have wealth. If a Donor could be as wealthy as even the poorest Recipient, maybe then there would never be any beggars in Donor gutters either.

There are more pastry shops than I thought possible, much less necessary. A Recipient with a white curly wig on his head balances a tray of small cookies on the tips of his fingers. He swings the tray around the market into the faces of passersby, tempting them. When his pale face spots us, he pauses, then grins widely, showing off teeth so white they're blinding.

The slender pastry Recipient makes his way toward us, pushing the ruffles of his long waistcoat out of his way as he walks. He bows over his pointed, outstretched foot, pushing the tray of food into the air. It makes him look like a pony. I bring my hand to my mouth and cough to hide my giggle.

"Your Highness honors us today. What suits your fancy?"

Marcus tries to keep walking and brushes the man off, but he only prances forward, somehow keeping the pastries in place.

"On the house. I insist! It's not every day we get to serve Master Marcus, much less his Donor friend to boot." He puts the tray in front of us and smiles.

The cookies are puffy and put together like little colorful sandwiches. Lime-green cookies with sparkling purple centers and a bright pink one that looks like it is embedded with diamonds. Looking at them makes me leery, but their smell, a kind of lemony scent I can almost taste, does something strange to me, and I find myself leaning in against my will. I'm unable to stop looking at them and licking my lips.

"No, thank you," Marcus pushes the tray away from me, and I shake my head. That felt weird.

"Come on," the store owner says. A crowd is forming now, watching the exchange. "I think your friend here wants to try one. She looks like she's unable to resist it. Just one." He whispers the last words, and the tray is before me again.

This time I notice that in between each cookie is a tiny dot like a pill. They match the cookies in color and design. "What are those?"

Marcus steps forward, forcing the tray to swirl away from me. "Nothing."

The pastry seller laughs, and though I step to follow Marcus, I look over my shoulder at him and pause. His face is so slender, when he laughs or smiles it makes his mouth protrude on the sides like a smiling frog. "Our Donor friend asks 'what are those?'"

"Cancelers are as simple as they get." The crowd laughs and he looks around at them. "Am I right or am I right? It's a pill dear, like from the old days. A pill that lets you eat what you want."

Marcus grabs my wrist now, and I'm too stunned and angry to pull away. I let him drag me through the circle of Recipients.

A man's low voice rings out loud enough for me to hear. "Donors don't want to cancel out their food. They need all the food they can get."

The Recipients laugh harder and then disperse. Marcus pulls me swiftly through the crowd. The Recipient market is larger than I realized, and we continue on forever while I let the situation sink in.

"I'm sorry, Aston. I'm sorry I didn't think about some of these things that would be so different. They know but they don't understand. These are the things I'm hoping to change. Educate the Recipients. I don't think any of them know how desperate Donors are. I know I didn't. I never knew why so many Donors donated themselves to death. I mean, I knew, I just didn't put it together."

Marcus chatters away, but I stop listening. Just across the street there is a cart full of flowers and standing by it is a Recipient I recognize. Her muddy hair stands out in the rainbow of colors. In any other situation I would try to ignore her and not give away anything that could lead to exposing the resistance. But there's something off about how she stands by the cart, looking at the flowers and talking to herself. Something doesn't feel right.

I navigate toward the cart and Marcus shuts up and follows. I try to sneak up so I can hear what she's saying but she sees me and pauses.

"Lovely flowers. Is this your cart?"

Sophie doesn't make eye contact and fidgets mercifully. She curtsies then rushes away from the shop without saying goodbye.

"Well that was strange," Marcus observes.

I nod in agreement. Strange indeed. I know we were not meant to know each other already, but something felt very off about Sofie's behavior. Maybe the resistance was not as accepting of their band of rebels. I hear Dustin in my head with his mean gravelly voice and wouldn't be surprised if he objected to the idea of them joining forces.

"Marcus," a small voice cries delightedly from behind us.

It sounds strange now to hear him not called Master. When I turn around, the mouseling girl from the dinner party that night is standing so close to Marcus that he has to lower his chin to look at her.

"Evangeline!" Marcus says, surprised. He steps back and bumps the cart, making a bouquet fall. Clumsily he lunges for it before it hits the ground, and when putting it back in the cart, he accidentally pushes his hand in too far and it splashes in the water.

Evangeline giggles and steps closer again. As much as I love seeing this display of his discomfort, I'm feeling antsy about moving. Something still feels wrong. I can't seem to shake it. Maybe I'm still just upset from the incident with the canceler pills.

"Marcus?" I don't really know what to say but evidently, it's enough.

"It was lovely to see you, but I must escort my Donor, eh Aston, uh, I have to go."

Marcus soon has his hand behind my back, moving me swiftly away again before Evangeline can protest. He wrings his other hand out into the air over and over again to dry it.

"We came for paints, remember? Let's just get them and get out of here," I say, feeling anxious to be free of this place. "Is there a trade store anywhere?" The invisible scars on my legs ache, and I'm sure Adakin is watching my every move.

"We don't have trade stores. Everything is new."

"Is there an art supply store then?"

"No. But we have eclectic stores with a mix of everything."

He steps up to a shop that has a bright rainbow sign. Inside it has glistening white floors and funny music playing, which feels strange and out of place in comparison to all the quiet shops. Who puts music in a store anyway? I wouldn't put it past Recipients to dance down the aisles in their party dresses each and every day. We pass shelves of glass goblets and plates and row after row of paper. So much beautiful, smooth paper. I let myself touch every single pack as we walk by.

When we find paints, I want to pinch myself. There's no "this just in" sign; there is enough stock to buy five of everything and come back for refills whenever I need them. Marcus insists I pick, but I could no easier pick a book. Instead, I explain to him all the different kinds of paint and what kind of paintings they are good for. Marcus answers by gathering everything he can. At the cash register, he tells the man to have even more delivered to the palace. I know I shouldn't be bought so easily, but my fingers are already twitching with excitement.

"Thank you, Marcus."

I stare at a package of new paints in my hand when the ground shakes beneath my feet. Glass on the shelves tinkles then falls, shattered, to the floor. A thunderous explosion rocks the store. The windows are blown in with an earsplitting whoosh. I instinctively crouch down and grab my ears. Marcus huddles over me with an arm over my back. Plates and bowls and mirrors fall all around us, making tiny pieces of glass bounce on the floor like it is raining tiny crystals.

My ears ring and everything around me moves like a silent movie. Marcus pushes himself up and runs for the door. Outside he disappears in the smoke billowing down the market street.

I get up and follow him. The street is utter and complete chaos. What was once white and orderly is now turned upside down with carts torn to pieces, their wares hanging from corners of the buildings. There is someone clapping long and slow, like a sick mocking joke to the scene before me. But then I realize it's the sound of debris raining from the sky and hitting roofs and sidewalks. Pieces of a building, tiles from a roof, curtains. Black smoke stains the brick, and a bright-orange fire blazes. Recipients don't care who I am now as they bump past me. I walk slowly to the wreckage where Marcus has a ripped piece of his shirt over his face as he runs toward the flames.

I don't know what to do. I just stand and stare. I'm confused about why there are people lying on the ground until I make eye contact with one of them. I gasp and feel sick to my stomach. One of them is the mouse girl from the dinner party. She is lying on her back, staring at the sky in a way that proves she is not seeing anything at all. She is gone.

"Donors!" A woman cries as she runs past.

Marcus pulls a body from the wreckage, and I run closer. It's a Recipient, but something looks familiar about him. How do I know this man?

"There are more," he yells. "There are Donors too."

"Donors?" Did I hear him right? Did he say Donors? He runs back into the smoke and brings another body. A young woman. I help him by taking the girl's arm and wrapping it around my neck. I pull her to the side away from the smoke as Marcus runs back in. The young woman is covered in soot, and I don't recognize her until she speaks.

"I thought you said this was the resistance." Sofie's voice is rough, tainted with pain and betrayal and exhaustion.

That's how I know this man. He was one of her crew. Her little rebellion. What did they do?

"What happened?" I lower her to the ground. Her hand holds her stomach and blood makes the soot on her clothes shine.

"I thought I could trust them," she says. Her breathing is loud and wheezy. "You told me I could trust them."

"Donors? These were Donors? That can't be."

Bright red stains the corners of the inside of her mouth, and her next words are slow and difficult. "Save. Us. All."

I wish the ringing from after the explosion would return and drown out the coughing and gurgling sounds of Sofie dying. I barely knew her. I don't know if she was a sister or an aunt or a friend. I don't know if she had hobbies like me or read books or was trustworthy at all. I don't know her motives for the rebellion, but at this moment I know that, Recipient or not, I have to hold her close and tell her it will be okay before she dies.

"I will," I promise her. "Sofie, I'm so sorry, but I swear I will."

She doesn't hear me. She is heavy on my lap. I'm suddenly so angry. Marcus screams as he pulls another person from the fire. He is gasping and choking. I lay Sofie down gently and run to help him.

"Marcus, you have to get help, you can't keep going in there!"

"There are Donors!" he shouts and turns back as the man in his arms starts to crawl away on his own.

"Marcus, no!" The flames are bigger than before, and the heat is unbearable from where we stand. His face is covered in black, and he's coughing and stumbling. I grab his arms with both hands..

It's too late now. The flames rise and grow out of control. Anyone still in there must be dead.

"There are Donors." His voice trembles as he yells, and tears make ugly smears of black across his face. "I have to save the power plant!" he shouts.

Power plant? I squeeze his arm so tight my fingers dig deep into his skin. He must have heard his own mistake as well, for he stops pulling against my grasp. He falls to his knees and sobs violently.

"There were Donors in there." He puts his dirty face into his dirty hands and sobs between each statement. "I didn't save them. I didn't even try! There were so many, and I didn't even try."

I squeeze his shoulder, and he grabs at my hand like it can save him. His head leans on my thigh and he cries harder.

"I'm so sorry. I didn't know."

I stroke his hair until he calms. Funny sirens grow louder, and soon there are swarms of droids everywhere. It feels like they took forever, but everything happened so fast.

The man Marcus pulled to safety coughs behind us. I recognize him. He's a tram car driver from my hometown, but I never said more than a few words to him as I paid for my fare.

"What happened here?" I demand. Marcus wipes his face and looks at who I'm talking to.

"It was a fair trade." The man chokes and then lays himself down like it is the perfect place to have a nice pleasant nap.

I stomp over to him and shake his shoulder. I have to know more. "What? What was a fair trade? What happened?"

The man coughs again and tries several times to talk but nothing comes out. When he rolls over on his side, he lets out a last crackly breath, carrying with it one final word. It swirls the dirt and charcoal on the ground away from his mouth as he speaks. "Dustin," he says and then lays limp and lifeless.

# CHAPTER 25

J anice ignores my protests and insists that I need a
bath. It is then that I first notice Sofie's blood on my
blue dress. My legs collapse beneath me. Janice
catches me before I hit the tile then holds me, soot,
blood, and all as I sob incoherent things into her shoulder.
I'm oblivious to her hold on me, unaware of any shushing
or stroking of my hair she may be doing. I'm only mindful
of the pain and terror suffocating me, like the flames from
the explosion are not only in my memory but in my lungs as
well. Repeating things like "I knew something was wrong,"
and "I never should have trusted Dustin," over and over
again like admitting the trauma and my ignorance might
make it all go away.

I don't remember getting into the bath or getting out,
but soon I'm in bed, silent and numb. I don't sleep for
hours. All I can hear is the applause of the raining debris as
I lay in bed and stare at the statue of the hands and the
droplet on the shelf.

Gannet doesn't come in person. Instead, it's just his

voice ringing through the room. I don't bother getting up. I just stare at the wall where it glows when he talks.

"Aston?"

I let him try a few times. Let him think that I'm asleep. Maybe I won't answer him at all.

"Aston? Are you there? Are you okay? Aston?"

"I'm here."

"Oh, Aston," Gannet says and then speaks so swiftly I don't have a chance to answer him. "I'm so sorry, we had no idea you were on that market street until we just saw the reports on the screen. Are you hurt? Is everything—"

I throw the blankets off and sit up in bed. "How would knowing if I was there have changed anything?"

"We would have—"

"So is it true? It was us? An attack on Recipients? Against the ones trying to help us?"

Gannet sighs, but Dustin's awful, gravelly voice comes over the speakers.

"Look, they were just Recipients, they were going to die someday or another anyway."

I stand so quickly my vision goes dark around the edges, and I yell into the room as loud as I can. "They were people!" Before they can say anything else I whimper angrily, "And Donors died too." The idea of Adakin eavesdropping flits across my mind but the risk is ruled out quickly. Surely I have enough anger to break any surveillance connection for miles around.

Something crashes, and I'm hoping someone punched Dustin in the face. Gannet starts explaining things rapidly again.

"I know, Aston, I'm sorry. There was a misunderstanding. We were trying to make a transfer and..."

"What were you trading?"

"What?"

I lose my patience with Gannet and yell at him again. "One of the victims said it was a fair trade, what were you trading?"

Dustin yells something in the background, but Gannet ignores him. "We were trading free blood for certain supplies."

"And did you get them? Your supplies?"

"Yes."

"Then what happened?"

"We weren't just transferring supplies, Aston. We were transferring... people."

I sit back down on my bed. So that's how Donors showed up in Bloomfield? I rub my aching head and pinch my temples together.

"Donors got there just fine but when they couldn't get back... Some of us panicked. Looks like it was just a glitch. Sofie was trying to fix it when..."

"Dustin," I whisper.

"There's no proof that it was a glitch," Dustin shouts, but there's a scuffle again.

"You're a murderer!" I yell. How can this be happening? How can the resistance be run by such awful people full of prejudices and blind to what is really happening? I think about things Marcus has said. His sobs over and over again into my knee. He didn't know. No more than I knew about the lives of Recipients in the dramatized movies. No more than Dustin knows from his sheltered, horrible life as a Donor.

Sofie's gurgling words haunt me. "Save. Us. All."

She knew. She knew that there was not a single wall that could divide us when everyone needed saving. Saving from the system, from the government, from ourselves.

"Anything else?" I ask.

There's a long pause.

"Aston, are you okay? We need to know if—"

"Anything else?" I say a little firmer.

"No," Gannet says softly.

I don't remember if he said goodbye. I only remember climbing into my bed and stuffing my face into my pillow.

Next thing I know, Janice enters and opens the curtains. She sits on the edge of my bed and strokes my hair away from my face and off my neck.

I open my eyes but don't move away from her touch.

"I have something for you, miss."

Why won't she just call me by my name? Janice brings something blue over to my bed, and I slowly get up. She holds in her hands a neatly folded pair of jeans.

I rub my hands across the top of them. "Thank you." When I pick them up, the pants legs fall to the floor. They have a crease mark down the center of the legs like formal suit pants and are a faded light-blue with darker edges.

"If you don't like them," Janice says, "it's okay. I can take them back. I confess I didn't know exactly what I was looking—"

Before she can continue, I hug her. Jeans in hand, I fling them around her back and squeeze her tight.

Her arms stretch around my back too, and she pats me between the shoulder blades like Grandma Bolgi used to do. "You're very welcome, miss."

The jeans are stiff and new but will break in soon enough. They fit like a glove, showing every curve of my hips and cling to my ankles. Janice hands me a shirt with the same fabric of my dress: a light-blue shimmering silk. I know there's no blood on it, but I can't help but see the image in my mind. I refuse it. "Anything but blue, Janice."

"But it brings out your eyes—"

"I'll not wear blue!" I yell. "I'm sorry. I didn't—"

"Don't apologize, miss. I'll see what I can find."

The only other shirt she can find is a white one that clings to my chest and waist yet is loose and flowing on the arms. When I look in the mirror, the shirt seems see-through, yet I can't tell if it's just the shine of the fabric playing tricks on my eyes.

There's a knock at the door and Marcus enters with a tray of food. The silence is so thick we could drown in it.

Janice leaves with a curtsy.

We sit and eat in silence.

"Where is Alex?" I say.

"No donations today."

The mood is so somber as we both revisit everything we experienced yesterday.

"If what you say is true about the serums, maybe they are a good thing."

"Marcus, how could you say that?"

"Because I don't want to feel what I'm feeling right now." He sounds close to tears again. "I don't want to remember the things I hate about myself. What do you do when it just won't go away?"

"Well," I say and then stand up when I make up my mind. "I paint."

It takes some convincing, but soon Marcus has found the paints we had ordered to the palace and stands in my doorway with aprons in his hand. I can't help but smile. I haven't painted in so long. It's like I'm about to be reunited with a part of my family. Another part of me that has been missing for so long. Art. Expression.

"This one's for you." He hands me the plain beige

smock, and I put it over my head. He's already down the hall, and I skip to catch up.

As we near the staircase, we turn left on the red carpet. I look over my shoulder at the large staircase as we head down the new hallway.

"Where are we going?"

"You'll see. I had this room made up for us to use... yesterday." His tongue trips over that last word.

There are three doors. One straight ahead and two on either side of the hallway directly across from each other. He opens the one on the right and steps aside for me to enter first.

The smell of flowers is my first impression, and I spot a table similar to the table in my room that has the largest bouquet of flowers I have ever seen. There are the hydrangea lilies that I love so much and orange ones and pink ones too. Every color of the rainbow is in this bouquet and small white stems shoot out taller than the rest like spikes.

I step further into the room and spin as I take in my surroundings. There are shelves lining the walls, and I can tell the furniture has been moved closer to them to make way for the two easels that stand on the other side of the table near the rear.

In other circumstances, I might have giggled at this sight. Euphoric at the thought of so many supplies before me. Instead, my eyes squint at the hint of a smile when I can't think of what to say. It feels wrong to be happy about something so trivial.

"I am hoping the most talented Miss Aston Vazeto will give me my first art lesson."

I turn to look at Marcus incredulously. I've never given anyone lessons on how to paint before. I just do it.

He motions to a small table connecting the easels that showcases several different kinds of paintbrushes and paints. I step toward the table with my hands behind my back and have to hold onto them tightly to keep from showing my excitement.

Oils, watercolor, pastels, acrylic—there is every kind of paint I've ever heard of and none of them are opened or used at all. I finally let go of my death grip on myself and let my fingers scan across the row of brushes still wrapped in plastic covers.

"Lesson one, which brush to pick," he says. "I like... this one." He picks up a thick-handled brush with a flat tip. "Feels manly and straightforward." He holds it up like he's brandishing a sword.

I can't help but laugh. "The kind of paint most often determines the kind of brush. And how big of an area you're trying to cover. That's a good one for oils." Our fingers touch as I take it from him, and the heat from his hand awakens me. "I like watercolors best," I say, stepping away from him. I pick up a nice round brush and play with the hair of it. I can tell it's synthetic, and I pull the bristles back to a point before I set it back down. "But acrylic is perhaps best for beginners." I quickly find a soft brush with a flat tip, hand it to him, and step away even farther.

"What should we paint then?" he asks. "Each other?"

My head snaps in his direction. I look at his face and see the lines of worry that weren't there when I painted him so long ago. We have both changed.

"I'm not sure you're quite ready for something like that," I say. "Faces are difficult to do. Perhaps these flowers would be a good start. Or we could paint whatever we want really. For me, it's a way to get out those emotions that I don't know what to do with. Give them a voice."

He nods and grows somber.

After a few basic instructions on my part, we are soon busy working, and conversation is lost in our concentration. I peek at Marcus and smile at how he focuses with his brow bunched up and his top teeth biting his lower lip with worry. I've decided to paint the flowers. I look back at my work. The large vase is planned out, and I begin on the first flower.

The feel of the brush in my hand alone is enough to make me sigh. Then the shape of the first flower as it comes together reminds me somehow of my sisters. So elegantly beautiful and graceful. They were all flowers, and what was I? A weed? I frown as I start on the next flower, a dark-red rose with sleek and firm petals. I can't take my eyes off the red petals. I don't always know what I'm doing when I paint. My hand has a mind of its own, interpreting what I can't put into words. Soon the rose petals are dripping, long and wet-like. Sofie. The Recipient I never knew but promised I would create change in a world trying to kill each other. As the bouquet comes together, I soon see the diversity in everyone I've ever known. These real and new-breed flowers only exist because of a controlling, masterful hand. Someone who wasn't happy enough with the flowers the way they were. Someone who couldn't just appreciate their singular beauty and dove into their genetic makeup to create something different.

Suddenly these flowers are a grotesque symbol of all those wronged by the system. My hands move at a feverish pace as I set my face in an angry scowl. The spikes of long stems that shoot out of the top with tiny white flowers on them as I paint them to look more menacing and angry than the frumpy sticks they appear to be. I am unaware of anyone else in the room, and my grip on the paintbrush begins to ache. There are faces in front of my vision now instead of blossoms. Torrin and Oliver with his poor hungry twin brothers, Shannon with baby Pip in her arms, Ari and Derek with their bratty son, Roylance, even Sybil flashes across my eyes as I paint. All of them would have been beautiful enough on their own. What could they have offered without the monopoly placed on their blood?

There is Janice too, and Trip and Sofie, Marcus and the little mouse girl. They deserve to be valued too.

"Whoa!" Marcus exclaims, and I jump at the sound of his voice. "I knew you could paint but this..."

"You've only seen me paint you. We are always our worst critics. Besides, I didn't have such nice tools as these."

"Are you okay?"

I shrug and wipe my face. I hadn't realized I was crying.

"Perhaps a look at mine will help lighten your mood?"

"Hmm?"

He motions me over and, with my face still tense with emotion, I step closer to his easel. My first glance at his painting at least removes the frown from my face. It's full of colors, only they're all blended together in watered down blobs, some of which drip and bleed into the other.

"It's..." I thought I could give a deadpan answer, but I quickly bring my hand to my face to hide my smile. Marcus laughs, a deep boisterous laugh that vibrates the tension loose within me.

"No, stop it," I say. "It's a really good first try. And it's not about what it looks like; it's about how you feel. It's an expression."

His laugh grows. "Is that the best compliment you can come up with? Tell me what you really think."

His laugh is contagious, and the more I look at his

painting, the more I can't control my own laughter. "Okay then, it really is a bit terrible, isn't it?"

"Hey! You can't blame me, blame my art teacher who left me all on my own." He jabs at me with his paint brush.

I lunge away with a laugh, but he gets me on my thigh, leaving a dark green mark on my new jeans.

I gasp. "These are new! You got paint on my new jeans!" I look at him with my mouth agape. We are frozen in place. His eyes twinkle. I take my brush in hand and wipe it across his happy little face, leaving a watery red mark dripping down his nose.

I'm laughing again at his shocked expression, and he retaliates with another jab with the paint brush. In a rush of movement, I grab my cup of water and splash it toward him, and he laughingly grabs a tube of acrylics and squeezes the entire tube in my direction. We are dodging behind tables and attacking each other with paint as we maneuver around the whole room.

Marcus grabs his own cup to dump on me as well. I grab his hand with both of mine to stop him and shout with a grin, "Don't you dare!"

For a moment the cup is suspended, but Marcus loses his balance and slips on the paint splattered floor. Grabbing my shoulder, he takes me down with him and the water spills on both of us. I'm flat on my back, laughing harder than I ever have, and he is groaning and laughing beside me. My arm is pinned beneath him, and I still can't stop laughing. Laughing so hard, releasing all the tension that's built from the attack, from everything. It's better than crying, but it still feels wrong. It feels on the verge of tears, like at any moment my cackles will turn to wails, when Marcus leans up on an elbow, and it sobers me. He is suddenly right above me, so close I could kiss him. Slowly, my laugh and smile disappear completely as I look into his eyes.

"About yesterday... How I fell apart—"

"It's okay," I say.

"I really am sorry, Aston."

"I know."

Our faces close, hearts racing, in this moment a peaceful refreshing balm spreads over my heart. "I know," I say again.

I freeze when he lifts a paint ridden hand. He moves the hair out of my face and leaves his hand there, his forearm resting on my chest. A tear leaks out of the crease of his eye. My heart hammers and my lips open.

But this is sympathy. I won't confuse it with love again. There's too much happening too fast. I can forgive him without loving him, can't I? My eyes drop for a second to his lips, open and ready. How in the bloody New world would it work for a Donor and Recipient to fall in love?

I shove his arm off of me and roll out from under him. He stares at me from the floor. My shirt, which was already tight, clings to me where wet. I look down at it and wrap my arm across my chest. Only our heavy breathing takes up conversation.

Marcus gets up without a word and moves across the room toward two doors. He slides them open, revealing a bedroom that I instantly know is his. The way he left his room with the bed unmade and books piled by its side makes me smile. He returns with a shirt, and I put it over my head without speaking. It's large and almost reaches my knees, but it's warm and smells just like him, fruity with a hint of musky soap. Now I know why he always smelled so clean. He's a Recipient who can afford all the luxuries of cleanliness. Lasers even.

He clears his throat before he speaks. "I'll take you back to your room so you can clean up."

I nod. We walk down the hallways in silence.

We are soon at my door, and he leans in front of me, putting his hand on the doorknob, but pauses. "Thank you for your help, Aston. The painting helped." He lifts up his messy paint hand and smiles. "I'm sorry that I..." He clears his throat and straightens. "I mean." His gaze is so intense, his turmoil and indecision sketched across his face like shadowing in a painting. "You know, I tell myself that I am just your Recipient, that you have every right to be angry at me, and that I'm going to prove to you I can be patient and the gentleman you deserve, but then when I'm around you, I can't help but want more of you. More of your laugh, your smile, your glances. I was raised with everything I've always wanted, but since I've met you, I've found joy in the work, trying to be better, being patient. I'm trying to change."

I cover my mouth with a messy hand and hide behind my hair.

"I'm trying to change more than just myself and the way I see things. I want this world to be different. To be better."

I risk looking at him now.

"I wish..." He lets it trail off and sighs heavily. "Will you join me for dinner?"

There's no explanation for how his blue eyes can shine in the shadow of this hallway. I'm suddenly drowning in the memories of his eyes yesterday, filled with tears, sobbing from remorse. I know he wants things to change even if I also know his ways are faulty. I nod without thinking. What excuse could I give? He smiles.

I step into my room and begin closing the door with one

hand on the doorknob, the other on the edge of the door, watching his retreating form down the hallway. Dinner? I shouldn't. All I can think about are the words of his letter and his grip on my leg as he sobbed all crumpled on the ground. He is trying to change and everything about him seems to prove he genuinely wants a better life for Recipient *and* Donor. When he looks over his shoulder at me and smiles again, I shut the door.

I lean on the back of the door and let my head fall backward against it with a soft thud. Sofie is dead because I convinced her to trust the resistance. Donors and Recipients everywhere are dying and confused and don't know what to fight for, and I'm going to have dinner, probably in a gorgeous dress.

I close my eyes and chastise myself aloud. "What are you thinking?" I pull my head forward and step away, only to freeze in place. The bee stings on my legs zing down into my toes like the bees are stuck inside my pants.

"Exactly what I was wondering, myself," Adakin Malloy says.

He sits in a chair in the corner of my room with his legs crossed and his hands interlocked around them.

# CHAPTER 26

The sound of his voice sends my heart into a panic. He stands and walks across the floor with the same *bump-click* of his shoes that sends a shiver up my spine.

"I would ask what you've been doing with my grandson." He eyes my appearance, covered in paint and sporting Marcus's big T-shirt. "But I'm not sure I want to know. Especially after your big show yesterday."

Adakin pauses at our tray of unfinished food and moves the cheese around like he is looking for a specific kind. "Your rebels made quite the spectacle of themselves." He tries to act confident, but I could swear there's a quick unsure peek to judge my reaction. He wants me to think he knows everything, but is there a chance he doesn't know exactly who I'm working with or how? He picks a piece of cheese and places it in his mouth with a pinky in the air and raised eyebrows. "Everyone get what they wanted?"

Recalling the conversation with Gannet and the exchange they were trying to make has my stomach twisting. Adakin knew? He knew and just let his own people die?

Or is he bluffing? Perhaps it's the way he takes my precious cheese from the tray, like he takes and does whatever he wants with Donors, that has my stomach boiling and rumbling mad. "Why do you let things like that happen? If you knew they were coming, why didn't you do something?"

"Oh, but I thought you valued freedom?" He claps his hands together with one terrifying sound and I flinch. He laughs as he starts walking again, pointing his praying hands toward me with each thing he says. "You can't have it both ways, Aston. Besides, how was I to know the Donors would be so jumpy?"

He studies the wall above the desk in the corner. "Enough about them and back to our lessons. I do love to teach, you know. If my expertise in medical research hadn't been so essential, I might have considered becoming a professor. Now, where were we when we were so rudely interrupted last time? Ah, yes." He places his decrepit hand on the wall and instantly, we are outside by the beehives again.

I hunch my shoulders and look around for the bees. I hear them even though I don't see them. A sound that has haunted me since that day.

"I always like to start with my bees," he says with a sort of perverted pride. "I believe we were discussing hive mind."

Adakin paces in front of me with his hands behind his back, making his belly stick out even further. He starts speaking like this is nothing more than a grade school class, and I am a yearning pupil.

"There's something called swarm intelligence. Individual identity is still very important, of course"—he bats his hand off to the side like he's sweeping it under the rug

—"but their sense of self is formed in the hive mind. There is a paradigm shift when we let go of our egos and become one entity." The way he gets excited with each word is nauseating. I'm half expecting him to wave his hands in the air like a raving lunatic, and half on edge for the onslaught of bees at any moment. Always on guard for the bees. He narrows his eyes for emphasis and almost whispers the next line of his speech. "We are our truest self when we swarm together for one cause."

Being completely serum-free, I find my voice easily, even if my mind still can't keep up with his lecture. "How is drowning the individual of existence in the first place the same thing as working together?" I point in the direction of the humming bees, though I still cannot see them. My voice shakes at the thought. "These worker bees work together because they want the outcome, Donors wouldn't really agree to the outcome if they knew the cost."

"Instincts, Aston." Adakin punches a pointed finger in the air and smiles like this is the most fun he's had in a long time. "These workers work out of instinct. They don't think, they just do it. They would die for the queen, not because they like her, but because chemicals tell them to."

"I'm no bee," I whisper. His words are as haunting as the buzzing behind him.

"Aren't you, though?" He tilts his head and grins. "Not much different, really." He smiles gleefully. "You covered up for Lazuli not because you liked her, but because fear made you desperate. Instinct kept you alive." A shiver down my arms leaves me feeling cold and alone. Does he really know how I hacked into the miniport to change her numbers? Does he know how Torrin helped me? Does he know everything? He steps away with a wink as if answering my worried thoughts.

"As fun as all this is, I didn't just bring you here to talk about bees or even to remind you of what these bees can do." Another shiver runs over me, making me visibly shake. It gives him too much pleasure, and I grind my teeth with determination to stand still. "No, I have gotten a bit off track again. One can't talk about the bees, however, without talking about the virus." He unclasps his hands and leans to one side, his elbow high in the air as he tries to reach into his vest pocket.

"One of the benefits of being in my position is having access to all the germ powders used in every war." He retrieves glass vials with red lids on them. "We have the progression of weapons as they became more sophisticated and led to Eva's ultimate creation." He holds up a vial until it is shining bright in the sun. "Why, right here in this sealed vial is the very powder that brought the world to its knees on that last round of violence." He gives a humorless laugh. "It's funny that we should be talking about the very thing that I had in my pocket, isn't it?"

My head hurts from the frowning. My legs wobble. He carries the virus in his pocket? My heart hammers, beats that drum in my ears.

"And funny that we should be talking about Eva, the very..." His smile drops. He never finishes that sentence and just stares at me long and hard. "We call it a powder when really Eva had discovered by this point how to make it invisible. An invisible airborne weapon." He looks at it in awe and with respect. "Now that's something to fear for sure. But as you well know now"—he spins his free hand around at our surroundings—"fear is in the eye of the beholder. Or should I say, in the mind of the beholder." He laughs again.

He steps toward me, bringing the vial down in front of

him until it is directly between us. My resolve to remain still and confident is wavering. My teeth chatter from the stress and anxiety building up through my chest. Is he planning to open it here in front of me and expose me? I am immune, aren't I? But what if a concentrated amount such as this would be too much for my antibodies? Is that even possible? Or is he hoping to have it in my system so as to infect anyone else that comes in contact? Like Marcus.

He seems bored with my panic and lowers the vial as he continues. "I took Eva Tabor's weapon a step further, though, you see. Using my trained officers as test subjects, we can now make this invisible powder personalized to its victims."

He stares at me so long and hard that my mind starts to reel and spin. Personalized? I can't take my eyes off him. I clench my jaws tighter to keep them still. He sees my gears working and waits patiently, hoping I will come to the conclusion he wants me to. And then it clicks. I suddenly don't hear the bees anymore.

"The personality test," I whisper in terrified shock. My jaw relaxes with distracted thoughts. He wanted me to find them, didn't he? Why does it feel like this news is more a distraction than anything else?

Adakin nods, pleased with himself. "See, your snooping did pay off. You and your little rat boy."

My head snaps up at him. He thinks I'm only consorting with a Recipient boy in the attic. He doesn't know anything about Gannet or the resistance at all, does he?

"With specific genetic adjustments and codes, this powder can be released into a sea of people and only affect those with the blood we program it to. Making it look as if one merely died of a heart attack."

"Or from their first week of donations," I say with a sneer, though I think I may be sick.

Adakin snaps his fingers and winks at me. "Ah, we are quick, aren't we. Yes, sadly there must be test subjects in every experiment as you are finding out so quickly. But don't worry yourself my dear, they were all low numbers to be sure. They probably wouldn't have lasted much longer anyway."

I make fists and my fingers dig into my palms. My jaw aches from grinding my teeth again. Numbers, never people. This is what Marcus tried to tell me. This was how he was raised. But he should have seen. Should have known better. "They were still people."

"I think you're getting mad at the wrong person, Miss Vazeto. Even I need to live, and it wasn't I who created this virus."

"How does that give you the right to kill innocent people? Surviving doesn't give you the right to control people as your little robots!"

"I don't think you understand my predicament clearly. I don't expect you to. War is still waging even if it is lulled into survival mode for a time. What I do hope you realize now, however, is the power which I hold and the precarious position you find yourself in." He twists the vial in his fingers close to his face.

"Your threats mean nothing to me!" It feels good to yell.

"Oh? Don't they?" He turns and reaches into the air. Our surroundings instantly change to a market scene. I flinch, reminded of the Recipient marketplace and the destruction I witnessed. This market, however, looks even more familiar. It is my hometown market, and the longing for it makes a cold empty place in my stomach. Home. I walk the street like I did innocently thousands of times, gulping the smells of my own market like the sweat and dust and sweet rolls are my only hope. My face falls slack at the sight of it, but something feels wrong. Too familiar. The people around me are moving too quickly, and I realize their motion is backward as if they're on rewind. They finally stop with a jerk like they just realized the funny dance they were all doing only to pick up their quick walking again. Something has caught their attention. I have a sick feeling of deja vu like I've not only seen this scene before but lived it. And then I see myself. My breath catches when I see the back of my hair, lighter from days spent outside and tangled without a maid to brush it every day for me. There I am, standing in the market crowd, holding a lopsided blue bowl.

"Sandy," I hear the other me shout. "Sandy, what have you done?"

The scene freezes, and I look at the face of the young girl caught in a painful red laser beam, her face contorted in suffering. Gloria. The only thing that gives me comfort is the fact that this entire footage is an aerial view, probably from a droid and not the eyes of a Recipient. I remember Janice's words—*you made others feel*—and realize I've broken that connection to surveillance before.

"See, I think you do respond to threats." Adakin weaves through the still crowd. "Especially threats on the innocent. Strangers even."

What does he want from me, and what does he plan to do?

Without taking his eyes off of me, he puts out his hand and the image changes again. We are suddenly standing in a school room. My head tilts back and I examine the high vaulted ceiling. It looks familiar, and I recognize it as my middle grade auditorium. Children of every age begin to gather and take their seats on the floor. An assembly of sorts, I suppose.

"This, in case you can't tell, is in real time again. Not a recorded file. This is live." His clown grin sickens me. His excitement is unnerving.

Another class is filing past me, right in front of me, so close I could reach out and touch them.

When I see him, I gasp so hard it hurts my throat, like I'm swallowing a boulder. I grab my neck as I screech, "Torrin!"

# CHAPTER 27

T yell and lunge forward to take his arm. "Torrin!" My hands make contact with his, but I have no effect on his form. I'm like a ghost who can feel his skin and the growing muscles of his forearm, yet I have no effect. My fingers go through him and slip over him whenever I try to tug. I don't have the ability or the clearance or whatever they call it. I can't interact with this scene how Adakin could with the beehives, but it doesn't stop me from trying over and over. I need to figure out how this tech access works. I need to get to Torrin. To be this close to him, to see him and do nothing about it, feels worse than a million bee stings.

Adakin chuckles and steps closer to the scene. "He can't see or hear you. His perception would need to be altered and connected to yours in order for that to happen. But you can see and hear and feel everything as if you were present in this room. That is essential for what is going to happen next, and I'm glad to see something of mine finally has the desired effect on you."

The children are all seated, and a woman stands at the

front of the assembly. Before she speaks, however, Adakin speaks over her.

"If I were to open this vial in the room, what do you think would happen?"

"Nothing." I square my shoulders, but I am anything but certain about my words.

"Come now, Aston, I know you're smarter than that. You asked the question yourself so you should know that I can affect and manipulate this scene if I wanted to."

I frown further.

He sighs and leans down to a young girl sitting cross-legged next to us. He picks up one of her braided pigtails and gives it a light tug. She spins around with a pout for the boy sitting behind her and slaps his leg.

"What?" the boy complains with two hands up pleadingly.

Adakin steps away from the children, closer to me, and I instinctively move to block Torrin.

Adakin whispers creepily as he comes closer, so very pleased with this performance of his. "I am here like an angel watching over the people. Always present. Never seen. Now what do you think would happen if I opened this vial into the air?" He pulls it in front of his face with two fingers pinched over the red lid, ready for action.

"This is a room full of Donors," I say. "We are immune."

He smiles as if he is waiting for me to calculate something. "Except for...?"

He is enjoying this way too much. My mind clumsily runs over the information he's given me. If I'm right, will this end? Will he take me back to my room? Will he keep the lid on that vial? I look out over the crowd of children. I recognize a few from my neighborhood, younger siblings of friends of mine, children of families I know. All of them are so different and unique but commonly pure.

Different. Unique. My head snaps to his waiting face.

"Except for the blood you've programmed to be affected." This was the reason for the science and tech lesson. He wanted to make sure I knew that whatever was about to happen in this room was of his making.

Adakin spins around, dramatically putting the vial out and over the heads of all the children like he will sprinkle it on them at any moment. My eyes follow his movements, and my hands fan out in front of me.

"Stop!" I yell, seeing the innocent faces ignorant to what is going on around them. He faces me again with his sickening grin. He puts the vial back down by his side. "What do you want?" I snarl.

"Give me a town. Just one city name. Tell me where Bolglarka is."

I look again at the faces in front of me. Grandma Bolgi said to tell them nothing, but what if she knew the innocent life of a child was at stake?

I close my eyes tight and squeeze my hands. What do I do? A child could die, but how many are Grandma Bolgi keeping safe that I would put in jeopardy if I give away her general whereabouts? How many more would the king kill if he found the resistance?

"If you only knew who you were staying loyal to," Adakin says disappointedly. I hear a pop like the sound Papa used to make with his mouth to make Pip laugh, and I open my eyes. The vial is open and Adakin throws it into the air.

"No!" I scream and lunge but it's too late. I know it's too late, yet still I charge down the small aisle the kids have created and watch the vial as it makes its descent. I try to catch the little glass and put my hand over the top like a stopper, but I can't make contact with it. My hand passes through the glass over and over again.

Adakin laughs, a deep throaty laugh, and spreads his arms out wide. "It's already out there, Aston. You're too late. Enjoy the show, and hopefully next time you will not let others die for your misplaced loyalty." He laughs again and takes a few steps. He opens an invisible door, the door to my bedroom, and then disappears out of the PR like a magician.

Slowly I turn in place. I can't keep the images of Donors and Recipients dying in the market the other day out of my head. Their screams. Sofie's blood. My ragged breathing pulses in my ears. Finally, I can hear what the woman is saying. "With that in order, the decision has been officially made to change the age of donations." The room is no longer silent as the children chatter, some excitedly, some nervously to their neighbors. "Quiet down. I know this isn't a shock to some of you since it has been rumored for so many years, but this new protocol will take effect immediately, and those who are already twelve years old—"

I shout, "Twelve?" into the room along with many other kids. I scan the room for Torrin. He will be a Donor before... before what? Before the resistance wins? Before I return? I don't know what to expect or dream about or wish for. I walk farther down the aisle, trying to not be distracted by this news. Someone here is going to die before then. I know that much. I inch closer to Torrin, internally chanting, "Please don't be him. Please don't be him."

"Yes," the woman continues, "Many of you have already been a part of the trials with little to no side effects. Those who are already twelve and older should be visited within the week to be tested. Those who are not yet of age can expect a visit now on your twelfth birthday. A B-mail is being sent out today to explain the new procedures to all families all over the New World."

Blurry from uncontrollable tears, I wipe at my eyes frantically to clear my view. I scan the crowd again, staying close to Torrin. My cheeks are wet, and my eyes are hurting from the strain of looking for the slightest movement, the smallest indication that someone is suffering.

"Thank you. That is all. We look forward to seeing some of our own students representing us at the auctions."

The classes are standing, and I can no longer see over the heads of all the children. I don't want to leave Torrin, but anxiety has me dashing to the front and climbing the stage to have a better view of the room. I hate leaving Torrin alone. The tears intensify of their own free will.

The children's commotion grows louder, sounding too much like the bees humming, and I wring my hands, then tear at the bandage on my arm. Maybe Adakin was lying. Maybe he was bluffing.

A scream echoes through the tall auditorium, and there's a curious hush that falls like dominoes away from a small circle forming in the back of the room. I run through the crowd, and though I can't push against the people there, I feel them. Like a cool mist, they tingle against my skin as I sprint through them.

Soon I am standing right above a boy that has collapsed and is grabbing at his neck. The wave of relief that goes through me that it isn't Torrin is quickly replaced with new panic and terror. This small boy looks no older than twelve. He is given a large circle of space as other children panic and begin to cry.

"What's wrong with him?" they say. "Help! Help him!"

Save us all! Save us all! Save us all!

A teacher pushes through the crowd and kneels down to him the same time I do. The teacher puts his face down to the squirming boy and listens.

"He's not breathing!" he shouts.

The boy stops wriggling. I reach out to the boy and can feel his soft skin and the absence of a heartbeat.

"He's turning colors!" A girl yells right as the boy goes completely limp. The shouts grow louder, but with a small snap the scene is taken away from me. I am kneeling in my bedroom with my hand on nothing. The boy is gone. Both in my perceived reality and in actual reality. He is dead. So many dead. Save us all!

The bright sun casts orange and yellow across my room like it's laughing at me with Adakin. The lack of screaming makes the silence sting my ears. I collapse on the floor and sob. The image of that young boy's face going lifeless won't leave my vision. He joins the torturous crowd of victims that haunt me. Sofie, Evangeline, the tram car driver, Greg —my list is growing, and I wish my name was on it, not theirs. I curl up on my side and weep for that boy who did nothing. Who was merely a part in this game between Adakin and me. Like a pawn in the game Marcus showed me.

I whimper into the cold floor andI don't care about the messy wet puddle I make beneath me. When I push my eyelids tight together, I can still see them. I cannot save us all. I cannot save anyone.

# CHAPTER 28

Hours later the tears have stopped. I can't move. The puddle of tears and drool beneath me has dried, and the far side of the room is dim. All I do is blink. My neck is sore, and the floor grows harder by the minute from where my hip digs into the wood, yet still I only stare and blink. My choices killed an innocent boy. My information killed Recipients and Donor rebels. If only I had kept my mouth shut. Or if I had just told Adakin. If I had just given the only hint I know—but I'm too afraid to even think it now in these walls.

Standing in my room I see everything differently now. The white sheets, the lamps, the new vase of flowers on my table. I hate everything in this room. Everything. I close my eyes and see the king's smile. The sound of the tinkling vial pings in my memory, and without thinking I grab the vase and launch it across the room with one giant guttural scream. Adakin will do it again. There will always be another boy.

I feel the urgency to paint again. If I don't paint now, I will go deliriously mad or break something else. Somehow I need to rid myself of these emotions, this guilt and ache, or I will explode. The paints are back at Marcus's room, and I have no canvas. No brushes.

I can't save us all. I just need to paint.

I walk numbly to my bed and pull back the covers. I don't want to be a Donor. I don't want to be treasured or valued, manipulated or used. I rip the white top sheet from the bed and tie a knot in each corner of it. I stretch two knots across the curtain rod of the window, the bottom two knots I pull tight over the protruding edge of the wooden windowsill. It's the largest canvas I've ever had.

My breathing is uncontrollably loud and my fists clench. The sheet is too white. Too clean. Too pure. I don't want my blood. I want this all to end. To stop now. The killing and the segregation, the viruses and the poor or rich blood. Oh, why couldn't I just have been born with different blood?

Would these people's lives be in jeopardy if my blood was out of the picture? What if the queen bee was gone and there was no ruler over the hive? I know the answer though. There would just be someone else found for the task. As Adakin says, he is with the people, always present but never seen. This will never end. But I have to do something. I have to stop something.

I look down at my veins. Precious blue lines. I don't realize I'm doing it until tiny dots on my skin prick with blood. I'm scratching at my wrists as if I could take these veins from my very body.

The vial that carried the deadly poison programmed for its victim sits oblivious on the floor. I feel a connection to it, like we took a great trip together. Like we understand each other and the pain we experienced. It's a memento of that horrible scene. I dip to retrieve it and shatter the end of it against the bookshelf.

Before I lose my nerve, I take the jagged glass and swipe it quick and straight across my skin. It surprises me that I don't flinch, and the jolt of pain draws attention away from my inner guilt, mourning, and chaos I can't control. My palm is greeted by a warm river of blood that glistens under the lamp light. I do the same to my other wrist, and when the blood drips from my fingertips, I lift them to my white canvas. It licks the blood off my fingers. I move my hands swiftly. Maybe one of my paintings will finally hold some value in this world when it contains my blood.

My own words from so long ago, spoken in a facility with a boy who was just a boy pretending to be a technician, comes floating back to me. *"This is my body. This is my blood. I should decide what I do with it."*

Tears stream down my face unnoticed as my hands move faster and faster. All I think about as I paint is how that small boy went limp. How Sofie grabbed her bloody waist. How the tram driver's mouth became moist with blood as he drifted beyond the realms of life. I picture them over and over again as I finger paint. Long dramatic lines, some of which I go over and over again to make a darker red. Some places I leave fingers in place longer to make a dark blot and then swipe down over and over again, making shadows and leaving some places completely white and untouched.

I chant in my head louder and louder. *Our blood. Save us all. Our blood. Save us all.* A chill blows through the room like someone opened the door to a wintery, blustery world. My arms grow weaker and weaker, yet I move faster.

It's hard to breathe and my arms start to slow. A sob tumbles out. For a moment I forget what I doing. Bloody arms dangle by my sides as I analyze the portrait. One last touch. Instead of signing my name across the bottom, I inscribe words that make another dry, tearless sob pour out. Or maybe that was the sound of the door, I can't tell. The "E" on the end takes the last bit of energy I have left. A voice shouts through the room, and I barely recognize it. I think it's the king screaming for help, and it reminds me of Mam in a sick way. "What are you doing, you foolish child! Maid! Officers! Quick, stop the bleeding! Save the blood!"

With his voice echoing through the room, it seems as if my painting has come to life. I fall away from my painting of Adakin Malloy, his large hard gaze watching my every move, and I can't tell if someone has caught me or if I've landed on the floor. Blood seeps from his portrait-eyes like tears, and his face is menacing and evilly happy. I faintly hear someone else yelling from behind me. My words at the bottom of the painting are what I see last, as dark spots cover my vision like the little red dots that pricked on my skin from scratching. "I bleed for no one." They blob and blend together and everything is lost. I have won. My blood is finally mine, and through death it always will be.

# CHAPTER 29

I clumsily grab my arms and feel the bandages that wrap them. I open my heavy eyelids. My canvas is gone from the window. My blood painting has been taken down, and I'm still a prisoner in the Recipient mansion.

Slowly, memories of what happened come creeping back to me. So much blood everywhere. So much pain. What did I do? I pull my heavy, bulky hands to my face and weep so gently I'm barely moving.

There's still so much sadness raging in my chest, and I don't know what to do with it. I picture Papa sitting on the edge of my bed, brushing the hair out of my face. The thought makes me cry harder. I'm glad, for once, that he isn't here to see me. What would he think of me? What would he say about what I did?

There's a tapping at the window. I sit up in bed and my head spins. There, on the ledge outside my window, is a small brown bird. A common sparrow with ugly speckled brown wings. There's nothing very beautiful about it. I remember being with my papa, wanting so badly to be the one to find a rare bird for him. I wanted to discover something colorful and exotic, not knowing then that few of such species survived the germ wars. All I kept finding were sturdy sparrows of every kind. There were song sparrows, chipping sparrows, field sparrows—they all looked the same to me, but Papa acted just as excited to see each sparrow as he probably would have if he saw an elegant trogon. As this bird ruffles and cleans its wings on the windowsill, my papa's reply to my complaining comes to mind now. *"Even common, ugly birds serve a purpose."* He smiled at me and continued. *"Even if it's to be the prey. Sparrows' ugly speckles protect them."*

At the time, I thought it such an out-of-character thing to say. Usually, he would have pointed out how remarkable the differences are, how a small variation of tufts or throat color or pattern on the wing creates this excellent challenge to identify it correctly. It's as if he told me those words for this very moment. There's a message there I can't quite decipher.

I lift my arms and look at the fat wrappings that make me resemble a boxer ready for a match. The pain in my chest melts down into my stomach with an intense sensation of shame. My ugly scars will not protect me; they will make me more of a target for attention and possibly popularity. Why didn't I think this through?

There's a small breeze like my window is open, and Adakin Malloy moves out of the shadows of my room. He steps to the window where my painting hung and stares out of it. The little sparrow has flown away, and oh, how I suddenly envy it.

"You do know how to put on a good show, don't you," he says without moving an inch. His back looks more hunched from this angle, and my lip curls at his words.

I lie back in bed, wishing I could disappear deep into the covers and wishing I could reverse time and change course. I close my eyes tight, recalling the thoughts that filled my mind last night. I don't really want to die; I just want it all to stop.

Adakin still addresses me without turning around, and his tone is just as bland and informative as ever. As if he were teaching a class instead of talking to his prey. "Oh, don't be so dramatic, Aston. You know, before the age of serum, everyone was depressed, sad, lonely. Often some said as you did, 'Why don't I just die'? In fact, depression killed more people per year than the disease or even donations."

"You're lying."

He turns and laughs sardonically. As he dips and shakes his head, he continues. "I wish I was, Aston. I wish I was. But sadly, no. More people killed themselves everyday than those who died from illness or murder." He shouts into the room like he is talking to an invisible person. "Wall one, show us suicide statistics for the year before the first germ war."

The wall across the room flashes white, forcing my eyes closed and then fades into images of doctors and physicians with lists of numbers scrolling upward. I stare at the numbers in shock. I can't tell if my head is fuzzy because of the movement and what I've been through or the sight before me as years roll on with numbers increasing on the right. One year, 275,000 deaths, another year 315,057 deaths, and the numbers go up and up at a terrifying rate. The fast-scrolling numbers make my wrists burn a little more. I gently wrap my arms around my waist and sink back against the headboard. So many lives. And I was about to be one of them. Again, just a number, a statistic.

"See, Aston? People in pre-serum America were plagued by sadness where they'd rather kill themselves than wait for disease to take them. One of the most selfish acts of our history." He clicks his tongue and shakes his head. "All that wasted blood. I couldn't bear to have our Donors suffer like that. If you reacted nicely to the serum, you wouldn't have had to suffer."

Closing my eyes, I push out the pain and try not to recall how easy it is to smile on the serum. I slowly lean back against the headboard. Did so many old Americans and Old World people really end their own lives on purpose? Like what I just attempted to do? Shame burns within me, replaced quickly by hatred. It was still their choice. As much as I don't agree with this act, the serum has still ripped an individual of choice. I wouldn't put that on anyone, no matter how happy it made them or how many lives it saved. Would I?

"That's the cost of freedom, I'm afraid," Adakin says.

It's too close to what I was just thinking. My stomach churns.

"Too much of it and you can't even recognize it. Too much of a good thing can blind an individual until they can't even see what they have. Even a kite becomes lifeless if there's not someone to pull on the string. Serum saved a nation from sadness."

Maybe the cost of freedom is too great. I look at my bandaged wrists and wonder. Would I have done this if I was on serum? I slump deeper into my bed. Maybe Adakin is right. About everything. Maybe the serum really is the protection from our own selves.

"Do you see now, Aston? We need each other. You can use my creations as a way to survive, and I can use you as a way to lead. A way to heal us once and for all."

"You mean control us once and for all." I sit up in bed again, feeling stronger by the second.

Adakin shrugs. "There's always a sense of control in order for any plan to work well. Without control, there would be chaos. When life is simpler, everyone is happy. Everything is given to Donors; they have no need to worry about the specifics or difficulties of life."

"But you killed an innocent boy!" I'm on my feet now and ignore the dark spots that bleed into my vision for a moment. "You killed him just because you didn't get what you wanted."

"It's not about what I want, Aston. It's about what the entire New World needs." His voice turns cold, and his face is as hard as stone. "It's for the collective good."

My eyes prick with tears again as the boy's lifeless body flashes across my vision. How can that be right? Adakin has to be the predator, but I feel so confused now. I put a bandaged hand to my forehead and look down at the floor.

Adakin all but pounces on the opportunity like he can smell my weakness, my uncertainty. "Your grandmother has the key, Aston, that could save an entire population." He steps closer to me with frantic enthusiasm. "Everyone. Think about it Aston, everyone free of the virus so there's no need for donations. No need for serum at all. Isn't that what you want? No more deaths? No more illness?"

Tears stream down my face, and I'm doubting everything I felt before. Of course it's what I want. I want it all to stop. I want protection for me and my family and Donors and the Recipients I care about. I can't give protection. I can't save us all. Everyone can see that putting trust in me because of my blood was a mistake. I open my mouth to tell him about Grandma Bolgi, about Dearborn, the tree she took me to and everything I know. I can't protect us. I look at my arms again—shame, guilt, weakness. I can't protect anyone.

"My grandmother—"

The door flies open. Marcus takes long quick strides to my side. "Aston!" he exclaims with worry etched in his voice. He steps right through the perception of Adakin, making the vision of the king disperse like smoke wafting through the air. His smile lingers in my room before I am in Marcus's arms. I let him hold me.

I lean into his strong arms, and I bury my face in his chest. I inhale his scent and make it completely a part of me as I sob giant, uncontrollable sobs.

"I want it to stop," I cry ungracefully loud. "I just want it all to stop."

He doesn't say anything, he only holds me and strokes my hair and lets me say and moan any scared thing I want.

My arms are wrapped so tight around his waist I feel part of him as if we are one lone tree standing tall and strong with waving branches in the wind. He is my roots in a way I never knew a Recipient could be.

"I don't know what to do," I say with a deep breath as the tears begin to dry. His shirt is wet beneath my face, yet he does not push me away.

"I know what to do," he says.

I lift my puffy face from him and look at his dear, sweet face with yellow corn-colored hair on top.

"You rest your hand on my shoulder, like so." He pulls a reluctant hand of mine from his waist and carefully puts it on his broad, strong shoulder. He runs his hand the length of my arm just as he did that night in the coat closet under the stairs where he first taught me to dance. "And put your hand in mine like this." Soon we are swaying and dancing lazily along the floor. There is no sound in the room, no music to dance to, but in my mind, I can hear his message.

When he moves, I move; when he turns, I turn. He is telling me in the rhythm of our movements and in the intense gaze we share as we twirl that he will always be there. That he has changed. That he is more than a Recipient just like I am more than a Donor. I hear his silent song. He is mine as much as I am already his. More than just blood. He will fight with me no matter the cause, no matter the side.

As we sway in the silence, I consider how wrong Papa was about some of the Recipients. What would he think of Marcus or Janice if he truly got to know them? Would he be able to admit he was wrong about them?

A blurry image warps the window. Adakin.

I rest the side of my cheek on Marcus's shoulder. Who is going to save us all?

I shut my eyes and picture Janice grabbing my shoulders, her slanted green eyes boring into mine. "You let your emotions soar, miss." My emotions. The very weakness I thought kept me from being valuable is what protects me from my predator.

I'm dramatic and loud and speak my mind. Maybe I'm a little bull-headed and blunt, and yes, I know I complain a lot, but maybe these attributes are actually what make me my own sort of powerful. They're enough to fight against the surveillance, maybe they're enough to fight against all Recipients like Adakin. My ugly brown speckles, like the bird, may be my power.

With a replaced focal point, the pain doesn't hurt quite so bad. My emotions aren't my nemesis, they are my strength. Adakin thinks he is everywhere and knows everything, but I can push him out with my ability to feel. I hug

Marcus a little tighter. I won't let those people die for nothing. Tears still pool in the corners of my eyes as I picture the young boy in the school going still. I have to do something. I can't give up.

Marcus hugs me closer as if he can feel the shift in my determination. "I am on your side every step of the way, Aston. Even if it's the side that will never accept me."

Our cheeks brush as he pulls back to stare down at me. I whisper to him as my hand moves up his shoulder and into the hair that reaches his neck. "They will accept you if I have anything to say about it."

The sparks that warm my chest don't make the pain go away completely. They don't keep the image of that limp boy from haunting me, or drown out Sofie's gurgling sounds, but they do give me something I haven't felt in a long time. Hope.

Marcus inches closer and I close my eyes. His breath is warm on my mouth, and I pull the scent of him into me with one giant sigh, as if I could gladly drown myself in him. Our lips touch in the most innocent of ways. Not with longing or urgency or even desire. Our lips move slowly, like we never want it to end.

A kiss of hope.

Hope for our future, our families, our people. I don't have to look at the window to know this kiss has conquered Adakin. He is gone. Is our love more powerful than one Recipient king, enough to defeat this long war against our blood? In my beloved books, love conquers all.

I fell in love with him for who I thought he was. Now I'm falling in love with the man he's choosing to be. I don't need my parents or a technician or a Recipient king or even a resistance leader to give me permission or freedom to choose. Right now, I give it to myself and ask deep within the valves of my heart that if I had the choice to love, who would I choose?

The kiss is over but neither of us want to pull away. Our foreheads rest together, and our noses rest side by side as we breathe deeply against each other.

If there were never any donations or auctions, no walls or glass cages, never a virus in the first place, who would I choose? I'm dizzy at the prospects, the freedom of it. My heart beats wilder at the freedom I allow it

"I—" I don't even know what I'm about to say. Marcus rubs my back, tracing the lines of my shoulder blades. I think I love him. I open my mouth again to tell him when Trip's secret knock shouts through the room.

Marcus's head snaps up. "What was that?"

# CHAPTER 30

I tense in his arms as the knock bounces through the room again, and my eyes are glued to Marcus's confused face. This time Marcus doesn't hold me closer to him, he steps away from me, taking my hand in his.

Another knock sounds louder and irritated. I can picture Trip knocking and cursing as he grows impatient with me. We've talked about this before. If I don't answer it means someone's in the room, but we've never had it happen. How could he forget? What does he think I'm doing? I silently plea for him to stop, but another knock and an audible curse is heard.

Marcus jumps a few steps closer to the wall. He pulls me with him, then stands in a defensive position in front of me, blocking me from whatever danger he fears is in the walls.

"Who is there?" He pulls his hand up to place it on the wall, I'm sure to call the officers.

"No!" I pull on the hand of his that holds mine. "No, don't."

"Aston, if this is another attempt to escape so help me—"

"It isn't. It's just not my secret to tell. "

It's the moment of truth. How certain am I that he will accept the resistance and the secrets I've kept from him? Is he supporting his grandfather or giving up everything he's known as a Recipient? Janice's words bounce through my head, though. "*Trip is not yours to risk.*"

"Aston," he turns to me and takes me by both hands. His brows pinch together in sincerity. "You are my life in every way possible. I would do anything for you."

His thumb rubs the top of my hand, and I feel the need to make myself clear that I am still very uncertain about where I stand even if I have given myself the freedom to choose. I'm not sure which one is correct.

I slip a hand from his grasp and place my palm on his cheek. It's warm and the small stubble feels like velvet as my hand shifts. "I care for you, Marcus." His cheeks relax in obvious relief. "But trust is something proven. I am still testing yours."

He nods and lowers his head. I'm testing Marcus's trust and testing Janice's as well as I step away from him to the bookshelf. "Brutis created passageways in the walls when he drew up plans for this addition. It's how he was able to get to me so quickly and to the library as well." Marcus stays close to me as I reach up to the top shelf and pull on the ruby red droplet. "You told me once Janice saved a boy from a horrible situation." His eyes grow wide as the shelf moves out of place and reveals the passageway and a shocked Trip scrambling to his feet. "This is her boy. This is Trip who lives in the attic."

Trip looks at me with terror in his eyes as if I have

betrayed him and sold him out. I hope to scars that I haven't.

"You're the Jones' boy," Marcus says. He checks the door, and I can't quite read his face. Is he worried about who will enter or trying to decide if he should call the Officers?

I wring my hands and doubt my trust already.

"I heard how badly they treated you. I'm so sorry our jurisdiction didn't..." Marcus struggles to find what to say. "Janice, you said?" He clears his throat. From emotion? Awkwardness? "I'm glad she was there for you when you needed her. I'm glad our home can be your safe haven now."

His speech is formal but well received. Trip looks around the room at both of us and then smiles a half smile. "Uh, thanks for letting me stay here?"

Marcus laughs and extends his arm, grabbing Trip by the shoulder and nudging him. "I like this kid," Marcus says, relieving the tension.

Marcus asks Trip all sorts of questions, and he is more than happy to oblige. Trip talks fast and motions with his hands as he paces my room. It's strange how quickly he opens up to Marcus when he took so long to tell me anything about his family. It's very clear how quickly Trip idolizes Marcus.

Soon we are all gathered on my bed, playing a card game Marcus teaches us and laughing when Lecky pounces on the deck. Holding my cards is awkward with the bandages. I balance them with the tips of my fingers, and Marcus helps place my card choices on the stack. Leaning back against my pillows, still weak from the loss of blood, I find myself relaxing into a soft, numb feeling. Better than when I paint. It's not quite happiness, I still see those who have died ready to pounce and haunt my thoughts, but there's a sense of companionship that helps me feel less helpless. Not being alone brings a natural sort of hope.

Janice plows through the door without warning and freezes when she sees us on the bed. Her eyes shoot from one face to the next, lingering on Marcus.

Trip stands up with his hands in the air and is the first to speak. "It's okay, Juice. He's okay."

She shuts the door behind her and approaches us. "It's probably best that you're here. I don't know if I have access, but you surely would."

"Janice, what are you talking about?" I say.

She looks at me without seeing me, and then turns back to Marcus. "Do you have media access in here?"

His brow knits together, and he stands then nods.

"Put *In With the News* on the walls. Aston needs to see this."

"But—" Marcus says.

"She has to!" I've never seen Janice so adamant.

Marcus takes two steps to the wall beside my bed and mutters for *In With the News* to show on wall one—the same wall Adakin shared with me the suicide statistics. My chest feels hollow at the memory and in anticipation of what is to come.

The wall ripples with white waves like it did before the resistance came, before Gannet spoke with me. I struggle to sit up in bed but feel the need to be closer to the news and away from Marcus at the sight of it on the screen. And then the whole wall shows the news anchor. A crowd of Recipients gather around Griffin Manny who has changed his hair and make-up since last I've seen him. His hair is cut more like a Donor's with longer sides, and his makeup is more subtle. I don't process his words because what has my full attention takes the air from my lungs like a punch to the gut. My painting is on the screen behind him. Not the flowers that reminded me of the diversity and creation of Donors. It's the dark blood portrait of Adakin Malloy.

# CHAPTER 31

I walk closer to the wall and don't hear anything else. Only Griffin as he laughs and slaps his knee.

"We've been told Donors don't have much else to offer us, but it seems our dear Donor that lives right here in Bloomfield has quite the talent. If my memory serves me correctly, and by memory, I mean my notes"—the audience laughs—"this is the same Donor that stood on the steps of the Ambassador's Ball and talked with me about the Donor deaths in her town in New Livonia." He sighs as if remembering that moment. "She has such a caring Donor heart and obviously loves our great leader. This portrait of Adakin is not just painted by the Donor herself, but it is painted with her very own blood. That's right, Recipients, the highest rated blood this new country has ever seen, and it's going for auction in a new special televised auction later this week. With our new Wallvision you should be able to palm in your bid from anywhere. Good luck to you all, and I'm excited to see more from this Donor." His laugh is choppy and short. "She never fails to surprise us, does she."

With a sigh he moves on to the Donors' deaths of the day, and I wonder if that boy I watched die will be reported.

The wall goes blank then ripples back into the fake wood panels they were. The room is still and silent. No one moves or says a thing. It hurts too much to make a fist, so I clench my teeth.

Janice finally mutters to Trip, "To bed with you. You will be shipped back home quicker than a wink if you're caught."

It's the first time I've heard her reference his real home instead of calling him her boy. I look at her then, and she looks so worn and frail. I don't know why I never noticed it before. Janice follows Trip to the wall and sees him up. When the bookshelf is back in place, she looks to me and meekly asks, "Will you be needing me tonight, miss?"

I shake my head and suddenly feel the exhaustion of it all. Like a crashing, capsizing wave, the attack on the marketplace, the young boy, the painting, the loss of blood —it all leaves me washed up, weary and weak. Marcus hurries to my side. His arms hold me up before I even have the chance to teeter.

He kisses the top of my head and whispers close to my skin. "We'll get through this, Aston."

"How?" A sob chokes me, and I feel weak and helpless again. "They'll never see."

Marcus shushes me as he holds me tight. "You made *me* see. We'll find a way to open their eyes too. There are more out there on your side than you think." He helps me to bed, and I put my hand out to him as he places the blankets carefully on me.

"Stay," I muster before my eyelids close.

"Forever," he replies, but when I wake in the morning he is gone.

A nurse is scuffling through the room, a different one than Alex. She takes my hand and begins to tend to my wrists. We don't speak, and when she is done, she gathers the dirty bandages and merely says, "Your donations are canceled for the day."

I stare at the window but see faces instead. The blood portrait of Adakin, trusting Sofie, the young dead boy. Marcus, kind and attentive. When Janice enters, I don't hear what she says to me.

"I'm not hungry," is all I say.

There's a pause, and for a moment I think she may have left the room but then she says again, "You may be interested in the bowl of cantaloupe."

I don't move, and Marcus's face glides across my vision again. I shut my eyes tight. "I hate cantaloupe, you know that."

"The bowl is lovely, though," she insists. "Perhaps you will like it this time."

I turn to her now. "Janice, what difference would it make if it was in a wooden bowl or a golden one. I don't like the strange fruit."

She raises her eyebrows and tilts her head to the tray just before she sets it on the table. "Very well, miss. Suit yourself."

I think about her hints as I stare at the platter. After she leaves, I drag myself out of bed, and sure enough, under the small white bowl of cantaloupe is another note from Gannet.

# CHAPTER 32

S omething about seeing that bird again makes my heart sink and stomach flip at the same time in an awful way. Makes me see the week's events in a different light. I slump in the chair and put my face in my hands. What am I going to do? I've only had one week with Marcus, and I've already helped connect a Recipient rebellion with the Donor resistance that led to an attack that killed people, aided in the murder of a young boy, and accidentally attempted suicide only for the act to back-fire and create a new unique demand on blood at auctions. Who knows the consequences my stupid blood painting will have on the market.

I also kissed Marcus. I have to at least tell Gannet that Marcus knows about the resistance and has shown signs of wanting to help. Maybe Marcus would be able to help more than Sofie could have. A lump forms in my throat. The gurgling sounds fill my ears, and I shut my eyes.

To drown out the image of Sofie, I picture Gannet and Marcus in the same room and wonder how each would react. What do they think of each other? Gannet believes that Marcus ruined his family farm, lied to me and put my life in danger. And knows that I kissed him. The memory of how Gannet growled and paced when he heard about our relationship makes my stomach tingle. What would I say to them?

I grumble at the empty room. What a predicament I've put myself in. For someone who's fought for freedom so much, I sure don't know how to use it well. Logically I want to be happy that Gannet is coming, but I'm still so upset over the incident. How they killed innocent people.

I take a handful of cheese cubes and muffins to my bed with me like a little squirrel hiding away her nuts. I'm still in bed like this when Marcus enters. The bandages around my hands are difficult to maneuver with and there are crumbs all over me.

His boisterous laugh as he looks at me makes me shrink in embarrassment a little. "Hungry, are we?"

He chuckles again and steps to the wall behind my bed. "The auction of your painting is on today."

The same wall ripples then shows Griffin Manny standing alone with all sorts of graphics dancing behind him in gray and black and red.

"We have here the exclusive auction of the famous 1342, although it's no secret anymore it's Aston Vazeto, the Donor from New Livonia who has new surprises in store every day. She is what some are calling the 'Recipient princess' who seems, to the chagrin of many teenage Recipient hearts, to have gained the favor of our beloved Marcus Malloy."

Marcus clears his throat and shifts in place. A strange feeling washes over me. I'm not truly happy to have the New World think of us as a couple, but it's not quite upsetting either. Marcus may have lied about being a Recipient, but I'm finding out every day that he has tried to be anything but who he is.

"I see walls all over the nation pinging in here. From the Givens' home of New Chicago, hello there Margie, and from the walls of the Southall house, welcome Janetta. So many Recipients on here to bid for this rare and precious piece of artwork. Now before we get started, some history of artwork. It's not something that came back in the New World very quickly, and there's been little to no market for it up until this point."

My eyes roll and I fall back into the bed. No market for it until now? That's an understatement. I recall the times I tried to sell my artwork to escape the donations. My paintings possibly still hang in Mr. Burke's trade store. I sigh as I think about what I've done. Should I be happy that I've made art popular again even if it's my blood that brought all the attention to it? This wasn't the message I wanted to portray when I painted.

"I heard," Marcus says, "that the reason this is broadcast in PR—"

I sit up and look at the screen differently now. He sees me looking and says, "Oh, perceived reality is—"

"I know what it is, remember?" A chill runs down my arms. "But this is still on a screen."

"Well, every person is probably seeing something slightly different behind him, it's personalized. I heard they had to do this instead of being public or with a live audience because of the amount of protesters."

"Protesters?" I look at him for more answers. Protesting my painting? Some don't like art or a Donor with skills?

Marcus smiles a proud sort of grin. "Your message across the bottom has since been cut off in the process of putting this on a canvas, but enough read your meaning and are protesting your being held prisoner."

I don't know what to say. A breathy laugh shoots out, and I look at the screen again. The gray graphic "x"s and black "o"s float behind Griffin. I think about what Marcus said. My painting got across to some. My talent, my blood, my life are finally not going unnoticed.

Something else Marcus said makes me wonder, though. "How does perceived reality work on Recipients? I heard that for Donors it has to do with the serum. The tech running through our blood interacts with the message being put out by the screens and the walls. How are Recipients affected?"

"Well," Marcus folds his arms and shifts his weight. "Donors get the serum from the donations. Serum that I was always told helped them recover." I nod, since this is exactly what we were told as well. "The serum runs through Donor blood and well, we have Donor blood in us."

Hmm. That makes sense, I guess if a serum is going to be personalized to each Donor, then how does that affect a Recipient?

The bidding begins and my stomach starts to roll as the numbers rise, reminding me of my blood auction where I lost my fill of caramel popcorn on the feet of reporters on my porch.

"I can't watch this." I excuse myself to the bathroom where I spend most of the morning. The screen turns off after the auction, and Marcus yells out the cost. $250,000. More than my blood. *Who gets the money?* Adakin probably.

I shout through the door that I'm going to have a bath. While I lie with the red bubbles tingling on my skin, I stress about tonight. When Marcus knocks on the door, I jump.

I've decided not to tell him about Gannet coming or my connection with the resistance. Not yet.

"I'll be back at lunch time," he says, and I give a feeble reply.

When he returns, I feel fresh and new. New bandages on my arms and new clothes on my body, except the jeans. I love the jeans Janice gave me. I smile more easily at him. The rest of our day is calm and uneventful, a pleasant change. The lack of donations gives me more strength by the minute and soon we are laughing on the sofa about him hearing Trip's knock and what he thought it was. We laugh about my first dance, and he turns somber when he tells me about his sister who died when she was ten. I learn about Marcus's mother and grandmother who are both also deceased from symptoms of the virus. His mother evidently went through four Donors and nearly exhausted his father's inheritance before she passed away at the age of forty-one.

I find myself moved by his stories. Throughout my life, I avoided the daily death toll counts as often as I could, especially the Recipients'. Yet here I am on the edge of my seat, listening to his stories about how his mother loved flowers and spent her time in this very garden, creating new species, blending new colors, and finding new ways to breed masterpieces. Here I am wishing I got to meet this person that raised such a kind, understanding Recipient and wondering if I, in the few times I rolled my eyes at the Recipients' deaths, heard the name Edith Malloy on the screen. In my mind, I piece together the woman she was, perhaps with eyes like his that help the mud-blue in Adakin's sparkle a little brighter, a little better. Corn-colored blond hair and high cheekbones.

Everyday, I'm beginning to doubt what I've been taught

by my papa. Recipients aren't the blood-sucking selfish enemies we thought they were. Just as we aren't the ignorant, good-for-nothing Donors that Recipients were taught we were. I tremble to recall my words just a year ago about Recipients. I would never wish someone as strong-willed as Janice and creative and inquisitive as Trip to die. And I would never look at the death of Edith Malloy as a victory for Donors. At least not now.

I don't notice the room getting dark. Neither of us reaches our hand to the wall to call the lights on. We are both twisted to the side on the sofa, facing each other, and our knees are touching and our heads on hands propped up on the back of the sofa are so close. His face is shadowed, but I can see his lips perfectly.

Maybe it's the lips that remind me, or the dark. Gannet will come tonight. I scoot and jump forward to the edge of the sofa. "My, it's getting late." I stretch and it's not very hard to make a yawn come. "Thank you for being with me today." I feel stupid the moment the words leave my mouth. He's supposed to be with me. It's part of the experiment. But our meetings seem more and more congenial than compulsory.

I place my hand on the wall and when the lights are on, I walk to the door. I still have two-and-a-half hours before Gannet gets here, but I don't want to take a chance.

Marcus stops at the door and pokes his head back in just as the wall ripples behind him. No! It's too early. Maybe it's Janice. Or is it Gannet after all? Are we going to have a repeat of the Trip situation where I shock Marcus with the lies I've been keeping from him all this time?

"Should we paint again tomorrow?" he asks.

It's not just the fear of Gannet speaking into this room any minute that has me shaking my head. It's the weight of what painting now means. The Recipient royals have a way of ruining things for me. I'm not sure I'll ever paint again. Instead of trying to explain any of this, however, I merely raise my hands with bandaged wrists. "I might not be painting for a while." I step closer to the door to both help it close quicker and hopefully block anything or anyone that may appear in my room at any minute.

He gives me a sad sort of smile and then leans in and kisses me on the cheek. With a sigh, I shut the door, lean on the back of it and close my eyes.

"Aston?"

I jump away from the door, and when I open my eyes, it is Gannet. Thanks to perceived reality, he is standing right in front of me with a girl by his side. She is looking the other direction, but Gannet's face is hard and sorrowful. How long has he been standing there?

When I notice the girl, my face turns to ice. "Sofie?"

# CHAPTER 33

"Sofie was my older sister. I'm told we look a lot alike, but no, I'm Sienna."

I'm hoping my shock is enough emotion to block any eavesdropping. Gannet's face doesn't change as he explains how Sienna had been a part of the experiment that turned deadly, the experiment that somehow sent her to Donor territory with no return, how Dustin has finally been removed from his position, and how Sienna offered to pick up where her sister left off in helping them defeat her kind. He looks at corners of the room instead of at me, and his mannerisms are stiff though cordial.

I should tell him. Tell him that Marcus knows about the resistance and wants to help. I should tell him I have feelings for him, and that Recipients aren't really the monsters we think they are. It is only an elite few that are the enemy. But with Sienna here by his side, maybe he doesn't need to know about Marcus to realize this.

Sienna speaks first in her thick accent that's just like Janice's. The more she talks, the more I notice differences between the sisters. Sofie had a firmer jawline where Sienna's face is rounder and softer looking. "We have discovered a way to get you out of Bloomfield."

I glance quickly at the window and around the room. Can Adakin hear them? Perhaps I don't need to work so hard for emotions if Adakin doesn't know about the many meetings with the resistance.

"Great," I say unenthusiastically, which only wins me another glare from Gannet. It's strange to not see his smile. I don't like it. The menacing look on his face leaves me colder than his hands ever could. But people died for them to learn how to trade people in and out of Bloomfield. People died for them to learn how to trade me. He can't expect me to be happy about that.

"We know how. We just no longer have the means to," Gannet says. Even Sienna looks at him oddly, possibly wondering why happy-go-lucky Gannet is all of a sudden acting so glum.

"Because of the attack?" I say with a glare of my own. My blood is boiling. What right does he have to look at me like this, making silent judgments of my life? He chose to keep me in the dark, he chose to keep the serum from me. The resistance has only made sloppy mistake after awful mistake. The blood bath and now the attack. How can this Recipient girl tolerate being a part of the rebellion that killed her sister? Recipients are more forgiving than I'll ever be.

"Right," says Sienna slowly. "Look, I know this is hard, but my sister did a lot to get us all here, and I believe in what she fought for."

"How could you?" I say. "How could you believe in something that murdered her?"

"Not just something, someone." She looks at me

sincerely and my heart feels broken. Me. The someone is me if you connect the dots. Is that what she's saying?

"Look, I may not know what it's like to be hungry, or to be coerced into doing something life-threatening every day, or have my family divided by numbers, but I don't think my life should be more important than someone else's just because I have something different in my DNA. I may never understand a Donor, or why they do the things they do, but that doesn't mean I can't still be understanding. My mother raised me to always be grateful for everything we have without realizing she was also teaching us to feel indebted to those who gave it to us." Sienna steps closer to me and looks right into my eyes. She puts her hands on my shoulders, and it feels just as real as if she was truly standing right in my room, speaking to me. I smell the same soap as Marcus, and in her eyes is the same innocent, or maybe naïve, gleam that was in Sofie's that night. "We see you Donors. More of us see you than you realize, and more are grateful to you than is relayed. But this is not right. We don't want life forced on us if its cost is the life of someone else."

I want to hug her but am afraid. I want to bury my face in this stranger's neck and tell her about my last moments with her sister and about the real message in my painting and about how her words make me feel like mush inside. Emotions are not just my talent; they are my expertise after all. They're never called on, yet always present for the slightest provocation. But controlling them is still a difficult task, and I don't want to frighten her. Instead, I nod, and she steps away, but it feels wrong not to say something. "I held Sofie. When she died." I can't think of anything more. It feels so stupid. I want to say something comforting and monumental, but I'm scared to admit out loud to the charge Sofie gave me to save us all and how it haunts my thoughts.

Sienna smiles. "I'm glad she didn't die alone."

How can she be comforting me? I nod and find myself smiling too.

"Now." She gets right to business and rubs her hands together. "There is a way to have things transfer between realities, but only in small amounts. Converters of sorts, like this." She lifts her hand with a smile, but there's nothing in it.

"I don't see anything," I say.

"Exactly. It's brilliant, really. Uses the same science behind chameleon's. Did you know they don't actually change hue like octopuses, they actually change the structure of their skin to reflect light—"

"Miss Flagmeyer," Gannet says impatiently, and Sienna looks at him.

"Right. Anyway, maybe it's easier to just show you than tell you. Give me something to send back with us to Dearborn."

"Sienna—"

"I mean, wherever we are, bloody scars, I'm not used to this, and the pressure you Donors put on me is not bloody fair."

Dearborn. I cringe at having my suspicions confirmed, not just about knowing where they are myself, but knowing Adakin possibly just heard that news. I open my mouth to warn them when another roll of nausea stabs my stomach. I check the window and scan the room. I was so caught up in the moment I shared with Sienna about her sister I didn't remember to protect the meeting. A smile spreads over my face as Gannet calms Sienna and reassures her to be more careful. I'm saving us without even realizing. Being my own emotional self should hopefully have been enough to secure this whole meeting. I think about my family together in Dearborn with Grandma Bolgi protecting them. I picture Torrin by the tree and Grandma Bolgi telling him about the answers that lie within his blood. Dearborn.

"I can send something back?" I say. "To Torrin? Did you get him out?"

Gannet looks at me and finally softens. "Yes. After..."

My eyes well with tears as the image is upon me again. Flashes of Torrin. Flashes of the boy going limp. "After an incident with a young boy at the school..."

"I was there."

"What do you mean?" Gannet steps toward me as if without thinking.

"Adakin used that boy to pressure me into telling him where you all are. He wants Grandma Bolgi for some reason. He wants to know where she is. And when I didn't tell him..." I pull my hand up to my face and Gannet gasps. He pulls my hands out in front of me, examining for the first time my bandaged wrists.

"Aston! What happened to you? What did they do?"

Adakin's words about suicide and the statistic rates come back to me, warming my cheeks and making my insides squirm. I don't want to tell Gannet what I tried to do. I only say, "I painted," and hope he gets the gist of what happened.

He lets go of me, and I don't look to see how he looks at me.

"The painting." He gets it. Enough of it at least.

"Everyone's painting now, you know," he says. I can't read his meaning. "Things are so different since the auction. Recipients are trying to come over the wall, and the officers' attention has been focused to guard it."

"Why would Recipients try to do that?"

Sienna clears her throat. "I told you. Not all Recipients want to live in a world where they are the enemy. Your painting opened a lot of people's eyes. We bleed for no one. We've sacrificed nothing."

"Your parents have been selling your paintings since the news of the auction got out," Gannet says. "Your father brings as much as he can of it to the resistance. And a trade store sold one of your paintings for over $150,000 this morning when the auction was over. A painting of hands." Gannet laughs at his own news. "Can you believe it, Aston?" I smile and am ready for him to say something like "you did it" or even further express what I am feeling inside, that my paintings, not my self-destructive attempt at freedom, but actual paintings, are being recognized. Instead, his next words bring a frown to my face. "A painting of dirty hands made more money than your blood!" He laughs at the ridiculousness of it. I know he's not laughing at me, but in this moment, it doesn't feel any different. Painting is more than just the image.

Those were not just dirty hands; they were the hands of my hardworking papa. My love and admiration wrung out of me and placed in each line, each stroke, and he thinks it's funny? Of course it should raise more money than my blood, because I did more than sit with a needle in my arm. Doesn't Gannet want to be recognized for more than his blood? Isn't that why we are both here?

"Anyway," Sienna says, and I cross my arms to keep them from shaking. "Do you have something to send back through?"

"Wait," Gannet says. "We need that Trip fellow here."

I'm grateful to leave the room for a moment. The darkness and closeness of the tight hidden halls is comforting.

Trip doesn't like being woken up, but after rubbing his eyes several times, he swats at me shaking his shoulder. Once he comprehends what I'm saying, though, he excitedly bounces on his heels at the thought of seeing Gannet again.

Gannet explains what the device is.

"A converter?" Trip says with sleep still making his voice deep. "How did you get one of those?"

"No matter," says Sienna. "Send something back so we can test it."

I look around the room and even in my drawer of stashed goods. Finally, I come upon the droplet statue that matches the one on the bookshelf. "Here." I hand it to Sienna.

She lifts her hand that holds an invisible object and makes a motion like she's setting it on the table. She shoves the statue forward and it disappears, as does the hand holding it.

She then places her hand in the air over the top of where the statue disappeared. It looks as if it's hovering in the air, but with a click and a beep, all at once, a large black metal box appears on the table. Trip lunges forward and starts to laugh.

"Worked like a charm. Oh, it's beautiful."

"Why, thank you," Sienna says.

"You did this?" Trip sounds like he is in love.

"It uses nanocrystal technology like the iridophore cells on a chameleon and transfers them for the cells of the object in hand." Her sentence slows down at the end as Gannet gives her a look. "Anyway, we lost our macro converter in the attack. We are hoping you can build another one. We need you to build one big enough for Aston to fit in."

"Me? That's impossible."

Gannet steps up and puts a hand on Trip's shoulder. I suddenly feel defensive of the pressure and responsibility they are putting on him. "Are you sure that's wise?" I say. "He's just a boy."

"It's the only choice we have," says Gannet. "I heard how you helped us with the transferring of those files, and I feel pretty certain you're the man for this job."

Of course Trip beams up at Gannet. When he looks at me, I give a weak, sad sort of smile. *He's just a boy.* Isn't that what I hated about the Recipients? Making Donor boys grow up faster than they should? Now Donor rebels are asking the same of a Recipient. My heart aches, but what can I do about it?

Plans are finalized. Gannet wants the machine or converter thing done in two weeks, but Trip convinces them to give him three. There isn't much of a goodbye, but my eyes are locked with Gannet's as he disappears like a mirage. The look in his eyes leaves my heart hollow. What have I done to him? I chose a Recipient over Gannet once without knowing what I was doing, but now I am doing it again.

Lecky bumps against the wall, and I hear the rattle of a toy ball. How stupid of me. What I really should be worrying about is how Trip is going to build this massive converter. And with Janice not finding out, because I know she won't support this kind of treason.

Suddenly I have so many questions regarding the plan. Like for starters, what happens to the object in the converter if it doesn't work? What happens when that object is me?

# CHAPTER 34

Donations started up as soon as my hemoglobin and general state of health were up to Recipient standards. In other words, I only got two days off. For two weeks Marcus has been by to read books with me and exchange small talk. Neither of us dares to mention the resistance or news about the rebellions now happening on both sides of the wall. Instead, we go over our versions of history, laughing at the humorless holes and lies laced through both. Every other day Trip has me risking my life in some way or another to get some sort of cable or flask or book from the library.

For once I'm awake before Marcus or even Janice. I stand alone in my dark room, staring out over the garden and the picket signs. I can't see the faces of the angry Recipient mobs, just their rhythmic pumping hands punching the air as they shout. There have been riots in the streets at night and protesters around the Malloy house since the day of the auction. I don't know exactly why their presence irritates me so much. Perhaps it's the fact that if Donors ever tried to protest, they'd be murdered on the spot. Something as simple as speaking up is still a freedom we've been denied. A freedom being flaunted across the wall right before me.

Tension is rising and the pressure for Trip's machine grows stronger every day. What used to feel like just a good idea to get out of here is now feeling like an urgent necessity to free me before the mobs put me in real danger.

Though I've never seen Trip's work-in-progress, the transporter he is so busy working on, I do my part to keep Janice ignorant of it.

A knock on the wall, three quick ones then two slow ones, lets me know Trip is there. I move the bookshelf out of the way, and Trip slides in quickly with two mugs in his hands. He hands me one and the warm ceramic helps soothe my nerves. I wrap my fingers around the whole cup, letting the heat soak through me.

"Still at it, huh?" he says, looking out the window. He drinks his lemon tea with one hand on his back hip and the sight of it makes me laugh. He's such a little grown up person sometimes. Talking of serious things like he understands what's going on and has firm opinions on topics he doesn't know anything about.

"What?" he says. "I liked your painting an' all and things ain't good how they are, but what's shouting all day going to do about it?"

I take a sip of tea to hide my smile. "How's it coming?" We rarely call it anything, avoid terms as best we can since we never know who will hear us.

Trip shrugs. "Slow."

Trip rarely says much about it. "Any more theories?" I ask, hoping that as he learns more about what he's making, there will be a better understanding of how it works. Like what could happen to the object inside the transporter if things don't go well. His theories aren't ever very pleasant. I could be stuck in a PR, invisible, suffer certain skin reactions to the heat of the transfer, or worse yet, split in two.

Trip shakes his head then takes another sip. "I don't know what you're so worried about. The way this Gannon fellow talks about you, I'm sure he wouldn't do anything that would kill you."

"His name is Gannet, and thanks for your confidence. I think."

"And I don't know why you think I know so much. You know, I've actually never tried to convert something living between realities before." He says it all so matter-of-factly, like I'm not just standing right here, worrying about being split in two.

"That is what has me worried the most," I admit.

"Oh, please."

The shouting grows as a ringleader I've seen around the wall before shows up. He stands on something so that others can see him and uses a device that projects his voice.

"They've kept Donors from us our whole lives."

The crowd cheers him on.

"Told us they could kill us."

"Yeah!"

"While their heir prances through their streets, picking out his Donor like candy. Do we want their hand-me-downs anymore?"

"No," the crowd shouts and boos.

I can't listen to it anymore. I take a deep breath and turn my back to the window. "Trip?"

"Hm?"

"Have you thought more about the size of this... thing?"

"Pretty big, I imagine."

"But remember my question? Could it take... more than one person?"

"I didn't write the blueprints, I'm just following directions, but the way it's looking, I don't see why not. Could fit a few bloody people in there, I imagine. Tight squeeze, though."

I let the hope of taking those I've grown to love back with me drown out the angry mobs in the background.

I thank Trip for the tea and the update then send him out before Janice starts looking for him.

Marcus enters as soon as the bookshelf shuts. He carries a tray of food and a book under his arm. "At it again, are they?"

I smile at how similar he and Trip sound.

"That painting of yours had quite the impact."

"I don't know, I've listened to this guy with a microphone, and one of the signs says 'equal rights to blood, make donations accessible,' so I doubt this is all my doing. I only gave them an excuse and platform."

"Whatever you gave them, there are a lot of very unhappy Recipients out there."

Marcus stares out the window at them, and I take advantage of his turned back to gather as much fruit into my pocket as I can.

"Well, they are in comparison to Donors, that's for sure."

I try not to take offense to his words. It's only the truth.

"But what difference does it make?" he says, turning away from the window with his hands in his pockets. "They're still able to go to auctions, we don't turn anyone away."

"But clearly they will have less resources and are less likely to get the Donor they need if they are not as wealthy.

Surely you can see that disadvantage." It surprises me how I talk about Donors. I frown and don't really want to have this conversation anymore.

Marcus must feel it too. He just makes a humming sound in reply and lets the conversation drop as he sits at the table.

We only have a few days left of our month together, and soon I will be escaping this place once and for all. I have to tell him about Gannet and the resistance and how we've been communicating. And somehow, I have to convince him to come with me. I rub my fingers over the scars on my wrists. There it is again. This hesitation. I don't know if it comes from not wanting him with me at all or not wanting my make-believe Recipient life to crash into my Donor life. Being here on this side of the wall, it's easy to have strong opinions and a loud voice about things. Here where I eat three-course meals and am bathed everyday by warm bubbles.

But what happens when I go back with a Recipient? Marcus said he'd follow me anywhere, but I also vowed to bleed for him. So much has changed. We have changed. Our world has changed.

We eat our breakfast in awkward silence, looking at each other over the rims of our glasses of juice and accidentally bumping fingers over the cakes without an apology. When we are done, we walk across the room to the sofa to read our books.

Though I still turn the pages, my mind is on the man sitting next to me. The man who has made wrong choices, who has done bad things but has repented. I've seen him change, not only his features as my donations finally gave color to his face, but his heart as he fought to save the lives of Donors to make up for his mistakes. I've seen him care

301

and play with Trip instead of turning him in or condemning him. I've seen him change his views about Janice and find peace with his past. Could the resistance see everything I see? Could my family?

Janice enters with a new tray. "Oh," she says aghast. "I hadn't realized you brought her breakfast already."

"I thought cook would have told you," Marcus replies.

"Yes, she usually does. I suppose she forgot. I will just leave this tray in case you two need a snack and take the empty one with me. I'm sorry, miss, but it seems cook forgot you don't like cantaloupe again." Janice dips a curtsy with the new tray and gives me a meaningful look.

"Thank you, Janice."

"I can't believe you don't like cantaloupe." Marcus leans forward and places his book on a coffee table before he stands. He makes a beeline for the little white bowl filled with mushy orange squares.

"No!" I shout and am by his side pulling on his sleeve before he can get to the fruit bowl. "I mean, go sit down. I'm more than happy to bring the nasty stuff to you."

Marcus chuckles. "It's okay, I can get my own fruit, Aston." He is soon at the table and picks up the small bowl of cantaloupe from the tray. There is the small, folded note underneath and I swipe it, hoping he doesn't notice.

"What was that?"

He noticed. "What was what?" I'm a horrible actor.

"That note…" He lunges around my right side, reaching behind me, and I swirl out of his reach. "That you're hiding…" He spins around the other side of me and I can't help but laugh at our dance around the room. "Behind your back." He fakes me out by going right but as I spin, he switches directions and snatches the note quickly from my hands. "Aha!"

He holds it up in the air like a prized treasure. When I jump to get it back, I accidentally knock the bowl of cantaloupe out of his hands. When we both try to catch it, we bump heads and trip over each other. I fall on my back, with Marcus on top of me, and sandwiched between us is the mucky, slimy fruit.

Marcus pushes himself up and looks at where it's soaking through my shirt, large watery spots circling around the flattened squares.

I groan in disgust and we both start to laugh uncontrollably.

"Well that'll teach you to hate on cantaloupe," he says.

"Or scar me for life."

Sitting on the floor, picking the fruit from my clothes, we find ourselves eventually entangled with each other. Marcus has moved behind me so I sit straddled in his legs and could easily lean back into him, against his chest. He brings his arms around me with the folded note in hand so we can look at it together.

I don't know why I'm waiting so long to tell him anyway. He's already pretty much proven himself trustworthy and on board with helping.

I open the note and expose the sketch of a gannet.

"A bird?" His mouth is right next to my ear. My heart is pounding from his proximity and from fear of how he will take this news.

I glance quickly at the window. Clear. I snuggle closer into Marcus, putting my head into the crook between his shoulder and his chin. Marcus reacts and his hand reaches out for mine, putting it on top, interlocking our fingers and then closing his hand around mine. My stomach feels like a red bath, zinging and tingly, but my thoughts are preoccupied by how handy this emotion is blocking out any eaves-dropping.

"It's a message," I say. "See, the ten toes on the bird's feet tell me what time the resistance will contact me."

He's quiet. His chest tenses slightly on my back and his hand holds mine tightly. I can't tell if I feel his drumming heart through my chest or if it's my own. Say something. Please don't be mad. Please come with me.

"Contacting you? How are they contacting you? Do you have the resistance hidden in your walls as well?"

I can't help but laugh. His shoulders relax around me.

"No, no one else is in the walls. It's with the perceived reality built into the walls. They got a hold of the manual."

"Do I want to know how they got a hold of the manual?"

"No."

"You should tell me anyway."

I sit up and turn to face him, kneeling in front of him and placing my hands on his kneecaps. "Marcus, look, you once said you wanted to help and would be on whatever side I was on and... well, I'm for the resistance."

"Yes, but look what these choices have already done." He points to the window with one hand where the shouts of protesters are muffled through the glass. His other hand gently cups one of my elbows. "Listen to the war that's already starting just from a painting. Is all of this worth another war like the one that slaughtered our families? I'm fine with supporting change, but I'm not too keen on how the resistance handles things. We need to be more careful. You need to be." He gently reaches for both of my hands, pulling them off his knees and holding them palm up between us.

I yank them from his grip and stand in one swift movement. "I don't like war any more than you, Marcus, but we don't even know the truth about our wars anymore. Donors are taught something their whole lives that would be shot down with one page of history found in your library." I stop by the window and turn around to look at him again. He is still sitting on the floor with his arms resting on his knees and hands clasped in front. "We aren't fighting to get back at anyone, we're fighting to be equal. To have a choice. To be told the truth. Donors deserve to be free and a few poor Recipients with signs saying they want a chance at life just as much as a wealthy Recipient is just the beginning of it. There is inequality all over this new land. The auctions haven't saved anyone."

"How can you say that?" He growls as he gets to his feet.

I soften as he puts his hands in his pockets and paces. "They didn't save your mother."

Marcus freezes in place, but he doesn't get angry. He just stares at the floor. The protesters' shouts of "free the auctions, free the blood" echoes through the room. Marcus tilts his head down even further, like he is about to pray, but instead cuts his eyes over to me. His face softens, and I see the boy I never knew at the knee of his mother in the garden wishing things could be different.

"Come meet the resistance with me, Marcus," I whisper. "Be in my room with me tonight and talk with them. Help them free both of our people."

Marcus sighs and now tips his head backward, looking at the ceiling as if now waiting for the answer to his prayer. The silence ticks on.

"Free the auctions, free the blood! Free the auctions, free the blood!"

I'm so close I could touch him, but I don't know if I should.

Marcus wraps an arm around me. "You really think they will care about a greedy, royal Recipient?"

I put my head on his shoulder, leaning into him more. "There is more than one way to bleed, and we are fighting for all lives, Donor and Recipient alike."

He puts both arms around me and hugs me close to his chest. I wrap my arms around his middle and am both relieved and worried. An image of Gannet glaring at me steals through my vision. I just spoke for the resistance without their approval. Scars above, I hope they accept Marcus.

# CHAPTER 35

T rip is on-call for when the resistance comes but is still away in the walls working on his machine. Marcus and I watch the sun fade from the window and then sit on the sofa and talk with only a small lamp on by my bed.

I'm as far away from him on the sofa as possible as I constantly check for the ripple against the wall that tells me Gannet is coming. I bore Marcus with all my stories, talking quickly with nervousness. He yawns in the middle of my story about the time Torrin and I used Mam's dentures to dig in the back yard and then simply replaced them in her bathroom. He lies on the sofa with a chuckle and soon his head is in my lap.

"What are you doing?" I stiffen underneath him and put my hands in the air like I'm afraid to touch him. The resistance could be here any second. And that means Gannet, and he won't be happy to see us like this.

"I'm tired. Are they coming soon?"

"Yeah, like at any minute, so sit up."

"Let me just rest my eyes until they come." He yawns

again and closes his eyes. His lids are slightly purple, and his brow relaxes so easily in front of me.

My arms hover in the air still, not knowing where to be as I look down at him. My stomach touches the top of his hair as I breathe, and it makes me suck in a breath to rid it of the excitement. His face is so smooth and perfect. The hard lines of his cheek and jaw and nose are like sketches, straight and purposeful. I want to trace them with my fingers and memorize them. What if he doesn't come back with me?

I rest one arm on the armrest but am uncertain where to put my other arm. It's uncomfortable to lay it on the back of the sofa, and I can't fit it by my side where he is lying. The only option is to rest my forearm around his neck on his chest like a giant necklace, my palm resting on his protruding muscles.

He makes a humming noise when my arm relaxes, and his hand comes up and pins mine to his heart. I stare at the veins on his eyelids and the perfect swoop of his nose. I convert everything to memory like the machine Trip is building, every detail sent to my mind, permanently recorded. Without thinking, I touch his hair. His corn-colored hair is surprisingly soft for how perfectly shaped it looks. My fingers glide through it easily and another humming noise comes from dozing Marcus.

I slip my hand from his chest and trace the lines of his matching light eyebrows. It feels more right than just intimate. I am an artist. I tried once to recreate this face, and I feel the lines as if I am painting him now. His full cheeks are no longer sunken in, and the tip of his nose looks square. There is an indent in his upper lip, and his bottom lip is full, so warm and soft. His lips part and my chest is on fire with pounding blood cheering to be near him.

His eyes open and his face turns to the side, brushing his cheek against my belly. "You're crying," he says, his lips moving against my ribs.

I don't have an explanation for why a tear goes down my cheek. Maybe the stress or the pressure. Maybe the fear of the unknown, of possible war all over again. But deep down I know it's because I don't see how this Recipient could ever fit into my world. I'm crying because I want him to. I want him to come to my family dinners and laugh while my father slaps him on the back. I want him to sit around the screen with us and anticipate the outcomes of something other than our blood and our fortune. I want to sit with other couples and friends and predict each other's movements. But how? I think of a movie we watched once in an abandoned basement. *Fiddler on the roof.* The words have more meaning than they ever have before. *A bird may love a fish but where would they build a home?*

With a pop, Gannet is in the room. His instant glare make the air feel thick and humid.

"Where's Trip?" He sneers. He backs up, nearing the bookshelf. I push Marcus off my lap and quickly stand.

"Gannet, this is Marcus. I think you've met him before. Marcus this is, w-was... my technician."

Gannet flinches when I call him my technician as if he was never anything more.

"I believe we met before the experiment," Marcus says, and extends a hand. Gannet looks at the hand in front of him.

"What are you doing here?" Gannet growls. His soft face reveals lines easily etched with anger and fear. It makes his face look older than before. More worn down. I hate it.

"I thought—"

Gannet doesn't even hear me. "Yeah, I met you before. Before you kidnapped her and used her like a test rat."

"I saved her life."

"Saved? You're the one who sentenced her in the first place!" Gannet lunges toward Marcus, and I stumble between them.

"Look, buddy," Marcus says. "I don't know what you think's going on here but—"

"I know exactly what's going on here. You're using your drugs and power and manipulation on poor, innocent Donors who are nothing more to you than a walking IV bag."

"Gannet," I plead. This is not going how I imagined at all. I knew Gannet would not be happy, might strongly disapprove even, but this outburst is so foreign, I'm not sure what to do or say.

"That's not true," Marcus says, but Gannet pushes further and we both stumble away from him in one close, tense huddle.

"Do you even know what happened to her family after you whisked her away?"

"No," Marcus says the same time that I say, "What happened to them?" I step away from Marcus, but the two of us are walking backward away from Gannet's marching determination.

Gannet only stares angrily at Marcus.

"Gannet," I yell, stepping forward and ending this march. "What happened to my family?"

He ignores me. He can't even look at me for his loathing of the Recipient by my side. This can't be Gannet. This angry monster in front of me can't be the same person who walked me through the donations and auctions with a cold, gentle hand.

Gannet doesn't take his angry eyes off Marcus, his face red and splotchy with anger. "Not just your family, Aston. Everyone. Do you know what Donors have been through since you saved one Donor's life and broke through Donor territory? Do you even know the suffering that went on while you sat here convincing her of how wonderful and different you are?"

"Gannet—" I'm not exactly sure why his words embarrass me. Perhaps because he guessed right at my thoughts earlier, that Marcus had changed. "Gannet, tell me about my family!"

He still ignores me and leans in closer to Marcus. He places a firm finger on Marcus's chest. "You don't. But I was there! I was cleaning up your mess. And I'm going to finish the job too."

He doesn't lean away, and my hands shake to see the anger in his eyes. The obvious torment and suffering he has had to endure being taken out on this one Recipient. Gannet's finger pushes harder and harder into Marcus, and I don't know what to do. I have to say something. I have to stop this.

"Gannet, he didn't kill your family."

I bump shoulders with Marcus so I'm facing Gannet and lean in between them, forcing Gannet to look at me.

Gannet steps back. He looks at me for the first time since entering the room and disbelief is etched in his tired face. He looks back at Marcus but says nothing.

I sigh and step away too. This is going over worse than I thought. I bet this would be a bad time to bring up how Marcus wants to help the resistance, and I'm sure mentioning Marcus coming with me is out of the question. I pick at the bandages on my wrists and arm.

I don't know what I expected. I somehow pictured the

topic of me leaving just coming up and having a nice discussion with the three of us of the pros and cons of having Marcus join us. I can see now just how delusional I was.

"Aston, I just came for an update." Gannet looks at me with sorrow-filled eyes.

"On what?" Marcus asks.

And here we go. I open my mouth, but nothing comes out. How do I bring this up now, after Gannet's warm welcome to the resistance?

"If it's ready, we should probably leave now," Gannet says, looking at Marcus, clearly enjoying the shock his news provides. "Before pretty boy here can say anything."

"Gannet, stop it. I think we can trust him. I think he should co—"

"Leave?" Marcus speaks over me. "What are we talking about?"

I put a hand on Marcus's arm but Gannet steps closer and speaks before I can.

"I'm getting Aston out of here." His voice holds too much provocation.

"Whoa." Marcus raises his eyebrows and takes his arm out of my grasp. "I'm not sure that's the best idea."

"And who says you have a say in this, huh? I think you've caused enough problems, Recipient."

I can't believe how bold and forward Gannet is. He grabs my wrist, and though he doesn't hold it very tight, just above my bandages, I suddenly see more Brutis in him than I could ever have imagined possible.

"I've made mistakes like the next human, I'll admit," Gannet continues. "But that doesn't mean I haven't learned from them. Nor has history been lost on me either. You

Recipients are starting a war I don't think you're ready to lose."

"Is that a threat?"

"It's a warning. Like all history is. A cry from the dust that we must take heed to not do the same stupid things again."

"Who are you calling stupid?"

"No one is calling anyone stupid," I say. "Let's just all take a deep breath and calm down."

"Aston," Marcus says, low and fervent as he steps closer and lowers his head like a wet dog in the rain. "You leave and there's no saving you from this. I don't know how I could protect you then."

Gannet's hand tightens on mine "She doesn't need a blood-sucker's protection."

"What about Lazuli?" Marcus addresses me, but it's Gannet who replies.

"She's got her own mission."

Both of our heads turn toward Gannet. I look back at Marcus, his face clearly showing panic and pain as well. Seeing his concern causes a pang of jealousy to roll through me.

"I'm not leaving you, Marcus."

Gannet's hand loosens.

"I'm not going anywhere tonight, Gannet. Let's just talk to Trip. He says there may be room for two."

"You wish upon me a quicker death than the virus?" Marcus asks. "If the Donors are half as gracious as this one, I wouldn't survive one night there."

"So the Royal Recipient does have an ounce of sense?"

"Shush, Gannet."

"I won't go with you, Aston. And I won't support this either."

"But you said..." He said he would be with me. I pull my hand free of Gannet's. I should have been braver and brought this up sooner. I should have told Marcus everything. Now, trying to convince him here in front of Gannet —everything is wrong about this. "You said no matter the side, even the one that wouldn't accept you. You said!"

"Recipients say a great many things," Gannet whispers and steps away, releasing me into the web he has created for Marcus and me. He must be satisfied enough with the torment he has put between us to leave us alone as he opens the wall and races up the stairs to check on Trip.

Marcus drops his head and puts a hand through his hair as he thinks. "I meant what I said, but Aston, this is too dangerous. A converter? Really? And not just a converter but one made from scratch by a boy?" Marcus takes my hands in his. "Your life is too precious to take that risk. Stay, wait, and let's find a different way."

I don't hear Gannet approach, already returned from the attic. "You mean her blood is too precious."

"I care more about her than her blood."

"Recipients always have been good liars. Admit it, all you want is her blood to keep you alive."

"Enough!" I shout. "That's enough. I've spent my whole life being told what my blood is and what I'm good for. If anyone in here understands what that's like it should be you two. Now quit it! Gannet, what did Trip say?"

He gives Marcus one last dirty look before he turns to me and frowns. "He says it's not ready."

Marcus sighs and spins away with relief. He walks across the room, far away from us.

"But it will be soon. And when it is, I'm bringing you back. Without any Recipients in tow."

Marcus throws his hands out in the air and leaves, slamming the door behind him.

I fidget with the bandages around my wrists. He has to come with me. I can't leave him here with Adakin. I just can't. "I don't think you get to decide that," I say.

"I do, I'm—"

"I'm not coming without him," I say firmly, looking down at the ground and still fidgeting with my wrist. "If he's willing to follow me."

# CHAPTER 36

I have only one more donation day before it's Lazuli's turn again. When Alex leaves, I plead with Marcus to understand our situation.

"Think about the good you could do for both our people. Think about the symbol you and I could represent *together*. With you representing Recipients taking the side of the resistance... I thought change was what you wanted."

"Not like this. It's a death sentence, Aston."

"No Donor would touch you. After my paintings, I'm almost as famous among Donors as you are here." I give him a soft punch on the arm, and he smiles.

"It's not the Donors I fear the most. If I were to vocally support the resistance, we'd have the most powerful Recipients on our heels."

"But what good are we doing here? The experiment is failing to get the kind of attention you wanted."

"So escape is your answer? Even if you live through the process, what keeps you alive once you're wherever the resistance is?"

"I don't know, but at least I won't be locked up like this."

"So that's what this is about again? Your treatment here?"

"No."

"I've had enough of this." He stands and stomps across the floor, making my heart ache at how much the sounds remind me of Papa. "I'll see you at dinner," he says over his shoulder as he opens the door.

*Please tell me I'm not being like Mam. What I'm asking for is reasonable, isn't it?*

"So that's it?" I say. "You can't just run away every time things don't go the way you like, Marcus."

"I'm not running away, Aston. You are! All I've ever done is run after you! But this is too far!" Our eyes plead with each other a moment longer. There is a message in his blue eyes, not blue like Torrin's or Papa's or mine, but a dangerous sort of murky blue that tells me he is never mine for the choosing. A Recipient blue, like serum. I'm not and possibly never will be free enough to choose him. He will never be welcome in my house. And I see now his fear that I can't ever do anything about it. "Too far," he echoes in a whisper. Echoing his words and my thoughts. We are too far from each other. There is more than a wall between us. There is a thick barrier of prejudices that will never be able to accept us, and we were stupid to try.

Marcus doesn't show for dinner. And when I wake the next day, the house is silent, and no one comes into my room. No breakfast can only mean one thing. Adakin. And I have been too distracted with Marcus at each of my meals to have stashed anything away. Marcus is with Lazuli now. Possibly where he should have been all along.

# CHAPTER 37

I'm surprised when Alex doesn't come for my donation. Although I'm hungry, I'm not as weak as having my blood drained would have made me. I pace the floor and step to the window. Marcus is already in the garden with Lazuli.

I pace again as my stomach growls. I won't spy on them. I'll let them have each other and leave the moment Gannet arrives. No. I have to convince Marcus to come with me. But how can I speak to him when it's Lazuli's turn? And Lazuli has her own mission? I pause in place when I remember what Gannet had said. What if Marcus *is* her mission? How will Lazuli get back home?

I walk briskly toward the door, but remembering what door handles can do here, I listen first, then touch the brass handle with a quick jab of my hand, then another quick one before my fingers rest on the cold metal with ease. I know where Marcus's room is. Perhaps I could sneak out and get to him.

I open the door, and I'm about to place my foot into the white hallway when I smell honey. Adakin is walking toward my room with clicking shoes just as tall, old, and proud as ever.

I leave the door open and back up slowly without taking my eyes off of him. He slams the door firmly behind him, and by the buzzing sound that pricks and tingles the hairs in my ears, I can tell it is no longer safe to touch.

At first, he looks as if he's in a hurry, but then he slows down as he eyes the books piled on the coffee table. My heart pounds as I see the book he is reaching for. Scars, I forgot that the book about the IPC I stole from his office is out. I clasp my hands behind my back to keep them from shaking.

"Doing a little studying are we? Funny, I don't seem to recall this book being in the library." He thumbs through the pages and stops to examine one. He gives a ragged sigh with a hum before he speaks. "Those were the good ol' days. There's Brutis, as smug and reckless as ever. You two have that in common, you know. Maybe I should have let him have you after all. You're both so bloody careless." He snaps the book shut and my shoulders hop in surprise.

He shakes the book in the air. "Did this answer all your questions, or do you have any more I can help you with?"

"I didn't donate today, you know."

"Oh, I know. The serum I used only needs one dose." He leans forward, replacing the book. "Any other answers you seek?" He moves toward the sofa, sits directly in the middle of it, and crosses his legs. Both of his arms stretch out the length of the top of it, and he gives me a foolish grin from under his sickly yellow beard.

"Come, come, have out with it. Don't be shy now. We've wasted so much of your time here with us. What's another day of discussion?"

"You think you're a god with all the answers to the universe."

"You *know* the one thing I want to know from you."

I search for my bandages, but there are none. My wrists have healed with nice shiny scars. Instead, I rub the glossy bumps on the inner part of my elbows.

"The IPC had no intentions to rally against the corporate world, did they," I say. "You were only after the shrinking of a thriving civilization. The goal was to dwindle the population of the world down."

"You say 'you' so confidently. How do you know it was me who created this goal and mission?"

"Eva then."

"Yes, yes, Eva." His laugh is childish and creepily merry.

"You were one and the same. But how did my grandmother fit into all this? What was her part in this group?"

"Ah, yes, you never cease to amaze me, Aston. The rumor of Donors being dumb would never work with you around. The IPC was an internationally funded program. It was never intended to be a killing mechanism, but a life-saving one. We were to study the sickest individuals, the rarest diseases, the largest causes of deformities. In the process of this study there were two outcomes expected. That some test individuals would die was a given, so the first goal was that it would in return save more lives than it was killing. Two, it would eliminate the problem of over-population."

"I already understand all this. You didn't answer my question."

"But you are not ready for the answer. How about we do this?" He brings his arms off the sofa and clasps his hands as he leans forward. "I will answer the question you so badly want to know if you answer mine."

I ball my fists and turn away from him. I walk to the bookshelf and lean the side of my shoulder on it for support. I've kept my mouth shut for so long it's beginning to feel exhausting. I just want to be done with it. What if he has created a serum for opening mouths?

"You see, Aston," he begins, and I look over my shoulder at him as he traces the piles of books in front of him, "I've been doing a little research of my own." When he smiles, his splotchy red cheeks covered in broken blood vessels protrude even further, and his purposeful smile makes him look as if he is high on happy juice. "And in my searching I've finally solved a mystery. See, our files say that Aston Vazeto is technically fatherless. Yes, according to our files, Patar Vazeto has never donated in his life, in fact, doesn't even exist." His face is round with joy. Loving every moment of this revelation.

"There is no Patar Vazeto on our records anywhere." He sits up and extends his arms out for emphasis. His eyebrows raise in mock astonishment.

My heart hammers in my throat and up into my head. My blood understands before I do.

*Tsking*, he shakes his head. "You know more than anyone that tampering with records is one of the highest offenses. Its penalty is death, though we have mercy on those we see fit." He scrunches up his face as if he's talking to an infant. I squeeze the wood of the bookshelf. I can't concentrate on breathing. Exhale, inhale... It's so loud in my ears.

He stands and places his hands in his pockets before moving to me.

"Actually," he shrugs and cocks his head to the side. "How could anyone really miss a person who doesn't even exist?"

"You stay away from my father."

"Tell. Me. Where. Bolglarka. *Is*!" He screams the last word so loud I flinch.

Looking out the window, I start to panic. What do I do? I recall the glances between Grandma Bolgi and Papa. It feels like ages ago when the only scary thing was telling my family a secret. What do I do now when my secret is what's protecting them?

Below me, Marcus and Lazuli are walking carefree through the garden. Fear. Outrage. Jealousy. All of it courses through me.

And then time stops. My heart stops. Everything stands still as Marcus, so far away from me with walls and glass and tech between us, falls to the ground, coughing and convulsing.

# CHAPTER 38

S creaming his name, I claw at the glass as Lazuli runs
to his aid and hollers over her shoulder.

I turn to Adakin. "Do something!"

He walks to the window and calmly looks out at the
scene. "Nurses will attend to him. It was bound to happen
eventually. You knew it, and I knew it. You said so yourself,
this experiment was doomed."

His carelessness shouldn't surprise me, but in this
moment of panic his words send my heart plummeting to
my feet, and I must move. I run to the door and don't care
about the shock that's there to block me. I need to get to
him. Pain shoots up my arm as I make contact, and I fall to
the ground, twitching.

Adakin steps over me. "I suppose you are right, though.
You've created an emotional frenzy about everything here.
The mobs will interpret this differently, and we can't afford
that angle right now. But don't think what I discovered was
meant for a pleasant little story time or family reunion. You
have until tomorrow to tell me, or I make a visit to dear
Papa."

323

The door opens and closes, and I push against the hardwood floor, wincing as I move. My legs are weak, but my arm that touched the door is the only thing still hurting. I'm slightly grateful for the ache that bounces through my veins like electricity and dulls the painful fear roaming in my chest. Sluggishly, I make my way to the window, groaning and sweating at the effort. Marcus and Lazuli are gone, and though I should be relieved that he's getting help so quickly, it makes me anxious to have him out of sight.

Pacing the floor with a limp and holding my right arm, I curse the silent floorboards. The absence of creaking wood reminds me of how alone I am, symbolizes the absence of Papa. Scars. How do I tell the resistance about the danger Papa is in? And how do I get to Marcus?

I stop. The walls. Trip. I'm at the bookshelf in no time, and the shelf has never moved so slow. I bounce in place as I wait for it. I pull on the railing of the tight stairs up to his room with my good arm, and as I move, the hollowness in my legs subsides.

When I burst clumsily into the attic room, Lecky hisses at me, and Trip turns around, removing goggles from his eyes.

"Trip! I need to get to Marcus's room! Do you know? Are there any passageways that lead there?"

He throws the goggles in haste and stands with a worried look on his face that ages him. "Why, what's wrong? You guys fight again?"

"Just tell me, Trip, it's important."

"Alright, alright. No."

I moan and pace his room. No sign of sound on his floor either. No help. All alone.

"There aren't any that lead to his room directly, but his sitting room has one."

"His sitting room?" I grab his shoulders, and the feeling returns to my arm. His sitting room. Where he took me to paint? "Take me there. Right now." I'm not sure what I can do even if I can just waltz right into Marcus's room, but the need to be by his side, to be as close to him as I possibly can, urges me forward without another care in the world.

"Ouch, okay you don't have to turn all president on me. What's the big deal?"

I follow Trip across the room and am surprised to find another set of stairs just like the ones that lead to my room. When we descend, voices raised in worry and panic jab at my insides like daggers as we shimmy down the dark, skinny hallway. Doctors talking about heart rates and temperatures.

"What's happened, Aston?" Trip finally starts to worry more.

"Shh."

Lazuli's familiar voice leaks through the walls. "He was just walking with me, and he collapsed. He just fell over and—" She shouts and sobs like a crazy woman.

"Someone get her out of here. She's probably the cause of all this in the first place!" the doctor shouts.

"I didn't do anything. I did everything I was told to. I—"

"Shut the bloody hell up, child." A rough, crass woman bellows. Lazuli's maid, no doubt. "It's your blood that done killed him, that's what he means, now get back to your room so the technician can do his bloody job."

"You rotten maid! It's *my* month! I need to—"

A loud smack like a tambourine being hit sends the room into silence, and then Lazuli sobs and clearly runs out. I press the side of my face against the wall, tensing and wishing I could show myself or do something. But Lazuli is already gone. I need to get to Marcus.

"Aw, now come on Martha, what'd ya have to go and do that for?"

"It's the only way ta handle them Donors. I'm the one that's had to deal with her nonsense, so don't you go disrespectin' my ways."

My fingers tremble at my mouth, and tears slide down my cheeks. Is this why Marcus was so supportive of Lazuli always outside? To escape her rotten maid? Poor Lazuli. I have to get her out too. She has to come with me through the converter, mission or no mission. She can't stay here like this.

"Remind me to give Janice a squeeze when we get back," I whisper to Trip.

After listening to the scuffling shoes and the beeping machines of technicians running tests and drawing blood, Trip leaves me behind to go work on the converter. I crouch, squished between the walls, listening to everything, wishing I was in there with him. Wishing I could give him my blood right now.

"What's it look like?"

I freeze at the sound of Adakin's voice. His feet shuffle with that same *bump-tap* of his shoe close to my spot in the wall, and I cover my mouth to make my breathing as quiet as possible.

"Switching between the good blood and the bad blood is making his body build a resistance to the cure. It's almost as if he's never had a donation in his life."

"If we get a donation from the other Donor now?"

"I'm not sure it would do any good. His body is fighting the virus and is susceptible to the triantacoccus that is already apparent in his blood test."

I squeeze my eyes shut. The virus. It's already in him.

"What can we do?" Adakin says.

"Honestly? Find another Donor. Does she have younger siblings? Maybe with higher numbers?"

"A brother. But higher?" Adakin chuckles a merciless laugh. "Not likely."

No! My eyes shoot open, but I stifle a gasp as dread fills my limbs.

"It's worth a try, but—"

"But what?" Adakin barks.

Their voices sound far away, and I can't tell if it's because they are leaving or because I am fainting.

"President, time is of the essence. We should let him rest and get him a new Donor as soon as possible."

"Fine. Get the boy. Test him. Get his blood." Adakin sounds more annoyed than concerned.

The door shuts and when I stand, my legs and feet tingle with numbness. I grope at the wall for some sort of opening. Uneven lines hint of a doorway, and I push. Soon I am in the dark sitting room lined with bookshelves and the double door to his bedroom is wide open. Beyond them, the foot of his bed pokes out and I run toward it.

I barely recognize him as his face glows among his dark burgundy blankets. I kneel by the bed and put my hands on him like they hold the magic that can heal him. I put one hand on his arm where his pulse is faint and weak. My other hand cups his cheek and then slides down to his chest. It barely rises and falls. So shallow, I'd miss it if my hands weren't on him. His brow is clammy and cold. My hands find every inch of him as I call his name.

"I'm sorry," I whisper to him.

His eyes flutter and then shut again but his hand is in my hair.

"You were right," he says, then coughs.

"Shh." I swallow a sob when I hear his voice. "Stop it. It's not about being right."

"Isn't it?" He coughs again, and his chest shudders under my palm. A strange crackling vibration is mixed with his breathing. He brings a hand to his mouth, exposing a dark purple bruise on his forearm.

"How did this happen so fast?" I whisper to no one in particular and grab his hand to kiss the top of it.

"How ironic that I brought you here to save, and now I'm the one needing saving."

"Again," I say sarcastically.

His laugh does more shaking of his ribs than his cough does. His thumb caresses my cheek as he looks at me.

"It was wrong, what I did. I'd change so many things if I could but none of them that brought me to you."

"You're talking like you're dying," I say, doing a horrible job at caging in my tears.

"No one lives with the virus, Aston. You heard him say so himself. Triantacoccus is already present." He doesn't look defeated, or even scared. Just blunt and matter-of-fact.

"I don't care. They're going to help you. You'll see." I gulp. "But Torrin.."

"I won't let them take his freedom like I took yours," says Marcus quietly.

Could I live with myself letting Marcus die?

Marcus closes his eyes. "I'm so tired," he says.

"I'll bring you with me, Marcus. The Donors can save you somehow. The resistance will help you, you'll see." That's it. I'll bring him with me and find another high-numbered person to help. As long as we stay far away from Adakin, we can make this work. I have to try. I can tell he's still breathing, but his eyes roll back and his eyelids close.

"Marcus?" My mind understands he's just resting, but my heart panics and skips. "Marcus?" I cry.

I lean forward and put my forehead on his and whisper against his lips. "I love you, Marcus Malloy."

"That wasn't so hard was it?" he whispers back. Even lifeless he makes jokes.

I smile against his face and then I kiss him. With hands on either side of his face, I kiss his dry lips and feel them move faintly against mine. I pull away and run my hand through his hair as I look at his partly open eyes.

Someone runs in the room, and I don't move. I don't care. I love Marcus and I don't care who knows it anymore.

"Miss!"

"Janice?" I run to hug her. When I make it to her arms, Gannet is there behind her.

His eyes are dark and hard. I thought I didn't care who knows I love Marcus, but Gannet's look makes me care, makes my heart completely shatter in two. I don't even know this man before me anymore. I'm losing them both, the Recipient I fell in love with on accident, and the technician I tried to love on purpose. The broken pieces of my heart grind into dust at the realization that Gannet will never help Marcus.

"It's time to go home, Aston."

# CHAPTER 39

"Gannet, I can't—"

"There's no time for that, Aston. The resistance is in danger. We overheard a plan from Adakin himself—"

"Papa!" In the drama of Marcus's illness, I forgot about Adakin Malloy's threat. Papa and Marcus and now Torrin. Scars, please don't take all of my favorite people from me. I look behind me at Marcus. He seems completely unaware of Gannet being here and one of his arms is covered in IV's and tubes transferring blood as quickly as it can. He's in no position to be moved. Stepping away from Janice but keeping my arms on her for support, I tell Gannet about the last visit with the president.

"Papa's in danger. Torrin too."

"All the more reason to go now."

He turns, and I reach out for him. One hand on my adopted Recipient mother and one on my Donor friend. That's what he is right? My friend? He used to be.

Gannet lets my touch stop him, but he doesn't look at me. I feel the urgency of our situation, the fear and adrenaline of needing to leave now, but it only dances on the side of my other stirring emotions that tell me to stop and look at him. To think about him and what he has been through. To touch him, speak to him, and he will listen, because deep down under his pain he is nothing like Dustin. He is kind and compassionate.

Finally, he turns and looks at me with the same warm eyes that saw me at the facility doors about to donate, rescued me from the serum, and brought me to the resistance when no one else fought for me. I take a deep breath, feeling assured that Gannet will listen to me, but before I can plead to somehow bring Marcus with us, the doors to his room swing open.

"Stop!" an officer shouts and a red laser brightens the dimly lit room.

Janice yanks me back to the sitting room and shoves me through the doorway to the secret passageway first. I don't understand right away what it is that continues to light up the dark hallway bright red. Janice is like a lantern glowing and showing the way to run, but her face—she looks right at me like she's apologizing, like she knew this would happen but regrets it all the same. A look that glows red and tattoos itself into my memory forever. The door shuts, slicing the red out of the picture, and Janice falls to the floor.

"No!" There is banging on the wall, but all my mind can register is the faint red glow that shines a hole in Janice's chest. In her hand she holds up the device that she recorded the files on from the raid of the office. Has she really carried that on her person all this time? Her mouth is stiffly open as she shakes, and only little grunts come out like her breath is stuck or maybe it's completely gone already. I try to ignore the sound the singeing hole in her is making, like crackling fire or the clapping debris hitting the ground.

I shake my head. "Janice, no," I sob. How can all this be happening? All the people I've grown to love. I lift Janice into my arms, the heat of where she's shot beats against my face, and I'm careful to keep my arms from the burn. She is trembling, but not breathing. I take the file from her stiff grip. Will all the people I care about always be ripped from me? I was wrong about Recipients. I was oh so wrong. This woman was more than my maid; she was my Recipient mother who raised me in this strange Recipient world and taught me how to change, how to forgive. I stare into Janice's face, and she blinks. We used to joke as a family that we didn't think Mam ever blinked. Never thought twice about a situation, never a second glance, everything was black and white with her, and she moved with precision and purpose. Blinking would have been a weakness: blink and you miss something. Janice blinks. For a moment in that blink, I pretend like there is nothing wrong in the world. Like there aren't officers chasing us or a resistance waiting for us to take a risky trip through a machine or a Recipient Prince dying on the other side of these walls.

Officers are shouting and clawing at the wall to find an opening. Gannet somehow comes up from behind me and stops when he sees us crumpled in the little dim hallway, or maybe it's the smell of burnt flesh and incoming death that makes him pause. Does he judge me for loving more than one Recipient now?

Janice puts her hand that's now bare and cold on my cheek. There is no breath, no sound, only one dying impulsive groan that sounds like Sofie and makes my legs go numb. "Trip."

"I'll take care of him!" I clench her shoulder as if my strength could reassure her of my conviction.

The banging grows and lasers heat up the wall my arm is on.

"Come on, Aston. Now!" Gannet yells.

"I'll take care of him," I say again, but she doesn't hear me. There is no life in her eyes anymore, and I fear the burning hole is contagious, because it rips through my chest now too—orange crackling flames eating away at my heart. Gannet helps me lay her down and pulls me to my feet. It doesn't feel like I'm really moving as we clumsily finagle our way around her. I look back one last time to her open, lifeless eyes, no more blinking. "I'll take care of him." My whisper makes me shiver.

Rounding the corner of the hallway, officers break through the passageway, sending light across Gannet's face. We have no choice but to move faster, no matter how numb I feel. Trip. I have to get to Trip before the officers do. The large officers struggle to fit through the small hallways.

I don't know where my feet take me or what I am doing. I only move. A hand grabs me here or pushes me there, and we are in the attic. Trip's excited and innocent face with his tongue sticking out from concentration make my tears run quicker.

He is pushing buttons and waving his hand over lights and running around.

"It's ready, Aston. Get in."

A large metal cylinder, like an elevator with red and blue flashing lights down the sides, whirs like a fan. An archway opening is in the center. I stare at it, trying so hard to process everything.

Crashing sounds from the wall are like an angry monstrous ticking clock. Officers are getting close.

Gannet steps forward and puts a hand on my back. "We're on the other side with you, don't worry. Now or never Aston, let's go!"

Shouts and grunts come from both sides of the stairs, and I step closer to Trip, grabbing his hand away from whatever device is making the fan in the converter get louder and louder. "Trip, Juice is gone!" I pull him toward the converter.

"What? No, I can't. What are you doing?" He looks down the stairs where I left her.

Gannet grabs the device from Trip's hands. Trip looks at Gannet like he has betrayed the young boy. How do I explain everything to him? There's no time.

"She's dead, now you have to come with me. I promised her, Trip. Now come on!"

Out of the corner of my eye, I see an officer halfway up the stairs.

"Now!" Gannet yells impatiently.

The officer aims his laser. Flashing red beams shoot through the room, and I pull Trip into the converter with me. I hug him close as wind whips up my hair and red stings my skin. My teeth ache, and for a moment I have a silly simple thought: "So this is what dying by laser feels like?" My vision fills with Janice, and then it's silent.

My eyes are sealed shut when I hear the whispers of angels.

"Who's that she brought with her?"

"Aston!"

My eyes flutter open, and before me is the face of my sister, Shannon. And beside her is a smiling Pip who hugs her mom's neck.

I let Shannon hug me but don't release my hold on Trip. Gannet is on the floor gasping, and a crowd of people gather around him.

"It's all in your head, Gannet. It's just a perception."

The officers must have gotten him. If only Janice had been a perception too, maybe she'd still be here.

"It doesn't scars-well feel like it's in my head," he grunts. I recall the bees and squint as I watch people help him stand. "Feels like it's rather in my spleen."

The crowd laughs, and I turn my head around at them. Why would they laugh at something like that? Why are they laughing at all? Don't they know Gannet will live with that dull pain the rest of his life like a bad memory that can't fully be erased? Don't they know what it really did to Janice? No. They don't know. I pull Trip closer to me to keep my arms from shaking. Looking down at him, I find his face is as white as the facility, and his eyes don't lift from the ground. What do I do with him now? The weight of responsibility is not exactly a welcome distraction from the pain.

I look around us. We seem to be in some sort of underground bunker. The ground of this elongated room is covered in dirt, and two lights dangle from the ceiling on either end. The walls are rounded and metal-looking.

"Where are we?" I ask no one in particular.

"Don't you recognize Dearborn?" a familiar warm voice says. The crowd chuckles, and from the other end of the room, people begin to move out of the way.

"Grandma Bolgi!"

# CHAPTER 40

"You brought a stowaway," she says in her gravelly voice. Her hug feels softer than I remember, better than the Recipient sheets. How could I have ever considered giving this person away to Adakin?

Breaking away from Bolgi, I notice the stares from the crowd. They are all wondering who this boy is too. "A friend," I say. Are they thinking 'Recipient'? Do they know? Their slack faces give me nothing to go on. "Another one who needed help escaping."

"Interesting," Grandma Bolgi says. "Come with me."

I follow Grandma Bolgi back the direction she came from, and people smile at me. Some touch me as I go by, but they all say the same thing. "Welcome home, Aston."

They all know me, yet I don't recognize any of them. We move through another room identical to this one, long and narrow like we are inside a medicinal pill. Even more people crowd in here; the small space makes it awkward to move with Trip hugging my waist tighter. These people greet me the same way. Like they know me.

"Welcome back, Aston." Those on the edges of the room

336

point and whisper loudly. "It worked," they say or, "It's really her."

Gannet grunts his way up to me. He gives me a sideways glance, perhaps seeing my discomfort, shock, and worry. He tries to put his hand on me, and I can't explain why I flinch away from it so quickly. Can't explain anything. I can't feel anything. My mind goes back to Marcus on his death bed and how I left him there. And Janice's cold dead eyes.

"These rooms were supposed to be empty." He dips his head close to mine as we walk. "It was the only place in the tunnels that the transporter had a good connection, but they were supposed to be kept empty." He repeats the sentiment a bit louder at the end of his speech and seems to aim it at Bolgi.

Grandma Bolgi ignores him. "We're all glad you made it. As you can see, you're famous now. Not something I support, really. I much rather my grand-daughter stay on the down-low, but what can I do? Teenagers these days."

Gannet scoffs like he doesn't believe a word she says. I always pictured Gannet half-worshiping my resistance leader grandmother. What am I missing? I don't have the energy to dissect another mystery. My eyes droop, and I wouldn't mind lying down right on this dirt floor and sleeping until the war is over. Trip grows slightly heavy and stumbles on the gravel, perhaps thinking the same thing I am. The reminder of this responsibility gives me a little more energy, and I heft him up, practically carrying him through his enemy's territory.

The third room is the same, only this one has drawings all over the wall. Some are black and splotchy, possibly done with charcoal or stones, others with actual colors. There are words and images at different angles and in different sizes. A large image catches my attention. The emblem of our New World: two hands holding up a droplet of blood, only these hands are depicted holding knives and needles.

"All tributes to you and what you gave them," she says as she continues to walk.

"What did I give them?"

"A way out, a distraction. A blooming desire to create something of their own. But mostly, Aston, you gave them hope."

Something bolsters Trip, and he lets go of me. I hold tight to his hand as we walk through the room. Just before we exit, there's a small tug on my free hand. I stop and look down to a small girl with smudged cheeks and imploring green eyes.

"I drew this for you," she says in a squeaky voice.

A mother comes running up. "I'm so sorry. I—"

"It's okay," I tell her.

I take the picture from the little girl and look at the scribbles, the little lines that make a face. It makes me think of my first drawings. Scraps of rough paper that would fall from Papa's work bag. Remnants and ashes from a fire for pencils. Oh, how Mam hated the way Papa doted over my drawings.

"*A regular Picasso!*" he'd exclaim.

"*Old World ways,*" Mam would hiss and try to throw away my drawings. "*Stop filling her head with nonsense the world cares nothing about.*"

"*Someday they will, Evelyn.*"

The little girl's voice breaks my memory-filled trance. "It's my daddy," she says.

I stare at the curvy little figure this small Donor drew. A young girl drew her papa, and because of me no one scolded her for it. Everything has moved too fast. Marcus, then Janice, now this new place that's cold and smells of dirt that people expect me to call home. Welcome home? This isn't my home. I shut my eyes to keep from crying. Marcus would understand why, but what will these Donors think of me falling apart like this? I take a big gulp and kneel down in front of the young girl.

"It's beautiful," I tell her. She smiles large enough for me to see her missing front tooth. Her hair is in braids down either side, but tiny hairs frizz around her head making a strawberry blonde halo. "A regular Picasso."

"My daddy," she says, pointing to the drawing again. "He died before you could get here."

Her words leave a weight on my shoulders that makes it hard for me to stand. *Save us all.* Before I could get here? I look around the room at all the eyes on me. What do these people think I am? How can they not think me a traitor for being in their enemy's land and working with them? For falling in love with a Recipient? Marcus. I did not think there was anything left of my heart to tear. Scars, I hope those scientists can save him. Was I wrong to not push harder to bring him? But he may have ended up dead more quickly here.

"Come on, little ash tree," Grandma calls out. People try to draw closer to me, give me things themselves, some even push a little when a man steps up to fend them off of us, arms stretched out like a human wall. "We have lots to talk about." Bolgi dips her head through the next small opening between capsules and disappears. I smile again at the little girl and shuffle with Trip by my side to catch up.

I smell the room before we enter it. A pungent smell that makes me think of roadkill. Trip puts his hands to his face, and I grip him to my hip again. The next room is different. Round and more light. More people too. Older people with less smiles and less congratulating. More sneers and glares. More wounded and dirty. We pass cots on the floor and some have white blankets over bodies, I assume.

"Grandma Bolgi, what's happened here?" I catch up to her and draw her arm back.

She pauses and looks down to where my eyes are plastered to the lifeless forms, unknown under the sheets, as if they're playing ghost. Janice's pleading eyes sting my memory, and I shield Trip's face, pulling him closer to me. Gannet puts a hand on my shoulder, and I'm too lost in my own trauma to react.

"We're at war, Aston," Bolgi says.

I nod silently. Trying to act brave. But inside, I'm aching and confused. At war already? I knew there was picketing and rioting, but has it already led to war? "I knew there were protests, but..."

"Protests are usually an early dynamic of war. But this resistance has been organizing for many years." She cups my cheek with her soft hand, and I smell her peppermints. Something I haven't smelled in so long. I want to sigh deep, heavy, healing sighs and wrap myself in her arms, but I know there is no time for childish things like that right now. "You, my dear, were what put years of scheming into motion. Years of calculating and deciding was all of a sudden done for us."

"But how? I didn't do anything."

Her quick sarcastic laugh shocks me. She ignores my question as she turns and continues onward. "The disintegration lasers have been used up to build your transporter. We'll be able to clean this place up in a bit."

The way she says "clean this place up" like these lives

were just pawns makes me think of Adakin. I've never seen this side of Bolgi before. Leader, commander, blunt dictator. But her words do give me insight. I look over my shoulder as we leave the room. The workers there still glare at my retreating form. Do they resent me for taking the resistance's precious time and material?

Gannet sees me looking. He looks back at the workers wearing matching brown shirts like the man who blocked the people from us. Soldiers?

"War makes a lot of people forget themselves," Gannet says softly. "Makes people angry."

"Angry at me?"

"Like I said, war can change a person. Make it hard to know who to follow, who to believe."

I don't really understand his words, but I let Gannet pull me back around anyway. Do they think I don't understand war? Well, I suppose they're right. I don't know the first thing about fighting, but I know what it's like to be angry, to suffer loss, to be confused about who to believe. Perhaps they are upset with me for spending my time reading books and eating cheese while they buried their dead. I hang my head a little lower.

Grandma Bolgi is now far ahead. I drop my hold on Trip and grab his hand. We jog ahead to catch up. Bolgi dips out of the room again and outside of this room is a landing ground, a fork in the road with three tunnels to choose from. Grandma heads for the one on the right, already several feet ahead of me. We're like little moles burrowing underground for safety. The damp smell of the earth and the closeness of it, being miles underneath the world, makes me feel claustrophobic and more caged-in than the Recipient bedroom.

"You get used to it," Gannet says from behind, reading

my mind. He looks different and is not the Gannet I once knew. The soft edges of his face have hardened.

The running has taken its toll on me. My head feels disconnected from my body, and I grab hold of Gannet for support.

"Bolgi," Gannet thunders, his voice echoing in the small landing. "They need to rest."

Grandma Bolgi spins around and takes in the scene. I try to stand taller and reassure her that I can do whatever she wants from me. I'm dependable.

She doesn't address me but Gannet with a hard gaze. "We need to get her farther away from the civilians and somewhere safe."

"She needs to eat and recover," Gannet protests.

There is a stand-off between the two of them. Trip teeters and leans on me, which makes it even harder for me to keep my balance.

"Of course," Bolgi says, pivoting to a different tunnel.

The next room we enter is cleaner. The smell of ammonia stings my nose, and the walls glow a polished white like the facilities and like my walls back at Bloomfield.

"Thanks to Torrin," Grandma says, "we replicated our own walls using the manual. It's not quite up to speed but—"

"Aston?"

The word feels strange, like it's coming from a stuffed toy from my childhood I've finally discovered can talk to me. I'm numb and alive at the same time. My body and mind both know and don't know what is happening, like a dream that I'm slowly waking up from only to realize the sounds and smells are reality. Like a fog that's starting to dissipate. Even still, my body reacts faster than my mind can. I let go of Trip without thinking and reach for the one he reminded me of. The real version.

"Torrin?" My throat cracks on the word. "Torrin?" I choke and each step is forceful and quick. These legs must get me to him as fast as I can.

# CHAPTER 41

He cries as we hug, his face squished in an unpleasant shape like melting clay. I realize he is not as much like Trip as I had thought. Torrin is no longer the little twelve-year-old boy that I left but is swiftly shifting into that in-between phase, not quite a man, not quite a boy. He is taller. I must not have noticed that when I saw him in the school. So tall I can no longer tousle his hair that is covered in mud. I can't even put my arms around his head, but instead I wrap them around his chest and his chin digs into my shoulder. Who is this boy in a man's body? What have they done to my Torrential Torrin, full of wonder and awe? He is grown. Faster than necessary. But was it Recipients who did that or the resistance? Or war? I'm crying in a raw way that I haven't in a long time.

I pull away when I remember. "Torrin, you're not safe! And Papa! Where is he? He isn't safe either." In incoherent strings of panic, I mutter about Marcus falling and what the technician said. I try to tell them all about Adakin's threat, but I speak so fast no one takes my words seriously.

I look at Grandma Bolgi with pleading eyes, which makes her pause. I recall her being in the photo with Adakin and see her taking it all in, calculating and deciding. Yes, she knows the king and what he is capable of. Looking at her face makes me sigh, and I yearn for those carefree days with peppermint and tree swings. I have so many questions for her. So much to learn. She looks over my shoulder and calls out to someone. When I turn around, I see more of those men with the same brown shirts. They move so silently I hadn't realized they were following us.

"Inform Dustin to take us to code yellow. All PR precautions."

I sigh, relieved that she's taking this seriously.

"And have my son meet us in the commissary." The soldier nods and rushes out of the room.

"We have Patar in another bunker," she says. Torrin gives her an unpleasant look, and I don't understand the obvious tension there. "He is in charge of new recruits. We will catch you up later. First you must rest and find your strength again." She says it like it was her gracious idea but there's a sense of impatience to her voice that makes me feel childish and weak for needing to be fed.

As we walk, she explains to me the four years of planning and recruiting that the small band of her original resistance leaders went through. The only thing they lacked was a way into any sort of Recipient territory. They needed three things: one, a way to spread the word about the resistance; two, a way to free themselves of their control; and three, a way to understand their tech.

"We figured out a way to block the effects of the serum pretty early on. But it was hard to tell who it was effective on and who it wasn't. And then with the help of your technician"—Grandma Bolgi turns to Gannet but not with a pleasant smile, only with a critical eye—"who took more risks and liberty than I agreed with originally, you were able to avoid the serum altogether. That is what helped others see. What helped others feel."

"Actually—" I break off because it shocks me how quickly I command the attention of the room. Gannet and Torrin stare at me, but it's the large group of strangers, brown-shirted soldiers mostly, that make me uneasy. How did I miss so many following us this whole time? Large men with hard gazes and women with strong, exposed arms. I pause and look at each of them in turn before I speak. "I'm immune to the serum."

"I don't understand," says Grandma Bolgi.

"He"—I'm careful not to say Adakin's name because they should know who I mean, at least Bolgi will —"couldn't get the serum to affect me the same way it affects other Donors." I speak slowly, waiting for my stomach to burn and double me over at any moment. I don't think I would have the strength to handle that right now. But nothing ever comes, and I continue on. "I can still think through it. And it wears off quicker on me."

Grandma Bolgi steps closer and looks at me with wide eyes and a half smile like I am a test dummy that she is admiring. "I wondered..." she whispers.

"He had to starve me and drain me with donations in order for the serum to be more effective."

Grandma Bolgi's eyes slant with concern, but I'm not sharing this for sympathy.

"Until he created a whole new serum to control me with. One that he says doesn't need repetitive injections." I'm not sure how I'm able to share this information, but I run my mouth as fast as I can, expecting any minute to be seized by nausea. Perhaps I've always been able to tell others about a working serum, just not what it does, exactly. I tell them vaguely about how Adakin visited my rooms and how I saved up cheese in my nightstand. I ramble on about unimportant information merely because it feels so good to talk about anything remotely related to the truth. When nothing happens, I begin to have confidence in their tech. Perhaps they are safer here than I thought. Grandma called for PR precautions. Protection from perceived reality?

"Do you know anything about this serum?" a dark-skinned man says from my right.

"This is Goru," Bolgi says. "He's our head scientist in the program." It bothers me how Grandma Bolgi says this —"program"—like it's a cult or government-funded project. And all of a sudden, I picture her with arms wrapped around Eva, the evil one who started this all.

She raises an eyebrow at how I look at her. I turn to Goru finally and answer him.

"No, not really. I only know it affected my ability to—" There it is. Nausea hits as I consider telling them about what the serum doesn't let me say. I choose my words carefully. "Ability to share information." I take a deep sigh of relief. "And to internalize the effects of the perceived reality. Like it messed with my ability to reason. My brain was easily triggered and hallucinations were stronger."

"What do you mean?" says Goru, who is writing everything down on his port screen as I speak.

"For instance, Gannet, you were in Bloomfield through PR right? What happened to you right before you came back?"

"Uh, you mean when I was shot by the officer's lasers?" He raises his eyebrows, and the room chuckles a little.

"Yeah. Did you feel it?"

"Of course I did."

"Does it hurt still?"

He instinctively grabs his chest. "No." His brow furrows as if he's trying to determine when the pain ceased.

"The PR relies on the serum that is already in our blood. My serum was different and created a long-lasting effect so that not only did my mind register pain long after I left the reality but any time I even so much as heard what hurt me or smelled the trigger serum, I felt the pain again. My body reacts without my permission based on what my mind tells it, not what's really happening." So many things I've tried to tell Gannet and Janice. What's so different now about how I said this compared to my other attempts? Before, I was trying to warn Janice and Gannet about Adakin. What he could do and what his plans were. I feel slightly bolstered to have found a way around Adakin's serum.

Goru looks shocked and sad. "And it was only a one-time injection?"

I nod.

He looks to Grandma Bolgi.

"I know you've been through a lot, Aston, but I hope you don't mind a few blood tests," Bolgi says.

I shake my head and feel a little defeated to be talked to like any other soldier instead of her granddaughter who made bread dough on auction day morning with her.

"After she eats," Gannet insists again.

Bolgi begins to lead the way again when I remember the device Janice copied the forms on and retrieve it from my pocket slowly. I'm unable to take my eyes off of it, and a lump forms in my throat, making it hard to speak.

"I don't know if any of this is helpful or what it all means. But I found odd documents in his office."

Grandma Bolgi turns back around and walks toward

me. I hand the device to her, and she hands it to a man that steps up from behind her.

"Thank you," she says. "We will look into it. No matter how you did it, without the serum or immune to the serum, you were suddenly the voice we needed and the key our resistance had been looking for. We all were dumbfounded by the invitation to the Ambassador's Ball. It was partly what gave way to our recklessness." She gives the stink eye that I know so well, that I've missed so much, to a short man with a beard who lifts his chin.

She returns her attention to me. "We were a little too overzealous to finally have access; we retaliated in a way that left even Donors skeptical of our goals, motives, and success. But you saved us all with the wonderful speech you gave at the ball. Some still reference it today as the first time they were able to really feel something. Using the St. Johns wort that spread quickly through the states, combined with your emotional words, they were able to see for themselves their inhumane treatment.

"And then the twist of your words when the Recipients used you for advertisement. Parents started ordering the flower's seeds to help cure their children. And we got new recruits by the hour instead of the month. War broke out when you were captured and people, including Recipients, saw the weakness of their government. Children were separated from their parents. Parents retaliated against the facilities and some broke down schools. Many were killed in public squares just for trying to get their children back. It's when we went underground."

"There was a boy," I say slowly. "That died in a school, Torrin's school."

Torrin's head is dipped and low. I can't see his eyes when he speaks. "That could be any number of boys."

The pain he feels is thick in the air, and I would instantly go through all the hardship I've endured all over again to erase the things Torrin has evidently seen.

"It was the assembly where they announced the age change for donations. A young boy fell and died of cardiac arrest."

"What does this have to do with any—"

I cut Grandma Bolgi off. "I was there for that. That boy's death is why so many Donors have been dying their first week of donations. They were test subjects for...his new virus. It's an invisible dust that only affects the genetic coded individual it's programmed to." With each new word I speak, my mouth runs faster and faster, as I hope that all the truth about Adakin can come out. That he knows everything. That he's everywhere, so please hurry and do something.

"And with Adakin's perceived reality, there's no predicting—" Nausea stabs my stomach, and my throat feels as if an invisible hand has pinched my airway closed. I reach out to support myself and cough.

The room is silent as I clear and massage my throat. It feels cold. Like it sucked all the warm air out of every living person in here until we are dead with shock and despair. Even Trip, who has hidden silently behind me, steps closer to my side as if to warm himself in my shadow. Will they get my message from the small, unfinished sentence? I can see the gears moving. Someone must get what I'm trying to say. What my story about the boy means. Adakin can be anywhere. I am his surveillance. Can the PR precaution, code yellow whatever, protect them from that? From me?

"How in scars..." The anonymous curse lingers in the air unanswered. One by one it's clicking and they're seeing how dangerous the situation is.

Grandma Bolgi rushes to my side, making Gannet move out of the way. "My granddaughter must eat. We will decide what to do about that later."

If I'm not mistaken, there is fear mixed in her urgency. She doesn't want to take me to the commissary because she cares about my well-being, she wants me out of this room to stop scaring her people.

Trip is dragged behind me and Bolgi hunches close to me as she whispers, "I can't trust even the people in this room with the conversation you and I must have. And it's becoming clearer just how vital it is we have our little discussion as to why you are so much more valuable. You and your blood are the biggest asset to this resistance."

What did she just say? My blood? I thought the resistance was about freeing our blood from such bondage. Why is it valuable to them? Do they just want to use me like the Recipients? Will they, too, use me as ransom or leverage?

We enter a musty tunnel that's narrower than the rest. Gannet follows close behind and soon we are in another room that seems more naturally lit. It's circular, yet larger than the burial room. This one has rows and rows of wooden handmade tables and benches. A large circle is cut out of the ceiling and plants drape down over the edges. A small bit of sky peeks through, and I take a deep breath. Judging by the color, I'd say this day is almost over. This morning I thought Adakin coming into my room was my biggest fear.

Grandma Bolgi sits me down and someone puts a plate of food in front of me. I'm starving. I could eat anything. Except maybe this. The boiled potato and carrot in front of me roll to one side of the plate, and I just stare at it. I'm ashamed at how much I miss the Recipient cheese.

Trip doesn't seem to mind. He doesn't even wait for forks or spoons and just uses his hands.

The food is bland without salt and when I wash it down with the fuzzy-colored water, it takes everything in me not to spit it out or throw up.

Half my plate is empty, and I can't continue. I notice people in the room watching me, how the soldiers stand around me. They are staring and pointing, so I put my elbows on the table and hunch further over my plate.

A man approaches the table and puts a foot up on the bench across the table from me. He takes a bite from an apple and leans on his knee. His hair is long and shaggy-brown. The dirt on his face and his smell suggest he isn't fond of showering.

"Who's the boy?" he says, and from his craggy voice, I instantly recognize him. Dustin.

Everyone looks at me for answers, including Grandma Bolgi. Trip finds my hand and grips tight. Gannet gives me a worried look and warning shake of the head.

"He's a friend."

"He's a Recipient!" Dustin sneers, pieces of apple flying from his mouth. The room explodes with murmuring. People at other tables leave their food on their plates. A couple men from another table join Dustin to see what the commotion about a Recipient is.

Goru is the one who speaks up. "Is this true? You brought a Recipient to our base?"

"He's just a boy who's—" I'm cut off by everyone as they take turns shouting out their concerns. I try to answer every one of them.

"He could lead them right to us if his blood has a detector in it!"

"Well, so could I," I counter.

"Now he knows everything about us!"

"Who would he tell?"

"Use him as a test subject like they used Aston!"

"No!"

Dustin stays quiet as he eats his apple, and a smile creeps over his face. Grandma Bolgi merely raises her hands and the room silences. How did she get such control? I remember the way the room shushed when Mam was in the room and shudder to think everything Adakin hinted about Bolglarka is correct. Is she really the woman I think she is? The woman I have defended? The woman I have let people die for to protect?

"I see the boy as no harm," Bolgi says.

The men behind Dustin and some of the soldiers give her a dirty look, then direct that look at me. The way they then turn to Dustin to see what he will say or do next makes something click. Gannet said war makes people angry and hard to know who to follow. Has Bolgi lost some followers to this Dustin creature? Do some appreciate his crass cynicism and hatred of me and all Recipients?

"In fact," Bolgi continues, "we are more harm to him than he is to us."

My shoulders slump. "Hadn't thought about the risk I put Trip's health in.

"But I agree with my colleagues and think it's best if we take precautions. Aston, he will have to undergo testing to make sure he doesn't have detectors in him."

"He needs to be locked up." A few men agree with Dustin with grunts.

"Locked up?" I say, exasperated, and stand with my hands on the rough table. "Even Recipients didn't put me in—"

Dustin moves his foot down, making himself stand

taller, and interrupts me. "I'm sorry we aren't as wealthy and gracious as your precious Recipients."

"Dustin," Grandma Bolgi chastises.

He continues. "But a cell is all we poor, awful Donors have to offer him."

Someone shouts, "More like a dugout hole," and the room chuckles.

Two men approach us, not wearing brown shirts but acting like command officers rather than soldiers. Why doesn't Grandma Bolgi do something? Why is she just standing there like she does not command these men? They come closer, and I turn to Trip. "Don't worry, I won't let them take you." I try to stay as quiet and calm as possible.

Trip puts on a brave face, but his puppy eyes are tormenting and innocent. "Don't worry, miss. I'll go. It'll be okay." My heart is strangled by the way he calls me miss, just like Janice. Just like Juice. I squeeze my hands on his arms a little more as the men put their hands on him. "It can't be worse than what the Recipients would have done with me. They would have sent me back home." His smile haunts me as they take him.

Gannet steps up and squeezes my arm. "I'll go with them," he says. It's a small comfort to know Gannet will make sure Trip is safe, but it's better than him being alone with all of these Donors who seem to follow a different leader than Bolgi.

Someone mumbles in the room. "He'll just get the virus from us and die." Others chuckle at the words.

"Is that what we're about, then?" I yell. I shrug Bolgi's hand off my arm. "Revengeful deaths for the suffering we've seen? Kill the innocent because they killed ours first? An eye for an eye? Blood for blood?" The silence in the room magnifies my heavy breathing as I turn and look at every long face. Every worn brow that has lost someone, loved someone, hated more someones.

"Resistance means refusal to accept!" I say. "Resistance is supposed to be about change!" I choke on the last word, remembering Marcus crying at my knees, wishing he could take back the things he'd done. "But you adorn the very attitude." I sling my hand at them, pointing with a circling, annoyed gesture. "The very hatred that put us here in the first place. If you accept their treatment and return it, then we are going nowhere." I step back, farther away from Bolgi, and catch my breath. I'm not finished. "Next time," I say a little quieter, "there won't be enough people to divide. Only a few short minutes ago that Recipient boy was on your side helping you. Without him I wouldn't even be here. And now you wish him to die?"

My face is sore and wet and raw, but I don't care. These people may be free of serum, but they still don't see what I see. They still don't feel what I feel.

A slow singular clap goes through the room. It moves faster and faster and Grandma Bolgi is clapping and smiling as she walks toward me. She slings her arm over my shoulder, like in the picture. Her touch, for the first time, feels unwelcome. "And *that* is why she will lead us forward." She turns to Dustin. "That is why you need her. One of the many reasons."

The whole room claps, but it makes me want to smack them. I'm not some talented puppet saying words put into my mouth for show or applause. Applause. The sound of the debris. Debris they made rain from the sky on dead Recipients.

There's a scuffle and a tower of benches along the far wall fall over. I jump over the bench and take off running. I don't know if I'm running from officers that have found me or Donors that hate me or Recipients that want me. I look over my shoulder, and there's a man with a salt-and-pepper beard that has knocked over the benches in his haste to enter the room. He is running after me without looking back at the benches, and something about his face makes me stop my escape.

"Aston," he says. The room is quiet, and for all I know it could be empty now for how that deep voice moves about echoing against these walls. Papa is pushing things and people out of his way to get to me. His face is rough with wrinkles, skinny and sunken around the beard on his face. His eyes are red, and his cheeks are wet.

I'm frozen in disbelief. How many times did I imagine him coming across the floor boards or being here to help me? It doesn't feel real to have him here before me. He doesn't waste a single second to pull me into his arms, and I let myself finally, truly sink into and rely on someone. I feel weightless.

"Aston," he says my name over and over again. Like my name is a balm that could heal all his troubles. "Aston." He holds my face in his hands, and his eyes take in every inch of my face, crying like only a papa can cry and laughing like only a father can laugh.

In this hug, I'm certain all will work out. I'm in my papa's arms, and it will all be okay. Somehow. Papa will know what to do.

# CHAPTER 42

No one takes my information about Papa's life seriously. Grandma Bolgi says to trust her. Says that she knows more than Adakin, which has to be true if he wants her so bad, so I let it go. After dinner, I take food to where they have Trip. I hold the blanket wrapped around my shoulders close around my waist with one arm, but the sight of Trip huddled in the clay mud avoiding the drips that rain from the poorly made ceiling makes my arms fall loose. I hand over the blanket and the plate of food to him.

"You might think this is just prison food, but this is actually what I grew up eating."

After his first bite, he says, "No wonder you hid our food away in your drawer."

I laugh. "And now you know why I was so reluctant to share it with Lecky."

He laughs and then turns somber quickly. Lecky. Janice. The memories of what we lost so quickly not so long ago hurts too badly to speak.

I tousle his hair, and the Donor guard beside me gives

me a look. "You'll be out wowing all these Donors in no time, you'll see."

He smiles. Torrin stops by, and I introduce the two. They get along in an instant, and I'm in awe that Trip reminded me so much of Torrin as they sit next to each other. I can see the differences so clearly now. Trip is now the younger version of what Torrin may have been. But the Torrin I knew is gone.

Torrin takes me back to the cafeteria of sorts where all the tables and benches have been removed. In the center, a giant campfire crackles angrily and people sit around it, drinking and laughing.

"Doesn't the smoke give us away?" I ask.

"Nah," Torrin says as we walk to where Papa and Shannon wave us over. "I've been playing with the perceived reality idea and tweaked it a bit. No one can see us from above."

The group starts to sing as Torrin and I take our seats. A song I only remember as a lullaby my mother sang to me. About diamonds and rubies, a children's song that has a deeper, sadder meaning to adults. About illnesses that leave one sore and ruby red blood that runs off the shore. A song about riches galore and mountains that fell but will rise again. Like tinkling diamonds, a joyous din.

Papa said Mam wouldn't follow him into the resistance, and he only grunted that he agreed she wouldn't be able to handle it down here. Said she's too refined or what not. Ari and her family feed the resistance intel from the lawyers and live undercover of sorts. Sybil and her family dropped all contact, saying it was the only way she could keep them safe if she didn't know where they were because she would turn them in if she did.

The song is on the second verse, and I stop singing to

look at the group. Pip is throwing trash into the fire, and Shannon is nearby ready to pull her back if little Pip with long ringlet curls gets too close. Derek comes up with a cup for Papa. And they all sing. Like children. Like sleepy-eyed babes unaware of what's to come. Unsuspecting of who's already here.

I sit with family, yet it feels incomplete. I frown as I realize it isn't Mam or Ari I miss most. I miss Recipients. Certain yellow-haired ones who may be dying this very minute without me. A proper Recipient criminal who loved me like her own child and died saving the enemy. Torrin puts his arm around me as I wipe at my face. I lean into his chest and find it odd that he should be the one comforting me.

I hear his childish voice from only a year ago when we laid in my bed. "Why didn't you tell anyone?" he had asked.

In that moment so long ago, I swore to him my hatred of Recipients. But I won't make the same mistake again. I will tell anyone and everyone about what I have learned. About what I have seen. About who I have come to love.

Papa hands me the drink, and when I put my nose to it, I smell honey. I drop the cup and sit up, away from Torrin.

"Aston, are you okay?" Papa asks.

The singing drowns out the sound—the bees. I hear them more than see them. I stand and turn rigidly one direction then the next looking for them. One by one the voices die off and stare at me.

"Do you hear them?" I say.

"Someone get Bolglarka," Papa says, moving next to me. "Aston, the singing? You don't like the singing? They've stopped, it's okay."

"No, it's the bees. I hear them."

"There're no bees here, Aston. Let's go see Grandma Bolgi, maybe she can help."

I let Papa put his arm around me, but then he's here. He stands just over Papa's shoulder, and at first looks just like one of the rebels. He warms his hands by the fire, but then turns to me with his wrinkly grin. Adakin Malloy is here.

# CHAPTER 43

"Papa no! Run away!" I push and shove against my father's strong chest. "Listen to me, h—" I can't say the simple "he's here." My tongue freezes out of my control with pins and needles. "You need to get away from here." I'm able to say this easily, but anything regarding the Recipient leader in the room my tongue will not obey. "You need to get away from this room."

"Don't worry, Aston," Adakin drolls. "No one can hear me or see me but you, and you aren't allowed to say anything about it. See, that same serum connects the two of us. It allows me to know where you are at all times. And that same connection keeps you faithful to my wishes like a devout spy should be."

"Papa, listen to me." I make him look into my eyes. "You must listen to me. Everyone needs to get out. You need to leave." I speak slowly and as firm as I can. "You have to trust me," I whisper, and fearful tears spring up in my eyes.

He looks at me a moment, and then straightens up and yells. "Everyone clear out. In your bunkers until further notice."

Some question him and Papa answers them as truthfully as he can as he looks at me. "I don't know, but there's something. We will let your leaders know when we have more, but just like we've practiced, bunker up."

"No, Papa, it's you. You need to get out of here."

He grabs my shoulders. "It's okay, Aston."

Grandma Bolgi pushes past the retreating crowds. "What is it, Patar?"

Adakin slinks forward. "Ah, Bolglarka at last." He is right up next to Grandma Bolgi, admiring her face and touching her arm.

"No! Get away from her!" I yell. She can't feel a thing but stops as she thinks about what I've just said. "H— It's —" I gasp from the effort of merely trying to speak, and sweat drips down into my eyes. I try again, grunting to get the words to come as red overtakes my vision, and my head pounds.

"He's here," Grandma Bolgi says. It isn't a question, and I gulp fresh air as I sigh. "To the control room, Patar, and get Goru."

"It won't matter," Adakin says.

"It won't matter." I find I'm able to repeat what he says even if I can't talk about him being here or know what he knows.

"Cheater," he snarls. I smile. Finally finding a crack in his plan.

"Why?" Grandma Bolgi says.

Adakin merely raises his eyes at me and dramatically pretends to zip his mouth shut.

At that moment, the open circle above the fire is drowned with officers and droids. I turn to run toward my grandmother, but an officer is in the way. The back of his hand swings toward me and hits me in the jaw. I fly backward at an angle that leaves me disoriented. My lip stings and my neck aches. I don't know which way is up or which direction my papa and grandmother are anymore. When I regain my balance, I spy a large stick someone had been roasting their potato on, and I pick it up, swinging at a droid just before it points its red light at me. I make contact and it whirs in unnatural flips, crashing into the wall. The officer in front of me connected to the droid grabs his head with the impact. I use the distraction to hit the officer over the head with the stick, but when going in for a second blow, a flash of red paralyzes me. With one jolt of electric shock, everything goes red. Not the kind of red from the sun shining through my eyelids, warm and friendly. The kind of red that speaks to my blood and commands it to be still. To disintegrate. To die.

# CHAPTER 44

My head is full of bees. Humming and singing and stinging me from the inside out. My brain is so full of them they push and shove against my skull and their wings have a ringing sort of sound to them when they buzz with all their might. Ringing and buzzing and ringing and buzzing and my hands grab for my head. I give a territorial sort of growl and shout for them to stop.

Someone's hand is on my elbow and I shake it off with another shout.

"Aston."

It's Grandma Bolgi. She's in my mind too, and I can't move my head, it's so full and heavy from the bees. When I blink, everything is blurred so I leave my eyes shut.

"Aston," she says again, and slowly I register that hers is the hand on my elbow.

Quickly, it is all coming back to me. The officers, Adakin, "Papa."

"He knows how to take care of himself. Aston, quickly, I need you to listen to me."

I try to pull my head from the ground. Pushing myself up, my backside in the air first and slowly my head that weighs a ton, I'm soon on all fours but can't hold up my head. It throbs and aches and buzzes. The pressure of the hard, cold mud floor feels better than free in the air.

"There's not much time, Aston, listen. You remember where I took you as a child?"

It's vague, but even in this bee-filled state I recall the place I remembered when in the gardens with Marcus. "The tree," is all I scratch out and then groan.

"Yes, the tree. Do you think you could find it again?"

My breathing starts to blur out the humming, and soon I can lift my head a few inches. I blink over and over and though my eyes water, I can slowly see a little more clearly. What is she asking? Can I find a tree in this wilderness? There are many to pick from. But that one was different, I remember. What made it different? I can't place it now.

"Maybe," I say.

"It's essential that you do. Do you hear me, Aston? It has all the answers."

"Special tree has some answers."

"This is serious, Aston!" Her shouting hurts my head but makes the buzzing clear even more, and I reach for her voice as I sit up.

"And I'm serious, Bol-glark-ah!" It stings more than my ears the way that I speak to her. The woman who comforted me and taught me. I used to think we were so much alike. I wanted nothing more in my life than to be like her. She always seemed so free as a Donor. Now I know why. "You know, I can think of lots of times through my life you could have told me a bit more. Clued me in a little more. Helped me out! Now you expect me to remember these code visits that I thought were just meaningful moments between a grandmother and a granddaughter? Time spent with me because I thought you loved me?"

"I do love you," she says.

"Yeah, well, you have really odd ways of showing it." I lean against the corner of the room we're in, pull my knees up and rest my elbows on them, then let my head fall back and hit the muddy side.

"Here." She scoots close to me and winces as she does so. It makes me feel wimpy to see how she moves when clearly hurt as well. She hands me something, and I lean forward to take it from her.

It's the statue I sent back through the small converter.

"It's the key, Aston. You found it, and you have the key."

"To what?"

"The answers. It's all in you, but you have to get to the tree."

With that, the metal door opens and in steps Adakin Malloy who straightens after ducking through.

"Ah, the Vazeto girls. See Aston, I knew you had more value than Marcus realized. You led us right to the queen bee."

"What do you want, Malloy?" Grandma says.

I look at Grandma Bolglarka. The fear on her face says it all. We are doomed, and she knows it. He has found us. He has found who he was looking for, and I am no longer of value to him. Not even my blood. His shoes no longer tap-click as he walks but actually squish in the mud as he steps, making protesting gurgling sounds.

"Just finishing up our history lessons." He turns to me. "See, over the past couple of months, Aston and I have rather enjoyed reviewing how we got here. Shall we continue? I believe we left off talking about the IPC."

Grandma Bolgi's panic makes me too curious to be

scared, looking at me, then back to Adakin. What is she so afraid that Adakin will tell me?

"Or maybe some reminiscing is in order first. See, I think Aston would like some answers in regard to a certain photo she found of you, Bolglarka." He retrieves from the inside of his waistcoat the photo, removed from the frame I had stolen from his office. He looks down at it and smiles. "Ah, those were the good ol' days, eh Bolgi? Of course, that's not what we called you then is it?" He grins an evil grin at me, then laughs.

"Stop it, Adakin."

It's my turn to look between the two. What is Grandma Bolgi so scared that he will reveal? I find it a little easier to lift my head now. I lean forward, ready to learn why my grandmother was in that picture, arms wrapped around Eva Tabor, that horrible person, the woman who started this all. What value does Grandma Bolgi have to the Recipients?

"Don't you know your grandmother's maiden name, Aston? Tabor. I knew her as Eva Bolglarka Tabor."

# CHAPTER 45

"You're a liar!" I shout, and the strain hurts my head.

Adakin laughs even deeper and turns to Grandma Bolgi. "Tell her, Eva. Tell her how genius we were."

My ribs are hollow like my lungs forgot how to breathe. They're not there, I can't breathe, I can't speak. That evil woman who started this all, who created the virus in the first place to kill innocent people just to make more room on the earth and become rich?

Grandma Bolgi looks at me with tears in her eyes and whispers, "I'm sorry, Ash tree."

Adakin laughs again. "Oh, aren't family reunions so fun. I love all the dirty secrets."

"She's no family of mine," I say, and Adakin giggles.

"Aston, things were different. It didn't start out that way at first, it was—"

"Now, now, there will be plenty of time to make up afterward," he says. "You two will be locked up here in the get-along room, but first you need to tell me, Bolglarka,

368

where is it?" His smile is so haunting but genuine. He loves theatrics. I can't take my eyes off of him. He has waited all this time, set things up so precisely, purely for the effect. To see me react and fall apart. He thrives on controlling others and when he couldn't control me so well he went about it the old-fashioned way.

"Where is what?" she acts like she doesn't know what he's talking about.

"The vaccine for this virus. The antidote!"

"You found your antidote with your scientists, I thought."

"Don't play games with me, Eva."

My face is suddenly lit up red, and the heat of a red laser has me plastered against the wall, trying again to remember how to breathe.

"I told you!" Grandma Bolgi sits up on her knees and puts her hands out toward me. "I told you, the virus got out of hand. I couldn't figure out a vaccine for this one, it attaches to the genetic code too quickly and travels airborne almost immediately. I tried everything I could to create a vaccine, but all it did was speed up an imminent death. Even the immunity couldn't save the infected when injected into them, you know that by now. The genetic missing antibody fought off the immunity too quickly."

She relaxes as she talks, like she's losing energy, and slumps against the wall.

"I don't buy it," he growls.

"You don't have to buy it. But it's the truth."

"Then why did you go into hiding?"

"Why do you think, Adakin? You saw how my own granddaughter looked at me just now. I became a monster not a savior. We lost sight of our goals quicker than the virus takes over. I wanted to be a new person. Start over. I thought the discovery of donations could be a new way of life. And then you enslaved the very people I tried to save you with. Treated them like cattle and circus freaks instead of heroes. Drove them into poverty with your greed and selfishness. I had to stand up somehow."

Adakin's image flickers, and he looks around him as if he's seeing things we aren't.

"You've always been a master liar."

"You would know best," she answers him with a smile. "Better keep me alive or you'll never know."

"Is that the lie then?" His image flickers again.

"You'll never know." She coughs and slumps further into the mud as Adakin growls and releases me from the red sting of the laser.

He shoots his hand toward Grandma Bolgi but pauses. His face, flickering in the room, speaks of something more than hatred. These two have history and for the first time, I see something I never thought I'd see on Adakin's face. Uncertainty.

A red beam flares bright and straight toward Bolgi. My screams surprisingly mix with Adakin's in an eerie dissonance that fills the cell as the beam hits the right side of my grandmother's chest. It leaves a burn-trimmed hole there just like it did to Janice. Adakin's cursing disintegrates into the air, and I lunge for my grandmother.

Her head is in my arms, and tears are on my face. Again.

"It's in you, Aston. Find the answers, my little ash tree, find them. It's in you." And then she is gone. The smell of burnt flesh is now my only companion.

My memories could all be a lie, but there's still a part of my heart that has a hole burned in it at the loss of the grandmother I thought I knew. I lost her twice today. Once at the discovery of who she really is and once as her soul slipped into nothing and her eyes stare back at me glossier than when on serum. I've cried too many tears to have anymore left for her. I only stare at her lifeless body and add her name to the list of people I once loved.

I don't know how long I sit crumpled on the floor, staring at the woman I wish I knew. The woman I wish I could ask all the questions I never knew I needed the answers to. It would be easy to hate her for who she was, but the grandmother I know couldn't be the same Eva Tabor that Adakin knew.

I stumble into the control room with my mind full of static and my chest numb from confusion. Dustin does a double take.

"What happened?" I ask. Movement in the room stops, and they all eye me.

Dustin speaks to me with the most respect I've ever heard him give. "The device you gave us has the IP addresses of every Donor on it."

I stare blankly at him until the man who took the device from Grandma Bolgi steps forward. "I was able to put them into the system and control the perceived reality. Reprogram each individual, so to speak. To not see or feel the presence of them."

"The attack on us wasn't real?" I say.

"Oh, it was real. As real as could be, but a few switches in the mind, and it's as if they don't exist."

"Bolglarka?" Dustin says.

I shake my head. "We need to talk." How do I tell them their beloved leader was once the evil ruler that began all the wars? The creator of all the viruses. Another day. Another time.

Torrin, Papa, Shannon, and Pip run in and greet me. They are accounted for on the ports along with the thousands of others that survived. Shannon's face is red and swollen, and I can see it in her eyes. How will we tell Pip about her father who died at the hands of an officer that was also a figment of our imaginations? Another day. Another time.

We hug each other close, and I breathe in their scent of fight and earth and blood. Gannet catches my eye from across the room and nods at me. I nod back. He is who I will tell first. About who she really was and what her last words mean. I don't know what she thinks is in me, but I know one thing. The love that's in me has grown, not diminished. I love more than Donors. I love Recipients too, and with that, my determination has grown. I will tell all who will listen. I will share the tale of how a Recipient gave her life for me, how a Recipient changed his heart. And I will fight all who get in the way of bringing the change Marcus foresaw.

I will save us all.

# ACKNOWLEDGMENTS

I wrote *Blood Numbers* before the pandemic and then was in shock when so many elements of my story came to life right before my eyes. As I began editing book two, the current events of George Floyd's murder were unfolding. I felt again this eerie sense of foreshadowing in my book as prejudices and hatred divided our country. The best thing about fiction is that it can point out errors and facts about our world in ways real life can't always accomplish. I hope others can find the truth in this fiction: we are all a lot more alike than we realize; there are always more sides to a story; friends can be found in the most unlikely of places.

I dedicated this book to friends and family who have over the years helped me see how wrong my perspective has been, who have changed my mind about topics important to me, and have given me insight into what it is like to walk in their shoes. Please always be curious before accusing. Seek answers and insight rather than judgment. I love this scripture verse, "...and he denieth none who come unto him, black and white, bond and free, male and female...and all are alike unto God."

A special thanks to my publisher and friend who has never given up on me and has been extremely patient with me as I have missed deadline after deadline. I owe much of my success to her vision and dedication.

# About the Author

C.F. Kreitzer is an award-winning author who loves to write angsty teenage romances because love and heartbreak often go hand in hand and love is definitely worth fighting for.

She didn't always love books. In fact, she hated reading as a child and timed the page turns just right to give the illusion that she was enjoying a book. Turns out, she was just reading the wrong books. When she stumbled upon Charlotte Bronte's *Jane Eyre*, she was smitten. Cary's journal entries while reading that classic novel are addressed to Charlotte and are quite dramatic and comical.

Cary lives in Orem with her husband, five children, three dogs, two guinea pigs, two goldfish, and a gecko (she's still not given up on convincing her bird-loving husband to get a cat).

9 781955 060202